O'Neil Ford on Architecture

Roger Fullington Series in Architecture

O'Neil Ford on Architecture

EDITED BY KATHRYN E. O'ROURKE

University of Texas Press ❮❯ Austin

Publication of this book was made possible in part by
support from Roger Fullington and a challenge grant from
the National Endowment for the Humanities.

Library of Congress Cataloging-in-Publication Data

Names: Ford, O'Neil, 1905–1982, author. | O'Rourke, Kathryn E., editor.
Title: O'Neil Ford on architecture / edited by Kathryn E. O'Rourke.
Description: First edition. | Austin : University of Texas Press, 2019. |
    Includes index.
Identifiers: LCCN 2018034567
    ISBN 978-1-4773-1638-2 (cloth : alk. paper)
    ISBN 978-1-4773-1860-7 (library e-book)
    ISBN 978-1-4773-1861-4 (nonlibrary e-book)
Subjects: LCSH: Ford, O'Neil, 1905-1982—Philosophy.
Classification: LCC NA737.F67 A35 2019 | DDC 720.92—dc23
LC record available at https://lccn.loc.gov/2018034567

doi:10.7560/316382

Contents

O'Neil Ford on Architecture

Introduction

The Language of O'Neil Ford

Kathryn E. O'Rourke

Why should we read what architects write? Because ideas drive great buildings. Written language, unlike visual or spatial language, requires no translation and therefore gives us access to ideas more immediately than do even the most affecting, powerful buildings. Great architecture, like all great works of art, is a form of knowledge itself. But the abstract nature of this knowledge and the sensory means by which it is received endow it with a different character than that rendered linguistically. Architects' words uniquely give us access to their authors' intellectual lives and the times in which they worked. They deepen and complicate our experiences of buildings and very often challenge our beliefs about history.

O'Neil Ford (1905–1982) spoke often and in many languages. One has only to call to mind a few of his major buildings to appreciate his agility in moving between architectural idioms to create an oeuvre that resists simple stylistic classifications. Diverse and forceful works, from the Little Chapel in the Woods, to the Texas Instruments Semiconductor Components Division Building, to the polylingual campus of Trinity University, reveal the architect's complete command of the grammar of modernism and his fluency in the languages of architectural history. They also show that he understood that a broad, timeless rationalism, well-chosen materials, innovation, and a firm command of proportion provide the framework of that history.

John Palmer Leeper, director of the McNay Art Museum from 1954 to 1990, was one of the first to summarize the breadth and complexity of Ford's built achievements. Writing when Ford was at the height of his powers, in the mid-1960s, Leeper framed the architect's work in terms of its "humility" and its "humanity," but he also found in it powerful connections to the titans of architectural modernism. Observing that the "harmonious and tranquil textures" supplied by rich materials and exquisite works of craft in Ford's buildings made his interiors "among the most sumptuous" in twentieth-century architecture, Leeper said that "often in richness of detail [they] recall Louis Sullivan, and in refinement of execution those of the Green[e] brothers." Muscular, rigorous compositions rooted in the architect's close attention to the relationships between program, structure, and form were at once tempered and enriched by the ways they nestled into the landscape. As an example, Leeper observed that "the Intercontinental Motors Building, as eloquent a structure as it is, is set in, is part of an important grove of elm and live oak trees"[1] (figure 1).

Ford thought deeply about architecture's capacity to convey ideas. He defended the singularity and authority of architectural intention repeatedly. The architect often quoted from Ralph Tubbs's book *An Englishman Builds* (1945), and suggested that Tubbs summarized his own view of the ways buildings communicate:

> I refer to contact of the mind of the builder directly through the form of the building itself. . . . The building alone . . . convey[s] to us something which could not be conveyed to us by any other means than by the building . . .
>
> Buildings appeal to us in different ways. . . . In each case, however, we see revealed to us something of the living man, for no architect can give his building a finer quality than exists in his own mind.[2]

Over the course of his life, Ford sharpened his mind and honed his eye through constant study, which he translated into

FIGURE 1. O'Neil Ford and Howard Wong; Stewart King, landscape architect, Volkswagen Sales and Service Center for Intercontinental Motors Inc., San Antonio, 1962–1963. Ceramic light fixtures by Martha Mood and Beaumont Mood.

buildings and words that helped define architectural modernism in Texas and contributed to an international conversation about modernity.

The texts collected in this volume allow us to hear O'Neil Ford's voice in a new way. They represent fifty-five years of thinking, reading, talking, and writing, from his formative days as a mentee of Dallas architect David R. Williams to his final years, when he ruminated on the lives of several of his collaborators. Many are transcripts or written versions of lectures. They range widely in their subjects but collectively show Ford's enduring convictions and concerns. Throughout them the great themes of architectural modernism resound: history, technology, nature, art, and social change. For Ford these manifested as a lifelong study of architectural history near and far;

a fascination with innovative construction methods; a profound concern with the landscape and its conservation; a multi-decade collaboration with artists and landscape architects, in which he played the role of a conductor directing a great, collective symphony; and a passionate commitment to civil rights, education, and the sustaining of well-functioning communities. Over and over they show that Ford's approach to architecture was rooted in his convictions that our treatment of the land is a mirror of our regard for one another and that a fundamental integrity of materials, structure, site, program, and form defines great buildings. These beliefs were buttressed by his long, close study of architectural history, were fueled by his worries about the future, and were shared with a world that he believed needed to be taught to see.

Ford was arguably twentieth-century Texas's most important architect and, in the 1950s and 1960s, a major figure in US architecture. He came to international prominence for his pioneering use of the Youtz-Slick lift-slab construction method at Trinity University in San Antonio in the early 1950s.[3] In the next decade, when both his writings and his buildings were richest, Ford's long-standing interests in history, society, and education coalesced into a powerful vision of what architecture should be. Through his travels, lectures, and teaching positions at Harvard, MIT, and the University of Virginia, Ford was in contact with a broad swath of leading US architects. At symposia he shared billings with, among others, Louis Kahn, I. M. Pei, and Pietro Belluschi. For many years he collaborated closely with William Wurster and Félix Candela, and he was among the elite architects whom researchers at the University of California, Berkeley, studied to discover the nature of creativity.[4]

Ford's words reveal that, far from being a regional modernist, he was at the center of a diverse and rapidly changing architectural modernism in the United States. A perhaps somewhat unwitting heir to the legacies of Louis Sullivan and Frank Lloyd Wright, Ford worked in and helped to shape a branch of American architecture distinguished by its intense attention to

FIGURE 2. O'Neil Ford talks to students and faculty at the University of Texas at Austin School of Architecture.

site, to nature, and to its role in shaping society. At the same time, many of his concerns—about planning, the fate of cities during a time of change, the proper uses of new technologies, the relationship of architecture to the other arts, and the value of the social sciences to architecture, for example—were shared by architects throughout the world. Two major invitations illustrate his stature and the breadth of his expertise: in 1960 he was a respondent to a keynote lecture by J. Robert Oppenheimer on a panel about technology and the future at the annual convention of the American Institute of Architects, and in 1968 President Johnson appointed him to the National Council on the Arts, where he served with Duke Ellington, Gregory Peck, and Charles Eames, among others.

Despite Ford's prominence in the 1950s and 1960s, nationally, he is relatively little known today. One reason is that, although they embodied defining qualities of twentieth-century modernism, most of his buildings were unlike the glassy International Style and modish New Formalist works that have been at the heart of the scholarly and popular vogue for midcentury architecture of the last twenty years.[5] Unlike many canonical icons, Ford's works were often modest in scale, rough rather than sleek, and marked by restraint rather than bravura. Ford has also been overlooked in part because he was a Texan and built chiefly in Texas, a state that has historically had relatively few architectural historians (compared to the number on the coasts) to tell its story. His omission from most histories of US modernism is in certain respects symptomatic of the tendency of Texans and non-Texans alike to imagine the state as different from all other places. This posture of otherness serves some aims admirably, but in historical analyses it risks blinding us to commonalities and blunting our capacity to critically articulate differences. Geography and form help explain, in part, why Ford is often associated with regionalism, even though he did not call his buildings "regionalist," nor did he participate in debates about regionalism, as many of his colleagues did.[6] Stephen Fox has shown that the term "regionalism" in Texas architecture was used as a means of asserting difference against a metropolitan center, an aim quite different from Ford's.[7] The architect's well-known admiration for vernacular Texas buildings has also undoubtedly contributed to the perception of him as a "regionalist." Yet, as scholars increasingly recognize, the work of many canonical "international" modern architects was informed by their study of vernacular buildings.[8]

Even during his life, that Ford worked in Texas almost automatically condemned him to a peripheral status relative to his colleagues in architectural centers. But in the 1950s and 1960s, Texas vividly typified the dramatic changes under way across the country and, in the person of Lyndon Johnson, was at the heart of national politics. Between 1950 and 1970 the population of Texas increased by nearly four million. In 1930 there were 7,300 miles of paved road in the state, and in 1950 there were 34,000, as highways began to slice through the still-young cities of Dallas and Houston, facilitating their sprawl.[9] Although Ford did not acknowledge the ways he benefited from suburbanization professionally, he fought tirelessly against sprawl and for preservation of the eighteenth- and nineteenth-century buildings of San Antonio, the state's most architecturally significant city and his adopted home. For Ford, the very real problems of a powerful nation in the midst of an extraordinary self-reinvention were also the problems of architecture. He spoke repeatedly and passionately in favor of civil rights and environmental conservation in a place and time when both were controversial. For some, Texas's vast, varied landscape seemed to cry out for protection against the onslaught of suburban growth, while others saw in it only profits to be gained or lost. Bitter hatreds stewed in many Texas communities, and although it was underpinned by the long, horrible histories of slavery and segregation, the lived experience of racial difference in parts of the state in some respects helped ease the process of integrating its urban public spaces. The 1960s—the decade when Ford was most eloquent about these matters—were the years in which Johnson, who had masterfully dominated the US Senate in the 1950s as Ford came to national prominence, signed the major pieces of civil rights and environmental legislation that are his greatest legacies. The intersections of and parallels in the two men's lives are notable because they illuminate the ways that Ford's words existed in a far-ranging, multidimensional national conversation. Johnson was three years younger than Ford and like him had grown up in very modest circumstances in a small Texas town. In the mid-1930s Ford worked for Johnson briefly when he directed the National Youth Administration in Texas. Ford's clients Marshall and Patsy Steves, who were friends of the Johnsons, later reconnected the architect and the president, and Lady Bird Johnson in particular admired his work.[10]

The typical Texan directness that characterized Johnson's speech marked Ford's as well. Seemingly more grounded in the real world of things and people than in debates about the abstract problems of architecture, Ford's prose is clear and accessible. In it we discover O'Neil Ford the reader, the historian, the architectural theorist, and the citizen. Ford delivered most of his talks extemporaneously, and the texts of those collected here represent a tiny fraction of the total. Some have been published previously; others heretofore existed only as handwritten or transcribed manuscripts of speeches or remarks at conferences. They are held at the Alexander Architectural Archives at the University of Texas at Austin. For nearly thirty years Ford kept a diary. I have chosen not to include his diary entries or examples of his voluminous correspondence in order to focus intensively on the ideas at the core of his intellectual and professional life.[11] Attending only to the texts that he intended for a public audience makes it possible to identify more clearly the ideas that he most wanted to communicate and the principles that governed his work. I have edited the architect's words only lightly so as to retain the character of his speech as fully as possible. The reader will undoubtedly note anachronistic spellings and word usages, a few of which betray latent and once pervasive prejudices. Jarring as some examples are, they powerfully conjure a different era. My occasional interpolations in Ford's writing are in brackets; any text in parentheses either appears that way in the original manuscript or publication, or represents marginal notes made by Ford, such as identifications of slides.

Others have chronicled Ford's personal and professional life. Mary Carolyn Hollers George's extraordinary biography of the architect relies in part on his diaries, and David Dillon's study of his works catalogues Ford's development, influences, and major projects.[12] In Texas, and particularly in San Antonio, Ford is something of a legend, and it seems that nearly every architect in practice in the city today can trace her or his professional lineage to him by one way or another.[13] Ford's legions of friends and admirers have long provided recollections and anecdotes of his work and his antics. George and Dillon relate many of these, and they are vital to the larger story of the architect.

The purpose of this volume, however, is to make it possible to listen to the architect alone, so that we may better understand the ideas that drove his work and assess more thoroughly where he fits in the history of architectural modernism. The architect's speech was as purposeful as his buildings, even when it was tinged with self-consciousness and self-deprecation. The texts gathered here are verbal iterations of Ford's career-long argument about the nature of architecture and its place in the world, which unfolded simultaneously in his built works. They help us understand why he was so influential, and they collectively constitute a critical component of his legacy.

In 1953, *Vogue* magazine, declaring that he was "one of twenty-two Texans who help run the place," described Ford as "a brilliant, fertile-minded, rangy-talking architect."[14] He shared the pages of the magazine with some of the state's major power brokers, including Houston business magnate and US secretary of commerce Jesse Jones; Dallas's Stanley Marcus of the Neiman-Marcus department store conglomerate; Houston arts patron and philanthropist Ima Hogg; San Antonio scientific and industrial-research patrons Tom and Earl Slick; and oil industry pioneer and philanthropist Hugh Roy Cullen. Ford was famous for talking people like these into patronizing his work, yet even as he depended on the rich and influential, he critiqued them.

Ford commented that he gave "many lectures, perhaps too many, for causes I believe in." He was certain that because of his words San Antonio's leaders counted him among the "obstructionists and nonconformists" and that they regarded him as a "belligerent and controversial reactionary" when he "protest[ed] their support of the expressway though a campus and parks," crying, "Wait, study this carefully, take time to be sure there isn't another way through a slum. Take time to be sure the extra money for a better right-of-way isn't cheap compared with the irreparable destruction of open areas." Speech, like buildings, was a means through which architects could shape the world, Ford believed, and he urged his colleagues "to speak loudly and consistently against the brutal destruction of the good things our forebears gave us."[15]

The architect's words were at times informal, irreverent, and funny, but he could also be eloquent and serious. Like Sullivan and Wright, he did not graduate from college and he had little formal training in architecture. But he often wrote beautifully, and he cared deeply about language, which he believed should be clear and straightforward, like a good building. Unlike the dense, florid prose of Wright, the sweeping, strident manifestoes of Le Corbusier, the rather opaque, philosophical musings of Louis Kahn, or the punning, studied informality of the language of Robert Venturi and Denise Scott Brown, Ford's writings and lectures were usually conversational and casual in tone. He criticized the "special phraseology" he heard in elite architecture programs and recalled with irritation his experience of serving on an architectural jury and having to endure "tiresome and almost repetitive," "hairsplitting declamations and exclamations" and said he considered the "language . . . abstruse and the manner almost diffident."[16] As early as 1955 he spoke of his suspicions that such language, particularly when it was used to describe technical topics, masked a speaker's ignorance of the core principles of architecture. Remarking on his interactions with young architects, he said,

> I was confronted with the students. I found that they talk of all kinds of momentum and end reactions and all of that, I don't quite understand what they are talking about. True, I am not an engineer, I am an anti-engineer, but the simple understanding of tension and compression is almost beyond them. It is lost in the slide-rule world.[17]

Of the writing in the architectural journals he was even more critical. In 1964 he told an audience at Rice University,

I do resent all the mishmash of adulation and flattering language, the omniscient *pronunciamentos*, the wise words of these journalistic oracles. . . . The style of writing in architectural magazines has become quite as laboriously devious as the writings of art critics who bend hard to explain a painter's three swift strokes of green thrown across two brave blobs of red.[18]

Rarely did Ford resort to such flourishes. His words flowed from an endlessly curious mind that wandered far and delighted in its work. Moving between optimism and outrage, sputtering fury and eloquence, they reveal an author who was idealistic, irate, and unafraid. We repeatedly hear implicit and explicit calls for restraint, selflessness, and attention to detail—the qualities that distinguish his best buildings and make them both so challenging for some to appreciate today and so relevant. In Ford the quintessentially modernist revulsion against affectation and imitation manifested as a deep personal frustration with a society that he saw as increasingly willing to destroy beauty in the name of profit, and it fed his dialectical understanding of love and anger. In his comments after Oppenheimer's lecture in 1960, speaking of those "who care not about the destruction of the wilderness because soon we will have no wilderness—soon it will all mix into a messy nothing where there is neither urban nor suburban nor country civilization," he told the physicist and his colleagues that "indignation for this callous destruction of our lovely land and our beauty is the first form of love—hate of these is love, hate of these is sympathy, hate of these is the daring to hope."[19]

THE ARCHITECT'S LIBRARIES

Before Ford wrote, he read, and the spaces of his daily life were filled with books. They spread across his San Antonio home,

Willow Way, and his architectural office, which first occupied a nineteenth-century house in the King William neighborhood and then a nineteenth-century commercial building on East Commerce Street. His colleagues recall seeing books piled high in his personal office, and his children, who retain some, remember them in his bedroom.[20] When archivists catalogued his professional library in 1983, they recorded more than 750 volumes. He gave books, lent them, and received them from friends and clients. They formed the backbone of his study of architectural history and helped hone his close engagement with language. Like David Williams, Ford loved and collected old, rare books, but he also had new ones. The vast majority dealt with architectural topics, but also among the collection were works of fiction by literary titans and books on Texas history, Native American cultures, Irish folklore, and antique cars. His library included magazines, journals, and government documents.

Ford read before, during, and after his many trips to Europe, Mexico, and the US East Coast. As he traveled, he bought books, and for him, travel, reading, and study were closely connected. Writing about his visits to Foyles bookshop and Maggs Bros. Ltd.—two of London's great bookstores—in 1958, he marveled that "there were all the unbelievable books—couldn't help buying the fine old first edition of Robert Adam's great book—have always wanted one."[21] And later, when his purchases made it to San Antonio, he recorded that "all the beautiful books . . . have arrived—wonderful things. Medieval architecture. Ancient buildings of Greece and Greek islands. Italy. Romanesque. . . . These are the world's riches—the knowledge we must have if we are to be good at our jobs."[22] He told an audience about his library and his reading habits in 1964:

When I am not working, I read. This reading is history of architecture and the other arts, history of religion and Western civilization, history of Texas and America. I have read every book on the architecture and art of Byzantium, on Moslem architecture, on the architecture of the Middle Ages, on the architecture of Latin America that I could get or crowd into air flights and the late hours of night. Two of my associates read more. . . . We are excited—that's the only word that describes our feelings—about our discoveries in books.[23]

Reading prepared Ford to see the buildings and landscapes he visited during his travels. His remarks on the experience of moving between books and buildings confirms that, as committed as he was to the kind of knowledge that comes from tactile exploration of materials and a basic understanding of the workings of the physical world, a deeply intellectual approach to architecture also shaped his work. They also reveal that Ford's well-known fascination with Texas buildings and landscapes was matched by his admiration for much older and distant ones, which he believed could become equally familiar through books:

I have felt ecstasy over seeing the great cathedral at Albi because it was the subject of one of our serious studies. In its presence I felt quite humble. I have devoted hours to seeing Giselbertus's great sculpture at Autun. . . . I know the back streets of London better than the front streets of Houston because I had seen the beauty of the good Queen Anne and Georgian buildings in books before my firsthand visits.[24] (figures 12 and 3)

Ford's interest in education was undoubtedly tied to his love of reading. His bookishness and appreciation of the worlds that reading can open up surely endeared him to the many clients for whom he designed college campuses, schools, and research institutes. In her charge to Ford and his colleagues when she commissioned them to design the new campus of Skidmore College, Josephine Young Case, the chair of the college's board of trustees, told them,

FIGURE 3. Denmark Street, London, near Foyles bookshop, one of Ford's favorites, 1964.

You will design a campus which will provide for both student and teacher a feeling of freedom and wide horizon. . . . For here the student must discover herself, and through herself others and the world, and through the world others, and though others, herself. . . . At the heart of the beating center . . . set the library where every book wanted is immediately at hand, and a thousand others wait beside them to be discovered.[25]

A library was also at the heart of Ford's largest and longest-running project, the campus of Trinity University in San

Antonio, where he and his colleagues worked for over thirty years. The university's George Storch Memorial Library was one of the first three lift-slab buildings Ford designed, and in addition to housing the university's books, it materialized the principles that governed the campus and that reverberated in the architect's words throughout his career (figure 16). Composed of two principal volumes stepping down the terrain at the edge of the escarpment that bisects the campus, the library and its terraces yielded to and helped make visible the rock face as the organizing element of the site. By placing the library at the point where Bushnell Avenue would have cut through the heart of the campus, Ford powerfully suggested that cars should remain outside of it. From the library's windows and terraces, views of downtown San Antonio reminded students of the principle at the core of their education—that their intellectual discoveries and habits of liberal inquiry honed in college compelled them to shape the world as engaged, active citizens.

In his commencement address at Trinity in 1967, which took the form of a letter begun when he was teaching at the University of Virginia, Ford spoke about the person whose life embodied the confluence of scholarly learning, public service, respect for nature, and engagement with architecture more than anyone else's in US history. Ford told the graduates,

As I write, I sit close by the case that holds the drawings and building specifications and letters written by the entirely remarkable Mr. Jefferson—a master of expression. I have read his beautiful words that gave direction to the shaping of a different kind of nation, and I have imagined what impact they had on those fortunate men who first heard them spoken. . . .

Not long since, I was privileged to hold in my hand his equally remarkable letters. Whether Mr. Jefferson was writing about seed or soil, or brickmaking or food, or just relating an interesting and provocative experience, he set down his fine words with a freedom of expression and with an enthusiasm that is entirely lucid, fresh, and stimulating.[26]

Reading, writing, and teaching in Thomas Jefferson's Academical Village (figure 4), Ford chronicled his memories of shaping one that was, quite intentionally, radically different in form and style from the president-architect's. And yet, just as he had found in the Albi Cathedral powerful lessons for modern architecture, in a time when the country groaned and strained with change, he was struck by the continued relevance of two-hundred-year-old words written by one of its creators.

O'NEIL FORD, HISTORIAN

Ford's first published work was an essay he coauthored with David Williams on nineteenth-century vernacular buildings in Texas, "Architecture of Early Texas." It appeared in three installments in *Southwestern Architect* in 1927 and 1928, shortly before the magazine ceased publication. While it is impossible to untangle the separate contributions of the authors, it is clear that they both sought to identify elements they believed were found only in Texas that might provide evidence that a distinctive "indigenous" Texas architecture had emerged in the collective works of Anglo settlers. (Notably absent is any interest in the ways that Native Americans had lived and built.) The essay combines boosterism about the quality of the buildings with a claim that they embodied the modernist virtues of structural "honesty," craftsmanship, and simplicity, and, importantly, that their builders were not concerned with "style." Unlike settlers on the East Coast, the early Texas builders, Williams and Ford claimed, did not copy older models. Situating nineteenth-century vernacular buildings within the social and political histories of Anglo Texas, the architects argued that a recognizable idiom had "developed to fit the economic, social, and climatic needs of the people in a logical way from unpretentious beginnings,"

FIGURE 4. Thomas Jefferson, campus of the University of Virginia, Charlottesville, 1817–1826. Photogravure by W. T. Littig & Co. based on a painting, 1907.

and that it reflected indirect influences from Spain, France, and England.[27] The authors did not offer a full-fledged argument for exactly how the lessons of nineteenth-century buildings might inform modern design, but the germs of one were present. Years later, writing of his mentor and their historical research, Ford recalled that he and Williams studied "building, history, and materials. . . . We began to feel the sense of native things and the respect for climate, and the development of a kind of style just grew. Dave kept pressing for understanding of these values and suppressing the idea that we, or anyone, should copy the old buildings and develop a new 'ranch style.'"[28]

In 1928 Williams published an essay in the *Southwest Review*, "An Indigenous Architecture: Some Texas Colonial Houses," in which he repeated many of the points (and in some instances phrases) that had appeared in the earlier article, as well as Ford's drawings of "pioneer" houses from the article and new buildings by Williams inspired by them (figure 7).[29] Williams now spoke not of "indigenous" buildings but of "regional" ones, a shift that Fox argues was made to link architecture with developments in other arts, which were increasingly described as "regionalist."[30] The *Southwest Review* had been founded by faculty members at the University of Texas in 1915, and in 1924 it moved to Southern Methodist University, where it became one of the most prestigious regional literary and cultural journals in the United States.[31] As the detailed notes Ford made about the condition and significance of buildings in small Texas towns around 1940 and his various drafts of an essay on San Antonio's architectural history illustrate, his interest in Texas architecture was lifelong.[32]

In Naples in 1964 Ford wrote a lecture on the architectural history of San Antonio. He probably never gave the lecture, although it seems he intended for his wife, Wanda, to do so. It was published with the title "Texas Idyll" nearly twenty years later, just after his death. In it he opined on the city's architectural icons, saying that the "old, singularly beautiful" part of San Fernando Cathedral was "buried" in the "undistinguished" nineteenth-century one and that the Missions San Juan Capistrano and San Francisco de la Espada, despite their changes, were "a surprise and joy as one comes upon them rather sidewise." He wrote of the "genuine sadness" he felt about "our losses, mostly absolutely useless destruction," in a city whose leaders were "sane, honorable, but unimaginative." Ford noted that he had no "sources . . . for dates and places" because he was traveling and the airline had lost the luggage that contained the original draft of the talk and his notes. Musing on the city's eclectic and rich vernacular architecture, he said that San Antonio's "unacademic history and character" made "any kind of labeling next to impossible."[33]

Departing from the position he had taken when he and Williams wrote their essays decades earlier, Ford in his writing in the 1960s showed that he understood the city's architecture in terms of the legacies of the Italian Renaissance and of Spanish colonial architecture throughout the hemisphere.

He delighted in the idiosyncrasies that the study of canonical architectural history made evident in Texas buildings. Like modernists in many places, he was keen to critique academicism, and San Antonio's eighteenth-century buildings provided plenty of opportunities to celebrate deviations from the norm. He wrote of one San Antonio mission:

> When you look at the façade of Concepción, which is my favorite building in this hemisphere, you will see that everything done was wrong, academically. It has a little pediment which is way too steep and reminds you of Romanesque churches in Ireland, Southern France, Northern Spain, and the less populated parts of Italy, and can even be seen in the Byzantine architecture of Greece. The clumsy little gable is made too steep. . . . Then a window is placed right on top of the point, which no good designer would do, with two more below.
>
> All of this is quite wrong. If you drew one of these things, you'd fail sophomore architecture.[34] (figure 5)

Ford's study of architectural history also convinced him that "certain fundamental things cannot possibly be improved," a point made, he said, by his own Murchison Tower at Trinity University (figure 16). The brick tower serves as the campanile for the Margarite B. Parker Chapel, and Ford loved the historicity of the construction technique: "It is fine Sumerian material. They built upward three feet a day and poured it full of concrete as they went. Just the way the Romans did."[35]

What could be improved, however, was the teaching of architectural history. Remarking on his admiration for Bernard Rudofsky's *Architecture without Architects*, Ford said that teaching architectural history chronologically "is the sil liest way to teach history I can possibly imagine. . . . Teach it backwards and you'll find the reasons for things and you will go back to beauty invariably."[36]

FIGURE 5. Mission Nuestra Señora de la Purísima Concepción de Acuña, San Antonio, 1755. Ford called it "my favorite building in this hemisphere." Photographed 1936.

His impulse to resist usual chronologies or attempts to classify San Antonio's buildings manifested, on a larger scale, in his capacious reading and unorthodox periodization of Western history. He declared in 1968,

> I do not agree with anyone . . . that the Renaissance ended way back in the eighteenth century with Sir Christopher Wren. It ended about 1890, I think. The real Renaissance kept right on going one way or another, because the Renaissance and the Industrial Revolution were actually one thing. . . .
>
> After that comes this mechanization thing and this absolutely confusing age of technology, which, I think, we don't quite understand and isn't at all identifiable with the cruder means of the Industrial Revolution of the nineteenth century.[37]

In the midst of the Cold War the possibility that technological development had outpaced the capacity of people to use it meaningfully, and possibly even to control it, ran as an undercurrent in debates in many domains. Coming as governmental and business patrons embraced the cool, detached technophilic vocabulary of the midcentury incarnation of the International Style, as scientists and philosophers discussed the doctrine of "limited war" in the nuclear age, and as the production of cars and appliances made of mass-produced materials underpinned the national economy, Ford's suggestion that architects, along with the rest of society, had to make sense of new technologies without historical precedents to guide them had a potentially unpopular and ominous ring. In responding to Oppenheimer eight years earlier, Ford had critiqued the failure of the United States to use the lessons of modern physics for humanitarian purposes, not just for building nuclear weapons. Before opening his impassioned plea to save the nation's landscapes from sprawl, he suggested that in failing to do so lay a question about whether society had lost its commitment to "the real meaning of America,"[38] by which he meant devotion to unfettered debate about difficult issues.

Worse than a disciplinarily narrow, chronological interpretation of the history of architecture was not studying it at all. Ford sarcastically noted the absence of historical awareness among contemporary architects and what he saw as their eagerness to ascribe newness to very old things:

> Just recently, the arch has been discovered. . . . The arch will soon be given much printed space, and it will be defended in strong philosophical terms as a fine, sound, new thing and a shaping force. . . . Examples will be shown of the Carmel and San José Missions, the Liverpool docks, and Richardson's big stone arches. Brunelleschi and Michelozzo will be given space and humble credit. Most important will be the gushy praise for the men or preferably the man who showed the courage, etc., etc. Precisely so have some architects discovered the Doge's Palace and Lincoln Logs.[39]

Ford's cynicism about his colleagues' and architectural journals' limited view of their profession's history paralleled his frustration with their unimaginative replication of forms that appeared first in truly innovative works by architects including Le Corbusier, Ludwig Mies van der Rohe, and Louis Kahn.

As the 1960s wore on, a dynamism even greater than the one that characterized Ford's understanding of architectural history defined his conception of the relationship between people and nature. He suggested that cypress trees might be explained as column-like sculptures so that students might "better understand the earth as sculpture." He evoked the lawn at the University of Virginia, "this wonderful thing that Mr. Jefferson did that hardly any architects have ever been able to do since."[40] His evocative image of an adult talking to a child about history proposed a nontraditional kind of learning that was, like his buildings, both raw and highly refined:

"If you pick up a board or see a board on the steps in your home and you look at the grain, you might say, 'Let's start here with the sinking of the *Maine*,' or, 'Let's start here with the beginning of the First World War and let's count back.' Those grains are very close together in the dry season. They were all grown slowly above six or eight thousand feet. And they get farther apart and that's where Lincoln was assassinated. This very board was alive. Here is the day George Washington died, and at this time, Thomas Jefferson presented his paper, the Declaration of Independence. It's all in the board, it's in my house, it's in San Antonio. The whole thing." What does this do to the child? It gives him another dimension in orientation, in history, in land, in lumber, in wood, and the respect for what that is, a piece of dirt, a piece of wood, growing out of the earth.[41]

Ford thought about history chiefly in four ways: as the thing that gives character and meaning to cities and towns and therefore makes them worthy of preservation; as a source of inspiration for new buildings, like the Murchison Tower; as something to be explored, bent, and played with intellectually, as one might with clay or concrete; and as a thing fundamentally entwined with the social order and with nature. The agility and open-mindedness with which he read, interpreted, and used architectural history also characterized his attitude toward design problems. Ultimately, Ford's holistic, long view of the past shaped his conception of architectural modernism.

FORDIAN MODERNISM

Rooted in his close study of the history of architecture, his engagement with multiple strands of international modernism, and his perpetual fascination with finding commonalities in buildings across time and space, Ford's architecture was driven not by an ambition to create a "regional" modernism but by a desire to shape buildings that, by their reliance upon principles he regarded as timeless, would belong to a vast, far-reaching architectural history. Perhaps because he was unencumbered by much academic training in architecture, Ford assimilated disparate ideas and understood the task of shaping a modern idiom with an unusual intellectual flexibility. As a very young architect, he absorbed the exhilarating, heady energy of early twentieth-century architectural theory, but he also recognized the diversity of built work in that period. In the 1960s, having honed the perceptive and discriminative powers that marked his early writings, Ford reached further across disciplinary, social, and professional boundaries to shape a vision of architecture characterized simultaneously by the visionary, aspirational qualities of early modernism and by a deep engagement with the urgent social and political questions of the postwar period.

In 1932, at the age of twenty-seven, Ford published the text in which he offered one of his clearest statements on the principles of modern architecture. He wrote the essay shortly after he left Williams's office and used it to politely but decisively distance himself from his mentor. His "Organic Building" constituted the second section of the article "Toward a New Architecture," published in *Southwest Review*. The first section of the article, "What Is Modernism?," was written by Thomas D. Broad, a Dallas architect and major figure in the Dallas arts scene, in which Ford and Williams were also key players. By borrowing the main title of their essay from the English translation of the title of Le Corbusier's most important text, Ford and Broad signaled their theoretical position in an evolving debate about architecture worldwide.

Broad's title suggested that the readers of *Southwest Review* might not have known exactly what "modernism" in architecture was. And indeed they likely did not, as no agreement on what constituted modern architecture existed. Ford and Broad would have known well the debates about it from reading national architectural journals. In 1928 Henry-Russell Hitchcock published two articles in *Architectural Record* in which he classified the architects of major postwar buildings in Europe and the United States as either "new traditionalists" or "new pioneers."[42] As Hitchcock argued, and as the streets of US cities made clear, even as architects rejected Victorian decoration and the high historicism of the nineteenth century, "tradition," particularly in the form of modern classicism, was still alive and well. It remained to be seen, said Hitchcock, whether "pioneers" such as Le Corbusier, J. J. P. Oud, and Walter Gropius would in fact prove pioneering or ultimately be inconsequential. Four years later, Hitchcock and his colleagues at the Museum of Modern Art answered that question when they enshrined them as the foremost protagonists of twentieth-century architecture in the famous *Modern Architecture: International Exhibition.*[43]

Together, Broad and Ford demonstrated a thorough understanding of the questions central to the evolving definition of "modern" architecture. Broad took a long view and, arguing against historicism, said that architects should not imitate the past but should "emulate" the "methods of logically solving the problem at hand with the best means available." Stressing the importance of adaptation and change in response to new needs, he wrote that "the history of architecture presents a continuous evolution of form in response to the demands of function."[44] With this statement he evoked decades of European architectural theory and Sullivan's famous articulation of the principle of form as emerging from structure and program. Broad's sentence established the meaning with which we should regard Ford's use of the term "functionalist" in his section of the essay. The authors' "functionalism" was not the kind in which architecture was reduced to "building," as Bauhaus director Hannes Meyer had proposed in 1928.[45] Broad argued instead that buildings should be typologically distinctive and, notably, that they should be "sympathetically" related to "local traditions" and responsive to climate. Anticipating the theoretical debates about "local" and "universal" forms that would animate architectural discussions in many places around 1950, he noted that "local traditions are gradually becoming less and less local, but they will probably always exist because climates and the physical aspects of different localities will always be different."[46]

Ford, for his part, began his contribution to the essay by remarking on "the present rather amorphous status of American architecture" and introduced the theme that would drive his work for the rest of his life. The chief cause of this "amorphousness," he argued, was not tired pedagogies, clients' bad taste, or incorrect understandings of history, but an "inherit[ance] from the frontier [of] an unconsciously hostile attitude toward our environment, toward the land, which makes it difficult for us to build in harmony with the landscape."[47] With a few sentences Ford aligned himself, as his title indicated he would, with Frank Lloyd Wright and set out an approach to architecture that understood building, landscape, and society as intimately connected.[48] As he would repeatedly throughout his career, he condemned those who would destroy the landscape. Like architects in many places, Ford responded to the dramatic changes that fueled urbanization, and he did so not nostalgically but with a nascent environmentalism tinged with Marxism:

> There is frequently in our architecture a hint of a will-to-power, an assertion at all costs of the individual ego, which is possibly connected with the individualism of the Industrial Revolution. And then there is that curious American humility which leads us to imitate European styles in every branch of art.[49]

In the passage from a frontier society to an urban one, Ford saw the formation of a national character that served well the conquering ambitions of Anglo-Americans as they moved across the continent but that had dire consequences for the earth. Even as he repeated his admiration for the material and structural integrity of the "pioneer" houses he had catalogued with

Williams, Ford dramatically recast their builders as the rapacious ancestors of those who were now building cities. He condemned their treatment of the "untouched woods of East Texas, lush and generous," which they "clear[ed] and burn[ed]," and castigated them for seeing "the rich and boundless prairies [as] land to be broken, farmed carelessly, and allowed to lose its topsoil, which ran into the rivers so that now we think of spending millions to make the clogged streams navigable." Ford's blistering critique of westward expansion by Anglos was unparalleled in US architecture and, insofar as it risked alienating prospective clients and colleagues, represented the first great gamble he made in print. As a new kind of environmental destruction unfolded in Texas with the rise of the oil industry, Ford declared that the pioneer "did not care how he treated the earth; for by the time his own exploitation could impoverish one region he could have escaped to a virgin area." He observed that "the obliteration of the land along the frontier was a waste comparable to the casual and needless slaughter of the bison" and argued that "this same spirit of the pioneer has gone into the making of our cities, and has become merged with the influence of the Industrial Revolution." Elsewhere in the essay he decried consumerism, ornament, sprawl, "imitation" of all kinds, and "our falsely romantic attitude toward skyline and countryside," all of which, he said, stood in the way of creating an architecture that was "clean and sensible."[50]

Ford's organicism was organicism in the tradition of Sullivan and Wright. It was a firm conviction that buildings should be suited to and expressive of their programs, users, materials, structure, and site.[51] Like Sullivan, he understood architecture as "evolutionary"—coming from and being of the problem at hand.[52] And like Wright, he came to see the relationship between a building and the landscape as paramount. At least as early as 1901 Wright began explaining his concept of "organic" architecture, which he related directly to the "simplicity" he admired in William Morris's art. Wright contended that a "work may have the delicacies of a rare orchid or the staunch fortitude of the oak, and still be simple. A thing to be simple needs only to be true to itself in the organic sense."[53] Wright continued to explain his vision and his conviction that the principles of architecture could be discovered by studying nature in writings throughout his life, including in the series of articles "In the Cause of Architecture," which he published in *Architectural Record* in 1927 and 1928 and which Ford probably read. In "Organic Building," Ford, in an unmistakable evocation of Wright's houses, longed that, in place of jagged rooflines, "the serene and static restfulness of our own horizontal landscape would dignify our rows of houses."[54] At the time of his death, Ford owned four books of Wright's writings, more than any other architect's. By aligning himself with two of the greatest architects the country had yet produced, Ford firmly staked out a position apart from Williams and the regionalist school of painting coalescing in Dallas.

Ford linked Wrightian modernism with what was then being christened the "International Style" in his praise of "functionalist" architects, who, he said, despite their "rather forbidding name," believed simply in "common sense."[55] This connection suggests either that he understood Wright's considerable influence on European avant-garde modernists, which Hitchcock had noted, or that he recognized the fundamental congruency in their aims. Either way, it distinguished him from the architects and critics who tended to view "functionalism" and "organicism" as oppositional.[56] Ford said functionalist buildings were organic rather than "arranged" and were designed by architects who "eliminate[d] extraneous forms" and "analyze[d] biologically." Although it was not widely popular, he said, he admired in functionalist architecture its attention to purpose, careful planning, and human need, as well as its architects' ambition to "help the entire community to become an organism."[57] These qualities characterized his best works many years later, particularly his campuses and the buildings he designed for Texas Instruments.

The germs of other long-standing interests appeared in "Organic Building" as well. Ford's discussion of skyscraper design made clear that he was already thinking about windows and how to manage sunlight, a persistent preoccupation in his work. As if anticipating his lift-slab buildings and collaborations with Candela, Ford wrote of his interest in innovative uses of concrete. Rhapsodizing about Eugène Freyssinet's hangars at Orly, France, which he thought were "superb," he called the parabolic arch the "perfect symbol of structure, the line that has its ends in infinity, a static, moving, and beautiful curve"[58] (figure 8). The form would later define two of Ford's greatest buildings—the Little Chapel in the Woods and the Margarite B. Parker Chapel (figure 19).

Just as Ford's vision of modernism in the early 1930s bridged Wrightian organicism and European avant-garde functionalism, his written and built work in the 1950s and 1960s crossed the boundaries established by champions of the International Style as the "true" modernism and by those who argued for a "regional" or "sensitive" modernism. These two camps were embodied on the one side by curators at the Museum of Modern Art and on the other by Lewis Mumford. In a 1947 essay in the *New Yorker*, Mumford attacked Hitchcock and his museum colleagues for "glorify[ing] . . . the mechanical and the impersonal and aesthetically puritanic" and argued for a "native and humane form of modernism" typified by the works of Bernard Maybeck and William Wurster, which he termed the "Bay Region Style."[59] In response, MoMA organized the symposium *What Is Happening to Modern Architecture?*, during which International Style partisans dismantled Mumford's case.[60] Although Ford's deep admiration for Wurster, about which he spoke in his commencement address at Trinity in 1967, and the importance he placed on site-sensitive design would seem to place him squarely on the western side of this coastal clash for cultural supremacy, his position was not as strictly delineated as the MoMA-Mumford argument.[61]

In the early 1950s Ford was known for his technical expertise, not his earthiness, even though he often relied heavily on the expertise of others, notably Richard Colley and Félix Candela, when designing complex structures. He was introduced to a group of architects, engineers, and contractors in London in 1951 as having "wide experience" using the lift-slab method, which he described in his highly technical address to them as a "a sound, logical, simple idea."[62] Three years later, along with George Howe, he spoke on a panel addressing the impacts of scientific and technological change on architectural education at the annual meeting of the Association of Collegiate Schools of Architecture (ACSA). Ford discussed technical matters at length, but he also emphasized the imaginative aspect of the design process. In an echo of Le Corbusier's claims in *Towards a New Architecture*, Ford stringently differentiated architecture and engineering but spoke admiringly of those few engineers—he named Frederick Severud and Pier Luigi Nervi—whom he considered "great artists."[63]

The proper relationship between humanism and science, and between intuitive and quantitative ways of understanding the world, concerned people in many professions at mid-century, but Ford's thoughtfulness about these matters was somewhat unusual in architecture, as conference convener Walter Bogner, then a professor at the Graduate School of Design at Harvard, made clear. Bogner opened the ACSA panel discussion by saying, "It seems that there was something very unscientific brought out this morning that there is needed something very human, particularly in O'Neil Ford's talk."[64] Ford's combination of humanism and technological experimentation attracted several of his major clients. While a marriage of the arts and sciences appealed to educational institutions for obvious reasons, it also appealed to the leaders of Texas Instruments, particularly Patrick E. Haggerty and J. Erik Jonsson, who shaped the design of the company's buildings and the company itself as models of benevolent capitalism in which corporate hierarchy was de-emphasized.[65] Even as cutting-edge engineering concepts informed the designs of adjustable spaces in the Semiconductor Components Division Building for the rapidly changing needs of technological invention, its humanely scaled courtyards landscaped by Arthur Berger and Marie Berger provided reposeful places for employees. The building included numerous works of art and fine craftsmanship by Texas artists (figure 20).

Ford is well known today for his collaborations with artists, but he wrote and spoke publicly about them very little. He was quite explicit, however, about his interest in sculpture and his belief that architects should understand materials profoundly and should have intense visual and tactile knowledge of the physical world. For him these things were intimately connected to his essential belief in integrity in the broadest sense and in architecture's fundamental connectedness to the land. One of his last significant speaking or writing projects was a television program organized to teach children about architecture, *Lessons in Looking*, which was published as a book. In it he discussed sculpture, buildings of the distant and recent past, the principles of tension and compression, and materials, including stone, metal, and glass. He told the children that "learning to look means educating your eyes and your hands."[66] In its emphasis on materials and in the wide range of comparative examples included, the volume closely resembles the compilation of Wright's writings on materials by Iovanna Lloyd Wright and Patricia Coyle Nicholson published in 1962 as *Architecture: Man in Possession of His Earth*, which Ford owned. Although Ford described the architect of the Guggenheim Museum simply as "a man who hates paintings,"[67] the parallels between the two volumes, published just after and just before the two architects' deaths, suggest Wright's enduring influence on him.

Ford's comments on other twentieth-century architects and buildings also help situate his approach to modernism in a wider field. His most scathing criticisms were of those presumably numerous but unnamed architects who mindlessly embraced fads or approached their profession primarily in terms of profit. More specific attacks included those on Walter Gropius's Pan Am Building, which "ruin[ed] a street," and the alternating pattern of vertically and horizontally oriented windows of Eero Saarinen's Hill College House, a women's dormitory at the University of Pennsylvania, "where the girls who stand up and sleep have rooms, and the girls who lie down and sleep have rooms."[68] Ford's admiration for Alvar Aalto has been widely noted, but his deep respect for Louis Kahn and Le Corbusier is less well known.[69] Of Kahn he said in 1964, "In his rich language, broad awareness, and personal capacity great things dwell."[70] And, having shared the stage with Kahn at the *Sculpture and Environment Symposium* at the University of Texas at Austin in 1966 and with Kahn's Indian Institute of Management (figure 15), then under construction, in mind, he said,

> I would like to ask Mr. Kahn to tell me . . . of his new building in India, the big brick buildings which are to me something very important in architecture at this time; they are the first really inspiring thing I have seen in several years. They don't seem to fit into any tight hierarchy or anybody's tight philosophy of what architecture is.[71]

Of Le Corbusier's Notre Dame du Haut in Ronchamp, France (figure 14), he wrote, "We saw its great strength immediately—brutal and rough and beautifully sited . . . and as we walked in, the synthesis of shape and light and sound froze us still and silent."[72] The architect loved Robert Zion's tiny Paley Park in New York City (figure 17), which he called "one of the most astonishing things I have ever seen." And he had unreserved admiration for Candela: "I doubt that anyone has so beautifully respected the land and made sculpture of the whole composition as Félix Candela did with his little chapel at Cuernavaca" (figure 18).[73] The very different buildings and spaces Ford most admired underscored his catholic appreciation of architecture, and they embodied the values he spoke of again and again—connection to the landscape, structural integrity, well-reasoned risk-taking, and, at its most profound, a capacity to respond to deep human needs and to help sustain communities.

CITIZEN-ARCHITECT

Ford's modernism was inseparable from his social conscience. Although architecture's society-shaping potential has motivated architects for millennia, and was a defining characteristic of twentieth-century architectural modernity in many places, few architects spoke as directly, specifically, and often as Ford did about the political and social issues of their times. Foremost among these for Ford were civil rights and environmental concerns, which he believed were closely entwined. Speaking at all-white Rice University in segregated Houston in 1964 he said,

> All physical ugliness and social ugliness have strong concomitants and roots. Incredibly, there is rampant today all manner of hate and fierce argument on the basic idea—of all things—of civil rights. Today our great privileges are so flaunted and license so condoned that in some of our cities 30 per cent of the citizens live in slums. . . . It seems, therefore, not a crooked analogy to lock hand in hand the bitter disregard for the rights of others with the callous notion that a man may put up anything ugly, vulgar, or trivial he wishes so long as it is "big enough" and he has the money. Can you think how seriously tragic it is that any . . . lawmaker, anywhere, can find a reason or the audacity to speak against the civil rights of any man or group of men?[74]

Speaking thus, even in the relative "safety" of an academic setting, meant putting at least some of the audience on edge and it certainly risked losing clients. Disregard for the landscape, for cities, and for people were one and the same, Ford said again and again.

Coming in the era when Jane Jacobs, Edmund Bacon, Kevin Lynch, and countless others raised their voices and took up their pens to debate and draw the future of cities, Ford's attention to planning and social concern was not unusual. Sullivan and Wright had both talked about architecture in terms of "democracy." Robert Venturi, another architect who loved history and critiqued orthodoxy, brilliantly entwined his calls for a new approach to architecture with allusions to the civil rights movement in several statements in 1966: "I prefer 'both-and' to 'either-or,' black and white, and sometimes gray, to black or white. . . . [Architecture] must embody the difficult unity of inclusion rather than the easy unity of exclusion. More is not less."[75] But Ford was more explicit. His blistering statements about urban sprawl and his connection of capitalism and racism challenged national norms and threatened cherished Texan mythologies about individualism and private property. For twenty-first-century readers they provide a window into aspects of the state's history and character that are sometimes hard to see.

Ford was part of a constellation of prominent and powerful Texans who held similar views. These relationships suggest that, at least in Texas at midcentury, architecture, civil rights, and environmentalism in the form of land conservation were closely connected. One of Ford's major clients was J. Erik Jonsson. As president and later chair of the board of Texas Instruments, Jonsson worked closely with Ford to shape the company's new buildings in the 1950s; several years later, as Skidmore College's largest donor to date, Jonsson pushed for Ford's hiring there. Jonsson was elected mayor of Dallas in 1964 and governed during one of the most difficult periods in its history. He proposed far-reaching new plans and helped the city navigate the racial tensions of the decade. Referring to images of the city's skyline in 1918 and 1968, Jonsson asked the Salesmanship Club of Dallas in May 1968, "What will Dallas' skyline be like in another half century? More important, what will be inside those big buildings that compose its skyline? Will its people be of the same competence, responsibility, and good will, and desire to build a better place for themselves and their fellows?"[76]

Arguing, as Ford had, that "the revolution of technology has been far too rapid for us to grasp,"[77] Jonsson spoke about the racial and social implications of the accelerated urbanization that new technologies had stimulated, as African American agricultural workers moved to cities. Certain that race relations would improve as a result of direct, individual contact, Jonsson told his audience of white businessmen,

> I want each of us to talk to someone he never saw before and find out how it is with him—what his problems are. The hand we shake may be greasy, sweaty, grimy, and long unwashed. There may be several reasons for that. . . . It may simply be that water to him is too expensive and not readily available for washing. Did you know that there are a lot of people in this city . . . whose homes have no running water? . . . Would you? Have you? Do you know what I am talking about? Or are you a militant on the other side? Don't be.[78]

With his description of the conditions in which some Dallasites lived, the mayor's questions give some idea of just how big the gulf was that he and civil rights leaders sought to bridge. As Mayor Jonsson urged residents to integrate the city one by one, President Johnson pressed members of Congress to pass the laws that would protect the rights of all citizens. Also on the president's domestic agenda were legislative and executive directives to conserve and improve the environment.

At the White House, the most powerful voice championing the vision of the harmonious integration of landscape, architecture, and society that Ford called for was Lady Bird Johnson's. Johnson explained her definition of "beautification" in a speech at the annual convention of the American Institute of Architects (AIA) in 1968, noting that it meant much more than "landscaping" and planting wildflowers. Practically evoking Vitruvius, she said beautification was "the whole effort to bring the natural world and the manmade world into harmony; to bring order, usefulness, and delight to our whole environment." Johnson spoke admiringly of Native American understandings of the land, saying that the first Americans "were users and sharers of their environment—not exploiters of it." She decried the "sacrifice of human values to commercial values" and said that "a preponderance of concrete and asphalt—of fumes, haze and screeches—go against our grain in a cultural way, as well as in a biological way." Johnson went on to outline the principles of the "New Conservation," which included banning signage, limiting vehicles in city centers, preserving historic structures, and building on a human scale to create places where "people's imagination and variety of choice can flourish." Like Ford, she spoke admiringly of the San Antonio River and Paley Park, lamented the "ugly, ragged city fringes," and asked, "How many shopping centers are monuments to our lack of imagination—to our indifference?"[79] In 1964 Ford had applauded the AIA's efforts to resist "this new urge to rip apart our cities" and called on his colleagues to "join in the desperate fight to save our land from the reckless, the willful, the selfish, the unimaginative, and the just plain ignorant vulgarians."[80] And as Ford did repeatedly, Johnson called on architects to "become thoughtful political activists" and to make architecture "a form of public service."[81]

In the Texas of Lady Bird Johnson, Erik Jonsson, and O'Neil Ford, modern architecture was a potent force for good. Realizing that potential, they all recognized, required the courage to take risks and to swim against the tide. Ford praised this quality in his most important client, Trinity University, whose

FIGURE 6. O'Neil Ford, William Wurster, Bartlett Cocke, et al.; Arthur Berger and Marie Berger, landscape architects, Trinity University, San Antonio. The Student Union, one of the first lift-slab buildings, is in middle ground to the right. Murchison Tower stands in the distance. Photographed c. 1967.

"spirit of positive, progressive protest—with its strong admixture of common sense and devotion, of generosity and courage" he admired deeply. One year before Trinity hired Earl Lewis, its first African American professor, who launched the university's widely admired program in urban studies, Ford told the graduates of the class of 1967 about the "sea of cactus and exposed rock outcroppings"[82] into which the first lift-slab buildings of the university were set and let them know that in his years working there he had seen

> happenings which . . . have made this university a place of freedom. For as the physical campus grew . . . there was an accompanying growth here of a spirit of enlightenment and respect for man. . . . Believe me when I tell you that there have been numerous incidents of defense

of the unorthodox and in support of the man and the idea. These are events that have truly shaped the style and character of this university of positive protest. . . .

The Trinity Treatment of things . . . that makes this a place for the different and differing drummer touches the intellectual and the builder alike. Thus the freedom to be different and have different thoughts extends to planning and building differently.[83]

At Trinity, "positive protest" and the freedom to be different were undergirded, Ford felt, by the client's basic sense of humility, the characteristic that Leeper had admired in Ford's work. Implicitly praising the Trinity board and administration, near the end of his address Ford summarized the values at the heart of his architecture:

Never have I been asked to do one single thing that was not honest as structure, as decoration, or in any way contrary to integrity of purpose.

Here I have never been told I must seek to make a building impressive or sumptuous or imposing—or one that would awe or evoke critical praise.

As an architect and builder, I could ask for no greater gift.[84]

At stake in this collection is the idea that O'Neil Ford was not merely a great regional architect and a typically outrageous, untutored Texan but an important modern architect and a deep, careful, well-read thinker. His words help us understand him as a participant in a broad midcentury humanism that retrospectively appears as the last great expression of the heroic intellectual project of twentieth-century modernity, with its emancipatory and universalizing aspirations. Speaking and writing at the dawn of what would later be christened postmodernism, Ford seemed at moments to anticipate later critiques, such as when he wrote in 1932 that "the modernism which began by stripping away columns and cupolas has developed its own mannerisms."[85] But he belonged, ultimately, to the older generation. While younger architects, including Charles Moore, Robert Venturi, and Denise Scott Brown, would also draw attention to the dramatic changes to landscapes and society under way at midcentury, Ford, unlike them, did not convert his insights into ready fodder for academic debates and theory-driven designs. The language of O'Neil Ford was perhaps too straightforward, too angry, and too hopeful for such things. It's time to hear it again.

NOTES

1. John Palmer Leeper, introduction to *O'Neil Ford, Architect*, exhib. cat. (San Antonio: McNay Art Institute; Press of Ozzie Baum, 1965), n.p.
2. Ralph Tubbs, *An Englishman Builds* (Harmondsworth, UK: Penguin Books, 1945). The full quotation is in O'Neil Ford, "The Condition of Architecture," in *The People's Architects*, ed. Harry S. Ransom (Chicago: University of Chicago Press for William Marsh Rice University, 1964), 50. Speaking at the *Sculpture and Environment Symposium* in Austin in 1966, Ford said, before reading the quotation, that he had "read [it] to almost everyone here, I think a dozen times. . . . I read it at Rensselaer—in Dallas yesterday, and in Troy, New York, the day before." "Mr. O'Neil Ford's Speech at the *Sculpture and Environment Symposium*," box 61, folder 4, O'Neil Ford: An Inventory of His Drawings, Papers, and Photographic Material, 1864–1983, Alexander Architectural Archives, University of Texas Libraries, University of Texas at Austin.
3. New York architect Philip Youtz and Trinity University board member Tom Slick developed the Youtz-Slick lift-slab construction technique that Ford and Bartlett Cocke used at Trinity in the 1950s. In brief, the method involved pouring the slabs of concrete that would divide a building's floors on the ground (separated by a wax coating), then, after they had cured, lifting them into place with hydraulic jacks and welding them to steel columns that had been placed in a concrete foundation. The technique was markedly less expensive than conventional concrete construction methods because of the savings of materials and time needed to make formwork and shoring.
4. Pierluigi Serraino, *The Creative Architect: Inside the Great Midcentury Personality Study* (New York: Monacelli Press, 2016).
5. For example, Alice T. Friedman, *American Glamour and the Evolution of Modern Architecture* (New Haven: Yale University Press, 2010); Elizabeth

A. T. Smith and Peter Gossel, *Case Study Houses* (Cologne: Taschen, 2002).

6. See Vincent B. Canizaro, ed., *Architectural Regionalism: Collected Writings on Place, Identity, Modernity, and Tradition* (New York: Princeton Architectural Press, 2007).

7. Stephen Fox, "Regionalism and Texas Architecture," in Canizaro, *Architectural Regionalism*, 209–210. Writers in the *Southwest Review* debated the nature and character of regionalism generally at least as early as the 1940s and into the 1960s. Margaret L. Hartley, ed., *The Southwest Review Reader* (Dallas: SMU Press, 1974), xii–xiv.

8. Maiken Umbach and Bernd Hüppauf, eds., *Vernacular Modernism: Heimat, Globalization, and the Built Environment* (Stanford, CA: Stanford University Press, 2005); Jean-Francois Lejeune and Michelangelo Sabatino, eds., *Modern Architecture and the Mediterranean: Vernacular Dialogues and Contested Identities* (New York: Routledge, 2010).

9. David G. McComb, "Urbanization," Handbook of Texas Online, http://www.tshaonline.org/handbook/online/articles/hyunw.

10. Mary Carolyn Hollers George, *O'Neil Ford, Architect* (College Station: Texas A&M University Press, 1992), 197.

11. Ford's papers are archived as O'Neil Ford: An Inventory of His Drawings, Papers, and Photographic Material, 1864–1983, Alexander Architectural Archives, University of Texas Libraries, University of Texas at Austin.

12. George, *O'Neil Ford*; David Dillon, *The Architecture of O'Neil Ford: Celebrating Place* (Austin: University of Texas Press, 1999).

13. Among the architects from younger generations who were shaped by Ford are Frank Welch, Larry Speck, David Lake, and Ted Flato. On Welch, see his *On Becoming an Architect* (Fort Worth: TCU Press, 2014), 79–85; on Speck's view of Ford, see his "O'Neil Ford's 'Caring Campus,'" *Architecture: The AIA Journal* 72.9 (1983): 58–61; on Lake and Flato, see Kriston Capps, "Lake|Flato Architects," *Architect: The Journal of the American Institute of Architects* (Aug. 10, 2011): http://www.architectmagazine.com/design/firm-profile/lake-flato-architects_o.

14. Allene Talmey, "Power in Texas: 22 Who Help Run the Place," *Vogue*, Jan. 1953, 140–144.

15. Ford, "Condition of Architecture," 46, 49, 48.

16. Ford, "Condition of Architecture," 42.

17. O'Neil Ford, "Imagineering," *Journal of Architectural Education* 10.1 (Spring 1955): 22.

18. Ford, "Condition of Architecture," 45.

19. O'Neil Ford, Burnham Kelly, and George F. Keck, "Panel Discussion," *AIA Journal* 33.6 (June 1960): 70.

20. Michael Ford to Michael Guarino, email message, March 17, 2017, shared with the author by Guarino with permission from Ford.

42 Introduction

21. Quoted in George, *O'Neil Ford*, 141. Presumably he meant Robert Adam and James Adam, *The Works in Architecture of Robert and James Adam* (London: Aux dépens des auteurs, 1778).

22. Quoted in George, *O'Neil Ford*, 141.

23. Ford, "Condition of Architecture," 46.

24. Ford, "Condition of Architecture," 46.

25. Josephine Young Case, *Skidmore: The New Campus*, brochure (Baltimore: Pridemark, n.d.), 4–5. In file 25, box 100, J. Erik Jonsson Papers, DeGolyer Library, Southern Methodist University.

26. O'Neil Ford, "The End of a Beginning," in *A Trilogy 1967* (San Antonio: Trinity University, 1967), 21.

27. David R. Williams and O'Neil Ford, "Architecture of Early Texas," pt. 2, *Southwestern Architect* 1.6 (Dec. 1927): 5–8.

28. O'Neil Ford, foreword to *David R. Williams, Pioneer Architect*, by Muriel Quest McCarthy (Dallas: Southern Methodist University Press, 1984), xi.

29. David R. Williams, "An Indigenous Architecture: Some Texas Colonial Houses," *Southwest Review* 14.1 (1928): 60–74.

30. Fox, "Regionalism and Texas Architecture," 209.

31. On the journal, see Hartley, *Southwest Review Reader*.

32. "North and West of San Antonio," box 80, folder 12, and "Early Draft of Speech Prepared by O'Neil Ford," box 81, folder 01002, O'Neil Ford: An Inventory of His Drawings, Papers, and Photographic Material, 1864–1983, Alexander Architectural Archives, University of Texas Libraries, University of Texas at Austin.

33. O'Neil Ford, "Texas Idyll," *Inland Architect* 26 (Sept.–Dec. 1982), 34–35.

34. O'Neil Ford, "History and Development of the Spanish Missions in San Antonio," *Stained Glass* 60.4 (1965–1966): 39.

35. O'Neil Ford, "Culture—Who Needs It?," 1968, box 81, folder 01001, O'Neil Ford: An Inventory of His Drawings, Papers, and Photographic Material, 1864–1983, Alexander Architectural Archives, University of Texas Libraries, University of Texas at Austin, 17.

36. Ford, "Culture," 4–5.

37. Ford, "Culture," 10.

38. Ford, Kelly, and Keck, "Panel Discussion," 71.

39. Ford, "Condition of Architecture," 39–40.

40. Ford, "Culture," 18.

41. Ford, "Culture," 4.

42. Henry Russell Hitchcock, "The Traditionalists and the New Traditionalists," *Architectural Record* 4 (Apr. 1928): 337–349; Henry-Russell Hitchcock, "The New Pioneers," *Architectural Record* 5 (May 1928): 453–457. Shortly after these essays appeared, Hitchcock further developed his arguments in *Modern Architecture: Romanticism and Reintegration* (New York: Payson

and Clarke, 1929; reprint, New York: Hacker Art Books, 1970).

43. Philip Johnson, Alfred H. Barr, and Henry-Russell Hitchcock, *Modern Architecture: International Exhibition*, exhib. cat. (New York: Museum of Modern Art, 1932). Even as scholars have reframed the avant-garde buildings of 1920s and 1930s Europe through new research grounded in widening perspectives of architectural modernism, this architecture retains a certain centrality in many narratives of twentieth-century architectural history. Barry Bergdoll and Leah Dickerman, *Bauhaus 1919–1933: Workshops for Modernity* (New York: Museum of Modern Art, 2009); Mardges Bacon, Barry Bergdoll, Jean-Louis Cohen, et al., *Le Corbusier: An Atlas of Modern Landscapes* (New York: Museum of Modern Art, 2013).

44. Thomas D. Broad and O'Neil Ford, "Toward a New Architecture," *Southwest Review* 17.2 (Winter 1932): 210. On the history of organicism in architectural theory, see Harry Francis Mallgrave, ed., *Modern Architectural Theory: A Historical Survey, 1673–1968* (New York: Cambridge University Press, 2005).

45. Hannes Meyer, "Building" (1928), reprinted in Ulrich Conrads, ed., *Programs and Manifestoes on 20th-Century Architecture* (Cambridge, MA: MIT Press, 1975), 117–120.

46. Broad and Ford, "Toward a New Architecture," 214.

47. Broad and Ford, "Toward a New Architecture," 215.

48. On Wright, see Neil Levine, *The Architecture of Frank Lloyd Wright* (Princeton: Princeton University Press, 1996); David G. DeLong and Anne Whiston Spirn, *Frank Lloyd Wright: Designs for an American Landscape, 1922–1932* (New York: Harry N. Abrams, 1996); and Barry Bergdoll and Jennifer Gray, eds., *Frank Lloyd Wright: Unpacking the Archive* (New York: Museum of Modern Art, 2017).

49. Broad and Ford, "Toward a New Architecture," 215–216.

50. Broad and Ford, "Toward a New Architecture," 216, 215, 217.

51. In their attention to site, Ford's ideas had some similarities with those of Wright protégé Richard Neutra, whose writings were ultimately more concerned with buildings' psychological and emotional effects on viewers than Ford's were. For example, see Neutra, *Mystery and Realities of the Site* (Scarsdale, NY: Morgan & Morgan, 1951).

52. Broad and Ford, "Toward a New Architecture," 219.

53. Frank Lloyd Wright, "The Art and Craft of the Machine" (1901), in *The Essential Frank Lloyd Wright: Critical Writings on Architecture*, ed. Bruce Brooks Pfeiffer (Princeton: Princeton University Press, 2008), 28.

54. Broad and Ford, "Toward a New Architecture," 228.

55. Broad and Ford, "Toward a New Architecture," 219.

56. Ludwig Mies van der Rohe's integration of technology and its image with

a theory of architectural organicism is perhaps the most significant example of the merging of these domains in twentieth-century architecture. Detlef Mertins, *Mies* (London: Phaidon, 2014); see especially 232–279.

57. Broad and Ford, "Toward a New Architecture," 219.
58. Broad and Ford, "Toward a New Architecture," 226. Le Corbusier also admired the hangars and published a photograph of them under construction in *Towards a New Architecture*.
59. Lewis Mumford, "The Sky Line: Status Quo ('Bay Region Style')," *New Yorker*, Oct. 11, 1947, 104–110.
60. Stanford Anderson, "The 'New Empiricism–Bay Region Axis': Kay Fisker and Postwar Debates on Functionalism, Regionalism, and Monumentality," *Journal of Architectural Education* 50.3 (Feb. 1997): 197–207.
61. On California modernism, see Robert Winter, ed., *Toward a Simpler Way of Life: The Arts & Crafts Architects of California* (Berkeley: University of California Press, 1997).
62. O'Neil Ford, "O'Neil Ford Lectures on Slab Lifting," *Architects' Journal* 113 (July 12, 1951): 51.
63. Ford, "Imagineering," 22.
64. "Discussion from the Floor," *Journal of Architectural Education* 10:1 (Spring 1955): 27.
65. Caleb Pirtle, *Engineering the World: Stories from the First 75 Years of Texas Instruments* (Dallas: Southern Methodist University Press, 2005).
66. O'Neil Ford, *Lessons in Looking: Dialogues with O'Neil Ford, Architect* (San Antonio: Learning About Learning Educational Foundation, 1981), 11.
67. Ford, "Culture," 14.
68. Ford, "Culture," 13–14.
69. Like Ford, Kahn particularly admired the Cathedral at Albi, which he visited in 1959. The architects' mutual fascination with the building is noteworthy in part because of Ford's admiration for Kahn. Further research on their reception of Albi may illuminate the formal and intellectual similarities between the architects' works. On Kahn and Albi, see Eugene J. Johnson, "A Drawing of the Cathedral of Albi by Louis I. Kahn," *Gesta* 25:1 (1986): 159–165.
70. Ford, "Condition of Architecture," 42. On Kahn, see David B. Brownlee and David G. DeLong, *Louis I. Kahn: In the Realm of Architecture* (Los Angeles: Museum of Contemporary Art; Philadelphia: Philadelphia Museum of Art, 1991); and Mateo Kries, Jochen Eisenbrand, and Stanislaus von Moos, eds., *Louis Kahn: The Power of Architecture* (Weil am Rhein, Germany: Vitra Design Museum, 2013).
71. Ford, "Mr. O'Neil Ford's Speech," 32–33.
72. Ford, diary entry, March 1961, quoted in George, *O'Neil Ford*, 153.
73. Ford, "Culture," 12, 18. On Candela, see Maria E. Moreyra Garlock and

David P. Billington, *Félix Candela: Engineer, Builder, Structural Artist* (Princeton, NJ: Princeton University Art Museum; New Haven, CT: Yale University Press, 2008).

74. Ford, "Condition of Architecture," 32–33.
75. Robert Venturi, *Complexity and Contradiction in Architecture* 2nd ed. (New York: Museum of Modern Art, 1998), 16.
76. Erik Jonsson, "Address by Mayor Erik Jonsson, Salesmanship Club of Dallas, May 1, 1968," file 25, box 100, J. Erik Jonsson Papers, DeGolyer Library, Southern Methodist University, 1.
77. Jonsson, "Address by Mayor Erik Jonsson," 7.
78. Jonsson, "Address by Mayor Erik Jonsson," 11.
79. Lady Bird Johnson, "The Vital Balance . . . Nature . . . Architecture . . . and Man" (1968 B. Y. Morrison Memorial Lecture) (Washington, DC: US Department of Agriculture, 1968), n.p.
80. Ford, "Condition of Architecture," 49.
81. Johnson, "Vital Balance," n.p.
82. Ford, "End of a Beginning," 24, 26.
83. Ford, "End of a Beginning," 26–27.
84. Ford, "End of a Beginning," 32.
85. Broad and Ford, "Toward a New Architecture," 222.

The Making of a Modern Architect

Architecture of Early Texas

PART 1
With David R. Williams

After their travels together to small Texas towns in the mid-1920s, David R. Williams and O'Neil Ford coauthored three brief essays, each with the same title, on the vernacular buildings they saw and on the history of Anglo settlement in the state. The articles appeared in three issues of the short-lived journal Southwestern Architect. *They include photographs by Williams and Ford, and some parts of the text bear similarities to Williams's article "An Indigenous Architecture: Some Texas Colonial Houses," which appeared in* Southwest Review *in 1928 and included drawings by Ford.*

To tell our native folk that their forebears have left for them a native architecture as beautiful in its purpose as anything that has been built on this earth is a very difficult thing.

To tell this same thing to a Frenchman or to a Spaniard who might know something of our early Texas history and something more of the antecedents of the peoples who built up our first colonies would be much easier. Spaniards, Frenchmen, Germans, Englishmen, and finally Gentlemen from the old South, fighting for the same things, building to suit their needs and to satisfy the exactions of conditions and climate and of the natural materials close at hand, created kindred indigenous things, naturally beautiful and vibrant with new, fresh life, until

---

Originally published in *Southwestern Architect* 1.4 (October 1927): 5–7.

we cannot say that this or that is Spanish or French or English in origin, but that it is native Texan with uncertain but honorable ancestry. The influence of the French, Spaniards, and Germans, along with the marked stamp of New Orleans and the architecture of the Southern States, is easily traceable—but the thing as herein most worthy, it is in no instance copied or "styled," but is beautifully and honestly adapted to the limitations that a pioneer country set upon its builders.

It is refreshing, in marked contrast to present-day buildings which are produced by transportation facilities that permit the easy moving of any material from any place, to see houses that are born of the stones and clay and trees that their respective localities produce; and one is moved to nothing less than joy to see these materials used in an honest structural way. Herein lies the beauty of the homes of Colonial Texas.

Present-day tendencies to draw upon Europe and Africa and Asia as sources of inspiration (and this is putting the thing most diplomatically, for many are blandly copied) is a deplorable practice and entirely without justification, since at home we have a native-born precedent naturally suited to our climate, manner of living, and landscape. New England is hardly so fortunate, in the very strict sense, in its heritage of good houses as is Texas; for prototypes of the buildings in our Eastern States are surprisingly abundant in England. This is, of course, hardly applicable to the very early houses of the New England settlements, for they, like the houses of the first Texans, were charming because of their naïveté and the near impossibility of translating an architecture of stone and brick into wood. Please think that we are in no wise being more than mildly critical of our Colonial architecture, for most of it is lovely and "at home" in our country; but rather are we criticizing the practice of building "things" that are as foreign to our soil and seem almost as restless here as would a Chinese pagoda. A few modifications of the European precedents are admirably done, but it is impossible for something that is not natural to a country to be as beautiful as something that was born in that country.

The first houses in Texas, aside from the Indian pueblos and crude stick and mud houses, date back to as early as 1698. The most of these were built very near the Rio Grande River and near San Antonio by the Spanish *gobernadores*, and are prone to follow more closely the traditions of the mother country (as was the case in nearly all Spanish colonies) than are any of the later settlements. Very little is known of their origin, and excepting four or five extant examples they have little other than an historical existence to offer.

The dependencies of the missions, which must have been very interesting, have long since disappeared without any definite knowledge of their exact form. The mission chapels or churches which now remain are not excelled for their beauty or form, detail, and handling of materials; but even these cannot be seriously considered as precedent for homes.

Shortly after the beginning of the nineteenth century there was a steadily growing migration to Texas from the States, and a few dissenting liberty seekers and adventurers sought to establish colonies without charters or the consent of the Spanish government and consequently were without protection from the marauding Indians. Only a few subsisted, and their conditions were miserable and life uncertain. They were constantly "at outs" with the Spaniards and never comfortably safe from these people who at first tried to hinder the settlers' advance. However, the Spanish government, growing jealous of the foothold France was fast gaining on the coast and throughout Southeast Texas, gradually became more lenient and finally began honoring the petitions by individuals to set up colonies of people who wished to make homes in Texas. There was still, however, a constant friction between these people, the culmination of which was the Texas Revolution.

The influx of colonists, after independence was at last a reality, was phenomenal. Broadly speaking, each colony was settled by some one or two distinct nationalities, and difference of construction and planning resulted. It is to be noted that people who had left their native countries seeking a freer existence would not be hampered by the traditional methods of building that they had known. They were whole-heartedly bent upon living as they wished, and set immediately to using, as best they could, and in the simplest and most logical manner, the materials available in their respective localities. The result was natural and becoming to the landscape, as comfortable and friendly as the dirt out of which they had grown—an honest, unadulterated expression of a people and a cause. Houses built by French settlers are in no wise identical or even at first sight akin to the houses which these people had left in France, as is also the case of the Irish, Germans, English, and Spanish settlers, yet each of them had an individuality that is unmistakable. The influence of New Orleans is notable throughout East Texas, particularly houses which drew upon the simpler types such as "Madame John's Legacy" on Royal Street. This type is found in many places where Frenchmen built, including the French Embassy in, and two houses south of, Austin. Another type of house built by Frenchmen and which still retains the delightfully French flavor is to be found in Castroville, which is twenty-five miles southwest of San Antonio. Will you believe that there is not a "bungalow" nor one bit of "gingerbread" in all Castroville? And after more than seventy-five years, a Castroville house is still a good house!

There are many Texas towns that have old houses which far outdo, generally speaking, those now being concocted in good architects' offices. From Waco to Del Rio—the names alone are music—Salado, Austin, New Braunfels, San Antonio, Castroville, Quihi, and Brackettville are an endless wealth of surprises. And there are in East Texas, in Old Independence and hidden in the woods near Houston, hundreds of houses that tell us again and again that we are ungrateful in that we have been glorifying alien things and blindly ignoring that which is— along with a spirit such as only an Austin, a Travis, or a Houston could bequeath upon his state—our greatest possession.

1927

Architecture of Early Texas

PART 2
With David R. Williams

As set forth in the first article of this series, the native architecture of Texas developed to fit the economic, social, and climatic needs of the people in a logical way from unpretentious beginnings, but was subject to strong influences in form and detail from a number of widely separated sources. These influences came chiefly, but indirectly, from France, Spain, and England, and the extent of the manifestation of each influence will be found to follow the order in which they are here named.

The first colonies that were able to hold out against the wilderness and redskins were Spanish, so that the first buildings were, quite naturally, Spanish or Spanish Colonial in plan and detail; and, since Spanish dominion continued and this style of building prevailed for more than a century and a half, it may seem strange that we should place the French influence as more pronounced in later work covering a period of less than half a century and long after France had given up all claim to Texas, but in tracing down the reason for this we unfold an interesting story of the history of the colonization of Texas and bring onto this page the heroic figure of a remarkable man of good education, fine taste, and high courage—Stephen Fuller Austin.

At the end of the eighteenth century it was evident that the attempts of Spain and Mexico to colonize Texas with their own peoples had failed miserably, so that Moses Austin, when he

---

Originally published in *Southwestern Architect* 1.6 (December 1927): 5–9.

came riding into San Antonio de Bexar from Louisiana in 1820 with a colonization plan in his head, found most of the country a wilderness overrun by savages. The existing colonies, at that time, were San Antonio, founded in 1718; Nacogdoches, 1716; La Bahia (later Goliad), founded about 1720; and one at Ysleta, near El Paso, founded in 1682.

But at the time Moses Austin arrived in 1820 these colonies, which fifty years before had peaceful Indians all about, were now reduced to insecurity and subject to raids by hostile natives, and all except San Antonio had a very feeble hold on existence. There had been for more than thirty years more colonists leaving than were entering the country. Now, Louisiana had been settled and built up by the French, and Moses Austin had been a French-speaking subject to Spain during a part of the forty years of Spanish dominion of that country. His son, Stephen, had been reared there. Moses Austin died from the effects of the exposure and hardship to which he was subjected on his return from San Antonio, but left to Stephen the fulfillment of his dream and the Spanish grant for his colony.

We will skip over the extreme difficulties encountered by Austin in realizing the dream of his father, brought about by the Mexican Revolution and subsequent changes in governments. The colonies were founded and established, and the work with which we are herein dealing was begun.

Austin's colonists were chiefly Anglo-Americans, whose forebears had settled under Spanish grants in Louisiana and who had learned something of the French manner of building there, but a more important cause of French influence in Texas architecture was written into the stipulations of the Spanish charter under which the colonists were permitted to settle. The charter insisted that all colonists be sober and industrious, and land was allotted in proportion to these qualifications; but if, added to sobriety and industry, the colonist might be well educated or skilled in the crafts, or an artisan, he would be given still more land in proportion to his ability, so that the premium paid to training and craftsmanship evidently brought into

Texas at an early date, from Louisiana and the South, numbers of skilled carpenters, stonemasons, and wood carvers, which accounts for the delightful refinement and delicacy of details and intelligent proportions that are at first surprising in houses built with hands in a pioneer country. The refined personality of Stephen Fuller Austin was built into these houses.

1928

Architecture of Early Texas

PART 3
With David R. Williams

Though San Antonio, since the arrival of the colony of Canary Islanders sent by the King of Spain in 1731, had enjoyed a slow and at times precarious growth, there were, besides the Indians, only a scant three thousand persons living in the whole of Texas when Stephen F. Austin established his first colony in 1822. His settlement comprised the present counties of Brazoria, Matagorda, Jackson, Wharton, Fort Bend, Galveston, Harris, Austin, Colorado, the most of Washington and Brazos Counties, and parts of Lavaca, Fayette, Burleson, Grimes, and Liberty Counties.

Certainly no system so thorough, honorable, and painstakingly executed has ever been known to have guided a project of colonization as was set down in the laws of this home-seeking group who had settled on the banks of the Brazos. The painstaking Austin set to making a code of Criminal and Civil Laws for his people, and certainly the thoroughness and broad-mindedness with which he heard each complaint of the colonists must have induced them to be "sober and industrious," which were the principal requisites of eligibility in his settlement. Life here had at last come to be little different from that of any other normal community in the States, and at last the move that awakened interest in Texas throughout Europe and America had been made—a successful colony [had been created].

Originally published in *Southwestern Architect* 2.2 (February 1928): 5–9, 16.

Prompted by this accomplishment, many more impresarios attempted the introduction of colonists into Texas, all of which were more or less complete failures, due to the unscrupulous and negligent way in which the people, once landed, were treated, and they had, it seems, overlooked the fact that Austin had instilled in his people a genuine loyalty to the Mexican government and had cared for his charges with a patience and understanding that was prompted by something bigger than a mercenary desire. By his manners and diplomacy he had been able without serious friction to make himself the arbiter and the agent of two very different peoples who could not understand each other.

A grass-grown street with only a few frame buildings and the ruins of an old ferry are the only reminders that here was once San Felipe de Austin, the center of Austin's Colony and the beginning of Anglo-American civilization in Texas. We were rather disappointed that this town (now San Felipe) and the immediate vicinity had almost nothing of architectural interest that dates back to the early days of this colony and Texas.

We had seen many lovely houses very akin in detail, plan, and handling of materials as far west as Lampassas, and, proceeding toward the coast, between and bordering the Colorado and Brazos, were Belton, Salado, Davilla, Round Rock, La Grange, Independence, Columbus, and many others, all having unmistakable sameness of feeling. The fact that the country immediately surrounding Austin's first colony has little evidence that there were skilled masons and carpenters among those first immigrants (although there are records showing that the wise alcalde, Austin, paid a premium of many acres of land to those who excelled in the various crafts) is not surprising at all when one reflects upon the strenuous means by which these pioneers barely kept from starving and were ever busy fighting harassing Karonkawas. There is, too, the probability that the feeling of insecurity and uncertainty kept them from seriously setting to making any kind of houses other than log cabins. It is true that when Austin returned from Mexico City many of his people had moved farther up the river and there was very little land in cultivation and no seed to plant.

These were the colonists whom Austin had recruited in and around New Orleans, and as most of his later colonists were also from this place, it is not at all surprising that, once they found insecurity decreasing and prosperity increasing, they set to building strong and permanent houses that bear the stamp of their mother town. His later settlements, which were west from the original colony, following generally the Brazos and Colorado Valleys, bear definite evidence that there was a mingling with the Irish from San Antonio and the Germans from Comal County.

Even the most pretentious of these earliest houses were no more pretentious than those snug and alluring shops and houses in the French Quarter of New Orleans. Their nicety of detail and refinement of molding is not found in any "features" and applied ornament, but principally confined to the beautifully proportioned dormers and cornices and the exterior casings around the openings, which are delicately molded and much wider than our present-day "brick-molds."

These "cornices," though they are really in most cases only a simple hand-carved *cyma recta* supported by one or two *fillets*, are alone a lesson in the elegance that can be had by simplicity in stonework and the pleasing refinement derived from a very sparing use of cut stone contrasting with a plain stone wall. We found a few beautifully paneled doors, but prevalent were the simple vertical beaded-board doors with the characteristic "Z" battens on their backs creaking on hand-wrought hinges.

We have found in surprising numbers as far west as Jones County, and in the general direction of the source of the Brazos, charming wellheads carved from single slabs of stone and frequently carrying beautifully carved running ornament around the edges. In Salado there are several of them, all carved by "Whiskey Jack" Green (and may we ask that you think that he came from "Irish Flats" in San Antonio and not from those "sober and industrious" souls in Austin's Colony, and to substantiate this we have searched for the name "Green" in the list of Austin's settlers and it is not there). Mr. Rigsby at the charming old "Shady Villa" Hotel in Salado can tell you much about "Whiskey Jack" and will show you the wellhead there with a chicken trough ingeniously carved in the same block of stone. It is ridiculous to suppose that these delightful houses with proportions and refinements that any architect will tell you are not easy to obtain were the expression of an uncultured people who accidentally achieved beauty. It would be equally as absurd to imagine the charming homes of the early New England colonists to have been built by aborigines. These are houses built by craftsmen exceedingly skilled in the various arts, whose work was better done since they were encouraged and urged to do everything well by men who were cultured and possessed of remarkable good taste, chief among whom were Stephen F. Austin and Baron de Bastrop, their alcaldes.

To the north of Austin's Colony and principally in the vicinity of Nacogdoches and San Augustine are the majority of the real plantation houses in Texas, in the sense that the land was worked entirely by slaves. These houses are, in most cases, rather pretentious and show the influence of the Greek revival and the plantation houses of Louisiana. The few that are built of brick are very like some of the long, one-story Carolina and Virginia plantation houses and were built principally by gentlemen from those states. Many of them, however, were not influenced very seriously by the uncertain Mexican government. This was due in part to their isolation and their trade with New Orleans and in part to choice, since several times they ousted an undesirable impresario or governor and ran the country according to their liking.

They were in many cases very wealthy and the holders of many slaves, and those who moved to Texas in later times unquestionably foresaw the eventual emancipation of the slaves and so hoped to hold their property by leaving the States. They, with their great wealth and immense holdings, were marked contrasts to the long-suffering home seekers of

Austin's colonies, who were in turn a contrast, though hardly so marked, to those who came from the countries of Europe, principally idealists and communists, in the years subsequent to 1842. The colorful ingress of the Germans, Irish, and Alsatians followed closely on the heels of the revolution and the recognition of the independence of Texas in 1837 by the United States and in 1840 by Great Britain.

For a long time preceding any of the organized migrations from Germany, it is said that the Germans were by far the largest national group, excepting the Mexicans, in San Antonio. Many of these returned to Germany with glowing accounts of the promised land, and immediately several German princes, for political reasons, set to the task of reducing pauperism by organized migration. With annexation almost a certainty, speculators who represented owners of large tracts began appearing in Germany and almost immediately were given a hearing by this group. These several nobles, most prominent among whom was Count Castell of Mainz, had seized upon this systematic and grouped manner of migration as a means of securing more tangible and lasting connections with Germans in foreign countries and also as a source of wealth and power through trade.

On April 20, 1842, at Biebrich on the Rhine, these princes organized a society, which they called "The Verein," and immediately dispatched Counts Boos-Waldeck and Victor Leiningen to Texas to select choicest lands. They failed to secure a satisfactory grant from Congress, but after long parley obtained one grant in Fayette County. They returned to Germany with accounts adverse to any extensive colonization scheme in Texas. In the meantime, however, the remaining members of the Verein had been induced by a wily Frenchman to buy an entirely worthless tract of land and had already made preparations for sending the first colony. Prince Waldeck objected vehemently and subsequently withdrew from the society.

Prince Carl of Solms-Braunfels, accompanied by the contriving Frenchman D'Orvanne, arrived in May 1844. The prince was astounded and grieved to find that they had bought a tract of land far beyond the frontier, which was lacking in protection from the Indians, was unsuitable for cultivation, and they had but eight months in which to exercise their colonization rights. His predicament was difficult, but, by constant labor, he obtained a temporary place at Carls Haven (now Indianola) where his people might be landed. He eventually obtained a grant on the Comal River, north of San Antonio, where he founded New Braunfels. The prince was an idealist and, not to be outdone by disconcerting facts and straitened circumstances, he conducted his colony with the determination to give it in every way the feeling and atmosphere of a medieval European town. Indeed, his block house on the hill overlooking the town was called Sophienburg and the palisade fort that was built where the old Catholic Church now stands was called Zinkenburg. This visionary colonizer transplanted many of the autocratic customs and ceremonies of ancient Germany, which created an air of militarism that impressed the Indians. It is said that he conducted the most pretentious ceremonies and military demonstrations and fired a salute each evening. This was, of course, a sensible bit of policy to discourage any Indian depredations, such as were suffered by the adjoining colonies. Little fault can be found with Prince Braunfels's methods of governing his colony, except that he did not have sufficient business ability to overcome the short-sightedness of the Verein in Germany, which failed to finance properly or to regulate the numbers of immigrants sent to his colony. Consequently, the prince exercised his borrowing power to its very limit, and when he finally became so indebted to Americans that his predicament was embarrassing, in desperation he left for Galveston, where he was later arrested. His friend and successor, Hans von Meusebach, came to his aid, however, and he was saved from disgrace.

When Meusebach arrived in New Braunfels in the spring of 1845, the conditions were deplorable and his welcome was in the form of a storming by creditors and the astonishing news that the unscrupulous directors of the Verein in Germany were sending four thousand more immigrants—and all this on top of an indebtedness of $20,000, which had been accumulated by reckless expenditures on the credit of the Verein. When finally Meusebach had evolved order out of the chaotic conditions in New Braunfels, he began making preparations for the coming colonists. He finally secured a tract eighty miles northwest of New Braunfels on the Pedernales River and here, late in the year 1845, laid out a town which was later named Fredericksburg. There was now—for this land was purchased on credit—the tremendous debt of $140,000 confronting Meusebach, who had the small sum of $24,000.

Those who landed the following winter suffered inconceivable hardships on the long journey from the coast and many died, and others dropped out along the way. With the few survivors Meusebach founded Fredericksburg. Once the intrepid Meusebach had cleared the settlements of all debt and saw them well on their way to prosperity, he resigned his office to H. Sties and Dr. Herff.

In Germany, H. Sties and Prince Solms were stirring the students of Heidelberg and Giessen with their enthusiastic writings and speeches which pictured Texas as a land of opportunities, where talent that went unnoticed in Germany would reap undreamed of rewards. In an address at Darmstadt, Prince Solms won for the enterprise a graduate of Giessen, an accomplished engineer, Gustave Schleicher; and a student of law, Wundt. Many more students and professional men were enlisted in this communistic group and in April 1847, the forty of them set sail from Hamburg and were landed the following July at Galveston. The eager group immediately proceeded to New Braunfels and Fredericksburg and thence to the land set aside for them on the Llano River, where they founded Bettina. Being communists, there was no recognized leader and no one worked but as he chose and when he chose, and we have it that few worked at all. The university students and professional men were determined to do the directing, and the laborers were equally as determined not to be directed—consequently, the colony fell to pieces. Bettina was abandoned and the members of the colony settled in New Braunfels or Fredericksburg, where almost all of them became community leaders and later leaders in the affairs of the state. The worth and significance of this group ([which] cannot be associated with the happenings in Bettina) is inestimably important because of the influence that its members, [who were] well educated and aggressive, exerted in the communities in which they later settled.

The most casual visitor cannot but see intelligence built into the clapboard and stone houses of New Braunfels. Its parks, the great plaza, and the studied layout of its shady streets put one immediately aware that here there was certainly no haphazard pitching of tents. The houses are surprisingly unlike those along the Rhine, which is easily explained by the fact that these were a people seeking betterment who knew that their prosperity and happiness would be doubly assured if all their former customs and environment were forgotten. The result was freshness and entire freedom from pedantry. The faded red tin roofs, soft green shutters, and white-washed walls of New Braunfels could never have found a place more friendly and embracing than the banks of the clear, green Comal River, with its valley of towering pecan trees and wide oaks covered with grey-green moss.

Nearly the whole town of Fredericksburg stands on one long street, erect and immaculate, gable-to-gable. The great trees arching high over the red roofs and the few remaining second-story balconies with the wide street below make the town as cool and clean and peaceful as a smooth river. There is no harshness, no sharp, cutting edges, and the eighty-three coats of whitewash have softened the sturdy stone houses to an incomparable friendliness. Fredericksburg was the most isolated of the early settlements, and protection from Indians was the main reason that the houses were built close together. The mile of packed dwellings is reminiscent of Europe and as colorful as the tales that you will be told of the early struggles of this colony. Those things, intangible and inexplicable, the

San Antonio–Laredo Street

FIGURE 7. O'Neil Ford, "San Antonio–Laredo Street," c. 1926, published with "An Indigenous Architecture: Some Texas Colonial Houses," by David R. Williams, in *Southwest Review* in 1928.

houses themselves, the great trees and well-kept surrounding fields, make one of the most restful and picturesque scenes in Texas; yet there is no more prosperous community in the state.

Texas is fortunate! The settling of any new country has usually been closely linked with the expurgation, from all the countries of Europe, of criminals and undesirables, of one and another sort, sent for purposes other than peaceful residence. A few of this type came from the notorious neutral ground between Louisiana and Texas, and in 1833 such a group was sent from Mexico. They were not tolerated in any of the established colonies and were severely punished, even to the death penalty, in most settlements. In Austin's Colony they were whipped publicly and expelled from the town with the threat of death if they returned.

Those who guided and fostered the settlements were in almost every case men of excellent breeding and education. Very often they were of royal blood, and, still more important, they placed the well-being of their people above all things. Austin, Prince Solms, Meusebach, Green-DeWitt, Baron de Bastrop, Henry Castro, and many others suffered great hardships and were untiring in their efforts to make good their promises to the colonists against the most adverse conditions and with small remuneration for themselves.

1932

Organic Building

This essay was Ford's first important public statement after leaving David Williams's office and was one of the most theoretically significant pieces of writing of his career. In it he professed his respect for functionalism and implicitly aligned himself with the modernism of Frank Lloyd Wright. Ford condemned the environmental destruction associated with Anglo settlement of the United States and claimed that the same impulses that drove it were responsible for twentieth-century sprawl and the over-scaled revival-style houses that he regarded as inappropriate for their time and place. Dallas architect Thomas D. Broad wrote the first section of the article, entitled "What Is Modernism?" The notes in this essay are Ford's.

It is not easy to account fully for the present rather amorphous status of American architecture, but at least some of the influences at work can be detected. For instance, we seem to have inherited from the frontier an unconsciously hostile attitude toward our environment, toward the land, which makes it difficult for us to build in harmony with the landscape. Again, there is frequently in our architecture a hint of a will-to-power, an assertion at all costs of the individual ego, which is possibly connected with the individualism of the Industrial Revolution. And then there is that curious American humility which leads us to imitate European styles in every branch of art. These influences of course do not explain everything, but perhaps they will repay a brief examination.

Originally published as the second section of Thomas D. Broad and O'Neil Ford, "Toward a New Architecture," *Southwest Review* 17.2 (Winter 1932): 209–229.

Historians have described vividly the dauntless courage of the pioneers, and there can be no doubt that the dark and bloody ground of the frontier required and produced men of more than ordinary stamina and enterprise. When it was a question of a struggle for bare existence against a hostile environment, a self-reliance was necessary in describing which the word "individualism" seems no more than a polite understatement. But as the frontier passes and cities grow up on the prairies, the traits which were necessary for the conquest of the continent survive as a cultural lag in a new environment which requires a considerable degree of group-consciousness if life is to be tolerable. And as this growth of cities becomes the dominant factor in our new civilization, the negative aspect of pioneering becomes evident. For the pioneers, while they have founded an empire, have also stripped the earth of its trees and grass. The untouched woods of East Texas, lush and generous, were for them land to clear and wood to burn; and the rich and boundless prairies were land to be broken, farmed carelessly, and allowed to lose its topsoil, which ran into the rivers so that now we think of spending millions to make the clogged streams navigable. More times than not the pioneer was on the make, and did not care how he treated the earth; for by the time his own exploitation could impoverish one region he could have escaped to a virgin area. There were exceptions, to be sure: in South Texas, for instance, particularly among such German towns as Fredericksburg, New Braunfels, and Castroville, the tradition of culture was applied to the land, and the towns are models of planning, with houses which, though old, are beautiful, and far better than the few bungalows that have sprung up among them. For the most part, however, the obliteration of the land along the frontier was a waste comparable to the casual and needless slaughter of the bison.

This same spirit of the pioneer has gone into the making of our cities, and has become merged with the influence of the Industrial Revolution. Unfortunately, our cities represent not an advanced stage of industrialism, but the crude early stages, which not only reveled in childish production of cheap machine-made goods apparently for the mere pleasure of seeing what machines could do, but also displayed an equally childish love of power for its own sake, a destructive expansion of the individual ego. The American tendency to present a positive statement of one's taste and well-being by outdoing one's neighbor, by possessing a more expensive motor car, a bigger and more costly residence, or a larger mausoleum, is a kindred phenomenon. An American house must be an expression of the owner's personality, and it must never agree with the house next door in either style, color, height, material, or physical orientation. The banker's house is Spanish, the bootlegger's villa is Italian, and the dry-goods merchant has an English cottage of twenty-two rooms. The banker and the bootlegger and the dry-goods merchant are the sons of the pioneers; and, like their fathers, they find in their environment a challenge to their respective identities, a stimulus to self-assertion.

The same impulse seems back of the absurd skyscraper-building programs of cities, which have no natural limits to expansion outward instead of upward. We are obsessed with mere bigness. From the top of any one of the ever-higher skyscrapers which line our business streets, the modern American city looks, to quote Louis La Beaume, "not unlike a vast neglected asparagus bed, with bristling stalks upstanding in crass disorder."[1] And he asks, "Whither is this frenzy of Bigness leading us? Why should we be so impressed with swollen magnitude? At the circus children gaze with wonder on the fat woman, and bumpkins marvel at the muscles of the strong man. But must life be forever just a circus? Step this way, ladies and gentlemen, and gaze upon the tallest building in the world. Ten million tons of steel compose its bones, ten thousand pairs of hands bolted it together . . ." We crane our necks in wonder.

When one adds to these forces the snobbish impulse toward imitation which strains our residences into distressing caricatures of older styles, a really alarming picture is the result.

Our falsely romantic attitude toward skyline and countryside is hardly less retardant to the development of a clean and sensible architecture than the spurious misrepresentations of modern advertising ballyhoo. The architectural romanticism of imitation is of the same vulgarity as Suitatoriums, Cleanitoriums, Hatitoriums, Shrines of Thrift, and Cathedrals of Learning. It is hardly necessary, however, to aim another blow at "period" domestic architecture.

But perhaps it is necessary, as a sort of appendix to this exhibit of pernicious influences, to mention the "modernistic" fad—really another manifestation of the impulse toward imitation. Any sudden advent of a new material is baffling, and the small minds that never grasp its deeper significance are immediately struck with the amazing tricks they can make it perform. Some joyously mold it into imitations of honest materials: concrete is made to look like stone blocks; steel is painstakingly made to look like "improved" wood. And some merely warp the new material into a different "style," new, unprecedented, unique—mannered, original, and in vogue. But shortly the fads are out of style. And though these false styles are short-lived, the sincere workers and true visionaries are not a little dismayed at the sudden popular versions that are presented as final.

May I place all possible emphasis on the difference between the eclectic who turns a hand to a modernistic decoration which is merely flashy, amusing, and eventually disgusting and the builder who bases his work on organic unity and spiritual expressiveness? The grotesque atrocities of show-window cuteness and the jagged meaninglessness of department-store *objets d'art* have done much to confuse the public attitude and to arouse the suspicion that these prettyfied things are concomitants of the new movement, whereas in reality they are antithetical.

Such a situation might well seem hopeless, especially when one remembers that it has resulted in the main from impulses which arise below the level of consciousness and has developed forms which, however ugly, have become part of the mores of the community. To object in the name of reason is almost naïve. But a few architects are objecting, and though they usually call themselves by a rather forbidding name—that of "functionalists"—at bottom their only platform and their only theory is common sense. Yet their program, though simple, is not widely popular. However fundamental a concept may be, however evolutionary its development, there are those who would close their eyes to analysis and logic and rely on the easy application of embellishment and complications. The word "architect" has come to mean designer and decorator, and our buildings are arranged instead of organic. He who has the courage to eliminate extraneous forms, to analyze biologically, and then to build is invariably labeled as eccentric, while the hundreds of architects who do not think, but are content to rely on tradition and to apply the obsolete methods of the past, are accepted because they are considered dependable and conservative.

Yet the attitude of the functionalists is in reality the one dependable attitude, for only the functionalists try to take into account the purpose before they plan the building. Ours, they maintain, is a civilization based on science; and the houses we live in, the offices we work in, the schools which our children attend must all employ the advantages of invention and development so that through their properly apportioned uses and their honest application human existence may be an intensification of living, with goals, order, stability, and direction. They hold that architecture must not confine itself to the conceiving, planning, and erection of separate working units, but must help the entire community to become an organism, conditioned by its relation to present needs of adjustment and a sound analysis of its possible future growth. They have not assumed that the building of isolated examples of functioning structures—honest machines—will be more than a temporary remedy for our pressure of congestion and obsolescence; they realize that only by a deep gash across the path of enterprising individual and greedy speculator can our towns be freed from declining values and makeshift plastic surgery. They defy particularly the campaigners who desperately boost and push to extend at any cost the limits of their city in competition with its neighbor. They do not ask how a city of three hundred thousand can swell to five hundred thousand, but begin at the roots by asking for a determination of how big the city must be to perform all its social, commercial, educational, and recreational functions, and look forward to the setting of a minimum and maximum for different kinds of communities depending upon their character and function. The functionalist ideal is a building that serves basic human purposes permanently, that is related to the community as a whole, that is free from ostentation and faddish "isms," that depends upon an honest use of materials, and yet gives scope to the architect's vision and imagination working over these basic elements.

Let us consider the application of these principles to the architecture of the business sections of cities. The problem of contemporary architecture is presented here in its most acute form. With the growing perfection of the machine and the parallel inflation of commercial values, there came in the last generation the most staggering surge of building that any age has ever known. Real-estate prices fluctuated spasmodically, and the amorphous process of boom building began. The real-estate promoter built his additions and sold them overnight, while within the city great areas were left to decay, worthless or given over to slums. In the business sections the architect was throwing up great steel frames and covering them with the dirty lavishness of borrowed ornamentation, on the mistaken principle that he must glorify the ugly skeleton.

Today we are paying for the rehabilitation of the blighted areas, and now only rarely do we see classic columns or cupolas stuck on our buildings. Their ugly presence in our skylines only accentuates the simplicity of the clean new buildings. Yet the mere stripping away of ornamentation, the new application of physical principles, and the use of new materials do not necessarily make a functional building. Actually, the wooden frame house is often nearer the functional principles of building than are our skyscrapers, and among industrial structures, only in unstudied warehouses and factories do we find a sheer and honest expression of truth, function, beauty, and order.

In fact, the modernism which began by stripping away columns and cupolas has developed its own mannerisms. The same insincerity that underlies modern exploitation-advertising of commodities is evident in the affectation and spurious emphasis of the new modernistic fashion of vertical lines on tall buildings. There is absolutely no structural reason or aesthetic excuse for such alternating vertical dark and light stripes. They represent nothing but a more or less feeble attempt to symbolize aspiration, to make a building appear to be what it is not—for a building, whether it be three or ninety storeys high, can never be anything but a series of horizontal floors, one above the other, each floor self-sustaining. A glance at some tall building at night, when it is lighted, when the scrubwomen are working, will furnish conclusive proof that the "rooms expand on the same floor level and require windows arranged horizontally." Each storey is a plane where man's natural relation to man is horizontal. These successive levels are reached by smaller horizontal floors moving vertically, and becoming, at each station, a vestibule and continuation of the floor.[2] Any exterior denial of these fundamentals is either a concession to the owner's desire for dramatic effect or evidence of the architect's ignorance or disregard of engineering principles.

One has only to look at buildings under construction to see the gradual process of covering an honest core with a fake facing. For example: first the steel frame is up, a light and beautiful pattern of bays and cubic voids, a beautiful silhouette; then the concrete floor slabs are poured, and the building has assumed meaning: its logic is evident. For structural reasons its horizontals, the floors and beams, are much more prominent than the columns, the verticals. All that need be done now is to glaze it—absolutely nothing more, except painting, etc., is necessary to make it a light and spacious place to work. The verticals are entirely secondary and could well be set behind the curtain walls of glass, or a combination of glass and stainless sheet metal, or glass and concrete.[3] But instead, wide, heavy, meaningless piers of brick or stone are hung on the sides of the buildings. These masonry covers hide the actual structural columns; and, as if to shut out more light and to accentuate further the shooting upward, more piers are set between these so that small windows similar to those in the usual residence or old brick-wall building can be set between them. These little glass holes, high above the floor, are actually set back into the floor space (with a waste of rentable, usable square feet), so that the screaming verticals will be made even more prominent by shadows. Then the existence of such a base thing as a floor is willfully denied by filling the vertical spaces between the windows with some dark material, preferably green, that weakly approximates the color of the glass area. Inside the building the result is dark areas where the pretty pylons rise; and unless it has occurred to the architect that artificial air-conditioning is worthwhile, the structure is even poorly ventilated: an inflexible bulk, orderless and stupid.

The owner has spent great sums to make his building a bad machine—an already obsolete structure, and a questionable investment if he is concerned with the next decade. Even the steel or concrete frame had to be made stronger in order to carry the extra exhibition weight. He has a soaring and irreparable example of impracticality quite in harmony with our recent standards of inflation; and possibly, if taste does change to sense, he may find that he has incurred a similar reaction. These fundamental mistakes are only magnified if the building is incrusted with faddish ornamentation—sunbursts and perfume-bottle flowers. For such decoration, like the gingerbread gewgaws of the Victorian manner, will go the way of all spurious things.

Yet I do not wish to seem dogmatic. Although it is frequently possible to say what is bad in contemporary design, it is not always possible to say just what will be the ultimate forms, which a functional architecture will develop out of the new materials available. Reinforced concrete, for example, is a flexible medium, stone that can be poured, like water, into any conceivable shape. Yet, except for its strength and relative density, architecturally it is no more than wood if it continues to be limited by wood forms. A few pioneer architect-engineers have built tremendous domes and vaults with no outside forms and only comparatively small movable forms on the inside. But a common lack of necessary mathematical knowledge among architects and engineers and the extra expense due to lack of standardization in forms and machines make this revolutionary yet simple method as yet unavailable. Concrete shot on by compressed air is almost twice as dense and strong as poured concrete; yet in Texas, for example, there is only one firm equipped to do this type of work. Though so far as I know it has never been done, it is quite possible to build tremendous arched vaults by supporting, on light posts, a fabric of metal lath and light reinforcing—by plastering the inside and then spraying the required thickness of liquid concrete on the outside. When the inside supports are removed, the building is plastered and complete. As a matter of fact, the largest domes ever built were done in a manner somewhat similar to this. They are the twin domes of the Great Market in Leipzig, 249 feet in diameter, made of shells of concrete only 3 ½ inches thick.

Again, there are few examples of the use of that perfect symbol of structure, the line that has its ends in infinity, a static, moving, and beautiful curve—the parabola. The great airplane hangar at Orly, near Paris, is a superb work, a parabolic vault 1,000 feet long and 385 feet wide, built of a concrete shell varying from 8 to 3 ½ inches in thickness and having no beams or girders [figure 8]. Are these simple enclosures of space less products of the creative imagination than the cheap "modernistic" shop-fronts that have recently lined our downtown streets—or such pompously sterile monuments to classicism as our post offices and city halls?

In dealing with domestic architecture, a common-sense program has an even more difficult task; for custom and

FIGURE 8. Eugène Freyssinet, hangar at Orly Airport, Paris, France, 1921–1923. Ford considered the parabolic arch the "perfect symbol of structure."

convention, as well as fad and imitation, are here even more closely woven into the texture of the emotions of the occupants. One easily understands that even though there can be no reasonable objection to functional principles of building, we who have lived all our lives in period rooms with flowered wallpapers, Oriental rugs, furniture scattered in decorated disorder, and mantels weighted with gadgets can but experience rising doubts and antipathies in the presence of any radical alteration of these things. The issue, however, goes far deeper than a mere wrangle over decoration, for the engineer-artist-architect holds it incongruous to hide scientific household accessories in a hybrid structure in adapted Spanish, Colonial, or Normandy-farmhouse style. He considers it ridiculous for us to swelter in rooms that in order to conform to a borrowed tradition have small leaded casements—and ludicrous for us to sun ourselves under arc lamps in dismal Tudor houses when sunshine, fresh air, and an integrated arrangement of rooms are the precise gifts of our new materials. These very gifts may serve a new decorative purpose in relieving the simple masses and lines, in saturating or lowering the key of the broad sweeps of color, and in heightening or retarding, by mechanical adjustment, the actual emotional stimuli that these rooms may evoke.

In fairness to the functionalist, it is well I emphasize that his stand implies no contempt for the various types of architecture of the past. In most cases—usually, in fact, except in the periods of revivalism—they were exact expressions of their respective periods, reflecting the steps of progress and the structural limitations imposed by lack of material development. In this connection I am reminded of the movement toward the perpetuation and development of an indigenous Texas architecture that Mr. David R. Williams has so successfully advocated and applied. Until a few months ago I was associated with him in this research necessary to the formation of a sound background upon which to develop a philosophy of architecture. We had not intended that our investigations should lead to reproduction of these old houses or imitation of their mellowed stone walls and their tumbledown picturesqueness. They are beautiful houses, and certainly, since they are free from all imported precedent, they are worthy of emulation in Texas; but even this was almost the opposite of our purpose. We sought and found in these weathered Texas towns a seed of good sense: houses built to live in, built of the best materials available—the most modern materials then available. In some locations there was stone, and it was carefully fitted together; other places yielded nothing but the mud itself, and so adobe houses were built; and where there were forests, wood was used. Openings in the walls were either arched with stones or bridged with great wooden beams. Roofs were pitched sharply to shed the rain. There were wide porches, ells that sheltered from the north wind and ells that caught the precious summer breezes.

These were the things we found in simple houses grown out of the soil. And this is what we wanted to show Texans— that these houses were as modern when they were built as a skyscraper is today, as purposeful as a piston in a motor—machines to live in. These houses, with the charm of their fine proportions, are the wealth that our forebears have given us, straightforward and honest, free from mannerisms and styles.

But today we have concrete, steel, and glass instead of wood and stone and adobe. Today great openings can be spanned. Concrete or steel can project to form wide, unobstructed porches, and the entire area of the lot becomes a garden since the attic is done away with and the roof becomes habitable.[4] This one thing is particularly significant, both economically and aesthetically, for it is possible to use this roof-terrace as a private garden or, one can imagine, as a sort of elevated street, a clean and quiet place for strolling [figure 9]. The profiles of our streets would then be free from jagged dormers and spiky gables and pinnacles, and something of the serene and static restfulness of our own horizontal landscape would dignify our rows of houses. The easy movement of our horizontal-seeing eyes would find resting places in a pure and simple outline.

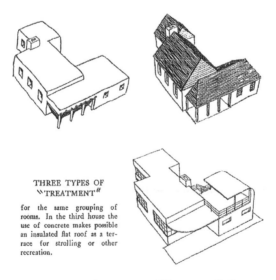

THREE TYPES OF "TREATMENT"

for the same grouping of rooms. In the third house the use of concrete makes possible an insulated flat roof as a terrace for strolling or other recreation.

FIGURE 9. O'Neil Ford, "Three Types of 'Treatment,'" diagram, published with "Organic Building," section 2 of "Toward a New Architecture," by Ford and Thomas D. Broad, in *Southwest Review* in 1932.

If one wishes, hollyhocks will bloom against these light-colored walls; ivy will trace its gossamer patterns on them; and these walls with their simple self-decoration will weather gracefully, gathering sunlight and casting subtle shadows. The living house is after all no more than spaces enclosed by walls, whether the walls be of logs, brick, glass, or concrete. They are covered with a roof, whether it be sloping or flat. There are great fireplaces, rows of books, teacups, and cigarettes. There is no camouflage. An ideal house is flexible, for it is not bound by rules of tradition; and it can have timeless beauty, for its beauty depends only on the nicety of its proportions, the fitness of colors and textures, and its inseparable union of function with form.

Tomorrow's architecture is here, and tomorrow will show us a way to a more satisfactory existence through building. It concerns everyone because all human experiences are related to walls and roofs. Home, factory, office, store, theater, and school are stages upon which life lives. Tomorrow's architects are not concerned with propaganda for a new style, but their stand shows conclusively how a new style will be formulated by meeting the needs of today with the scientific developments of today. It follows, incidentally, that the corollary is proved that style is "unity of principle animating all the work of an epoch," and that our own age is determining its own style as surely as the zeal of the Middle Ages produced the soaring cathedral spires or the Colonial years of Texas produced the simple stone houses which we admire today.

NOTES

1. L. La Beaume, "Our Own Adult Education," *Architectural Forum*, February 1931.
2. Naturally, when elevator shafts appear on the face of a building, there is a resulting vertical line, or absence of horizontals—a stem that, incidentally, is pleasingly contrasted with the horizontal floors.
3. It is interesting to notice that lighting engineers have demonstrated the value of large lighted areas of less brilliance in preventing eyestrain.

According to A. Lawrence Kocher and Albert Frey, "One of the most astonishing discoveries of lighting experts is the fact that the room flooded with daylight from an entire wall of glass is more satisfactory for working and less disturbing to the eye than the room with light from a single moderate size window. In other words, the greater the glass area the more favorable the working conditions will be. This phenomenon is checked by daily experience. There is no significant eyestrain in reading on a porch that is open on three sides, but there is an eyestrain in typing or reading in a room with light from a single window that is surrounded by dark wall areas. It is essential, therefore, to seek daylight intensity that is evenly distributed without excessively bright or dark spots. Lighting engineers offer the rule: the brightest spot in any building should not have more than three times the illumination of the dimmest spot in the same building. It is an easy matter to design shades with metal blades that would deflect the sun's rays, let in light, and at the same time exclude summer heat. Almost invariably office-building windows, though there may be only one in each room, are equipped with Venetian blinds which perform this very function" (*The Architectural Record*, February 1931).

4. These flat roofs can be insulated better against the burning heat of summer or the cold of winter than any pitched roof. Either a free, well-ventilated space between the ceiling and the roof or one of the various scientific insulating materials is far more efficient than a semi-closed waste space between the ceiling and a sloping roof, where the pressure downward is often great enough to break plaster or make ceilings sway.

PART II

Growth and Synthesis

1940

Review of *Williamsburg—Today and Yesterday*

While he was working on the restoration of La Villita in San Antonio (figure 10), Ford read a new, illustrated book on Colonial Williamsburg and wrote a very short review of it. The re-creation of the Virginia city as a historic site had begun in 1926 and was largely complete when the book appeared in 1940. Because he had almost no other precedent for how to restore and reuse old districts than Williamsburg to guide him as he worked in San Antonio, Ford's review is notable. One line, in which he makes clear his disdain for "lush sentimentality" in preservation, stands out particularly. Throughout his career Ford and his colleagues worked to stabilize and preserve many of San Antonio's most significant eighteenth- and nineteenth-century buildings.

Williamsburg was made the capitol of the crown Colony of Virginia in 1699 and for many years after was the epitome of the excitingly glamorous life in the new Americas. It was, literally, a section of England transported bodily across the Atlantic, and there was little concession to the problems encountered in the New World. The resources of the Rockefeller dynasty have restored the physical Williamsburg to its original state, and Mr. and Mrs. Rose have made this publication a super deluxe guide book. Mrs. Rose, in her text, fortunately avoids the lush sentimentality which is the general treatment of this subject by

---

Review of *Williamsburg—Today and Yesterday*, by Grace Norton Rose, with drawings by Jack Manley Rose (New York: G. P. Putnam's Sons, 1940), unpublished, box 80, folder 12, O'Neil Ford: An Inventory of His Drawings, Papers, and Photographic Material, 1864–1983, Alexander Architectural Archives, University of Texas Libraries, University of Texas at Austin.

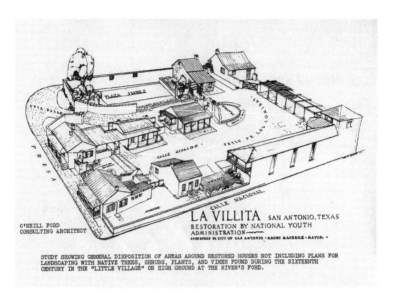

FIGURE 10. O'Neil Ford, La Villita restoration plan, 1939.

the house and yard magazines, and there is no mention of "the old antique secretary's desk." The book is beautifully printed and the typography is excellent. A brief but interesting and complete historical survey is followed by detailed descriptions of the important buildings and gardens, enlivened by gossipy tidbits concerning the original inhabitants and their courtly gayety, and enhanced by remarkably good wash drawings of the buildings and their surroundings.

1951

O'Neil Ford Lectures on Slab Lifting

In June 1951 Ford was invited to London to lecture on the Youtz-Slick lift-slab construction technique to a group of architects and engineers gathered at the Waldorf Hotel. His remarks were published as an article in the Architects' Journal *the next month. News of the new method had reached Great Britain through the architectural press only six months before and had generated great interest just as the first buildings at Trinity University, where the method was first used, were rising.*

We have in Texas, which is where I come from, an Institute of Inventive Research, part of the Southwest Research Institute. A young man named [Tom] Slick, a resourceful and wealthy young man, gives the money: an enormous amount—I think, some $600,000 a year.

One day Mr. Slick said to me, "This concrete of ours is a miraculous material, but what are we going to do about the carpenters?" Our carpenters get about £1 an hour. He asked, "Do we always have to build a wooden building before we build a concrete one?" So we went to work. It took a long time and a great deal of money. When we hit on slab lifting, we felt we had a sound, logical, simple idea, and when we designed our first building, we were determined not to mess it up; instead of using the minimum amount of steel, we over-designed. In spite of that we saved $26,000. We were 9 per cent under the cost of conventional construction.

Of course, we had our troubles: we had a fight with the authorities, but we did it. A lot of my fellow architects doubted

Originally published in *Architects' Journal* 113 (July 12, 1951): 51–55.

the thing; we doubted it ourselves, but we satisfied our doubts in the laboratory; they doubted it just because it was different. So when we decided to use slab lifting at Trinity University, it was predicted that it would cost not less but more than the conventional system. They asked me what I thought it would cost, but I refused to guess. When we got our tenders, a company from New York, which is eighteen hundred miles away, took it a little under the local contractors, not at $12 or $13 a square foot, not at $8, which I hoped for, but at $6.37.

I'm now going to show you a film of this system in action; afterward some of you may care to ask me some questions. Mind you, I'm not an engineer, but we had some good ones working on this. We had Frederick Severud, who came from Norway. He is an excellent engineer, one of the best we have in America.

(A film was then shown of the slab lifting at Trinity University, and, as it ran, Mr. Ford described this method of construction, as follows.)

The stanchions are set up, we pour the ground slab, and we put down the separating medium, which is something like you put on the backs of imitation leather notebooks. Steel collars are set down on this paper, on the slab. The steel is tied in to it. We use little wire bipods to support the steel reinforcement. Approximately 40 per cent of the cost of steel tying was saved by doing the work on the ground, where it is easy and comfortable, and there is no hoisting of bars. We mostly used 3,000-pound concrete. The method of transporting the concrete is fairly crude. (Special deep wheelbarrows were used.) On a very large building we should use a highway machine, with a traveling horizontal crane taking the concrete where we want it.

We built a small machine at the Institute, which gives a smooth surface finish to the concrete. It has revolving plates made of plastic, and does a good job. No hand troweling is necessary at all.

We do not vibrate the normal concrete, but where we use a lightweight aggregate, we find it necessary to vibrate. When all the slabs are poured, the jacks are set on top of the column. The jack reaches down with two rods and picks the slab up, pulling the rods through the jack. There is a piston in the center of the jack with a two-inch stroke. It is operated by a ten-horsepower electric motor, which also drives the locking nuts. What happens is this: As the piston goes up, the lower pair of locking nuts—the ones on the cylinder—are driven round so the rods pass through them. Then they are locked and they hold the slab while the piston is pulled down by the springs. The springs hold the whole assembly together and help force the fluid back into the compression chambers.

The boy at the control panel lifts, unassisted, 400,000 pounds of concrete. After the slab is lifted, two blocks of steel are welded under the steel collar to take care of the dead load, and after the jack is taken away, two more are welded on to take care of the live load. It takes two welders two hours to weld eight columns. As the second lot of blocks are being welded in place, they turn the jacks through 90 degrees and wind the rods down, through holes in the collars left for the purpose, to pick up the next slab. The rods are sticking high in the air; so we hook up all the screws to the motors, get them all revolving together and run the rods down. We tried to do it by hand, but it took all night. At first we inserted the bushings in the collar before the slab was poured and lifted, but that tied up our bushings. Now we use split bushings, which we put in after the slab is cured.

You might like to know some more about this building for Trinity University [figure 16]. We saved some £3,500 by the foundation system. We had no beams in any direction—I am against forming and shuttering entirely. We put in substantial bases for the stanchions and we graded the earth level. Then we drilled through the earth, at some 2s. or less a foot, to a depth of five to ten feet, to rock. We poured in concrete and a little steel and we had a thin ground slab with thousands of cheap links to the rock.

For the curtain walls—there are 1,300 running feet of windows—we shoot a steel angle onto the ceiling with a gun and weld the windows to it. Under the windows there is a light steel bulkhead faced with aluminum. This has all the plumbing, heating, and wiring in it and fiberglass for insulation. We are still learning. We don't plaster our ceilings now. We don't use paper for a separator; all we use is paraffin thinned with benzene. Instead of 5 cents, it is ¾ of a cent a foot. Then we sprinkle it with talcum and when the slab comes up, the underside is smooth like marble. We got another idea, too. We make snap lines on the floor with colored chalk, through the paraffin, to show where the partitions and the plumbing and the fixtures go. When the slab is lifted, the imprint on the ceiling is clearer than on the floor. It is a great saving in plumbing and follow-on trades.

Our most interesting job to date is a knitting mill we built for some people from Vienna. It was 26,000 square feet, but the day we finished, the owner—who has a factory in England—said, "Double the size"—just like that. We did something new. Instead of using any separator, we put down fiberglass fourteen inches thick and poured our slabs on it. We had a fine acoustical material for almost no extra money. It was separator, acoustical material, and insulator.

This [showing a photo to the audience] shows you that I am interested in a great many things. Some wall slabs were poured on the ground for a warehouse; after three days' curing, they were lifted by the best hydraulic system I have ever seen. The jacks lift 140-foot-long slabs eighteen feet high, in twenty-five minutes.

We take building like this for granted now; we think we know how to do it, so we are going right on with it. There are some extraordinary modifications of the system—we hope to start lifting concrete domes in some six months' time. The domes won't require much reinforcement—just some around the edge, which we will post-stress.

I want to pay tribute to the men who sat up all night when we lifted our first slab. Two thousand people came to watch, and most of them came to see it fail. Dr. Everett, the president of Trinity University, agreed that we should absorb the shock on this first occasion. He said to me, "It seems to me we had better get on the slab." Then he said, "Perhaps we had better get underneath it as soon as it is high enough, because if it does fall, you and I will be vastly better off there!"

1953

Statement on Behalf of the San Antonio Conservation Society

In 1953 the City of San Antonio proposed building a parking garage under Travis Park, one of the most prominent green spaces downtown and one of the oldest municipal parks in the United States. Ford drafted this statement on behalf of the San Antonio Conservation Society, which successfully opposed the building of the garage. His efforts to resist the encroachment on the city by cars and to preserve parks were lifelong. They culminated in the ultimately unsuccessful attempt to stop the building of the North Central Expressway (US Highway 281) through a park, a university, and historic San Antonio neighborhoods.

The San Antonio Conservation Society is not opposed to downtown parking. It is opposed to the destruction of our parks. The issue is not whether we can have downtown parking, but whether we can have parking and have Travis Park as well. If the City Council or the Planning Commission had taken the time to investigate, it could have found that projects for parking were actually being planned in the very area around Travis Park.

I repeat, we are not against downtown parking and we are not against parking in the Travis Park area. Any attempt to tell the people of San Antonio that an underground garage under Travis Park is the only solution to parking or that the

"The San Antonio Conservation Society is not opposed . . . ," untitled, handwritten text, unpublished, box 80, folder 12, O'Neil Ford: An Inventory of His Drawings, Papers, and Photographic Material, 1864–1983, Alexander Architectural Archives, University of Texas Libraries, University of Texas at Austin.

destruction of Travis Park will solve our downtown parking problem is a gross deceit of the people.

People ask what is the city giving and what is the city getting. The city is giving away a property value that can be estimated at a million dollars or more (two or three million). This is being given away without the city getting one single penny in return. The city is giving away a great number of trees, which aside from other values have a definite property value. It is not getting one penny in payment of these trees.

You may say that the city is getting $30,000 a year back. This is not in payment of the capital value of the subsurface projects. This is called a rental. It isn't even a rental but actually a payment in lieu of taxes because the city has agreed to deduct whatever taxes may be assessed from this so-called rental. You can make your own figures, but it can be shown that it is possible that the city will not get one penny in "rental."

You might say that the city is getting back some taxes as payment for the trees to be destroyed. The truth of the matter is that the city is making a bad deal. Compare this proposal with the Los Angeles underground garage. The City of Los Angeles is getting $200,000 a year plus 25 per cent of the rights for twenty years—$200,000 in Los Angeles, and we are supposed to get $30,000. Even as business, the city has not made a good financial deal for the people.

There is great talk about restoring the parks. According to the proposed figures, the park can never be restored. According to the figures of the proposed plan in the *San Antonio News* of October 15, the parks will be reduced from 112,225 square feet to 52,675 square feet. This is a reduction of the park of just over 50 per cent of its square feet area.

We shall later go into the legal and other aspects of the deals, aspects which will be of great interest to investment houses and their bond attorneys. We now say that we can have downtown parking and have Travis Park as well . . .

1955

Imagineering

Ford's remarks at the annual meeting of the Association of Collegiate Schools of Architecture in Cambridge, Massachusetts, in 1954 were published the following year in the Journal of Architectural Education. *In his talk he showed slides and may also have illustrated his ideas by sketching. Although he was invited chiefly to discuss the Youtz-Slick lift-slab system and, with fellow panelists, to answer the question "How should the impacts of scientific and technological change be reflected in architectural education?," Ford also ruminated on the relationship between architecture and engineering and on architectural education generally. Lamenting that young architects often lacked an understanding of materials, fundamental structural principles, and the design and construction processes, Ford argued for an approach to architectural training that emphasized the timeless, unchanging aspects of architecture and the importance of imagination to design, ideas to which he returned throughout his career.*

I have a seven-day lecture to give in twenty minutes. That is quite true. I am going to do it. I don't know if anybody will survive. I am pretty sure I will not.

But I have, as you know, a vast formal education behind me, and I got out my I.C.S. [International Correspondence Schools] books, every one of them, I looked through them and I found out a few things; I found out some very good things. I had not looked at them for twenty years. So I have decided, having had students who are graduates of Yale University and

Originally published in *Journal of Architectural Education* 10.1 (Spring 1955): 21–23.

Massachusetts Institute of Technology and Harvard and other universities working for me, that no teaching is any good at all. I don't like saying that because some brilliantly educated men have come to me, but somehow or other, in this great and ponderous curricula which they suffered with, the teachers at the school lost spontaneity, lost awareness, lost alertness. I don't know quite why, except that with the size of this place here, one is lost physically, mentally, and a lot of other ways. It looks to be too big a practical place or way of teaching.

So I started a series of lectures on Saturday mornings. They last four hours and I do the talking. Each man in our office is a registered architect; all of them except one has the master's degree. So I was confronted with the students. I found that they talk of all kinds of momentum and end reactions and all of that, I don't quite understand what they are talking about. True, I am not an engineer, I am an anti-engineer, but the simple understanding of tension and compression is almost beyond them. It is lost in the slide-rule world.

I just start simply—this is compression generally (illustrating)—this is tension and that is a wall and that wall supports nothing. . . . I want all this compression in abundance. I don't want a thousand columns. I want all of this abundance in the middle. I want this bent because I believe bending makes it function very beautifully, instead of simple span or cantilever. Let us bend it and pull it down and weld our sash, the mythological curtain there. No manufacturer has made one yet. We start with a thing just as simple. We discuss it and we design a barn like that.

We talk about tension. A piece of sheet metal, like this and that, with a column, all in a bend, where they begin and this in tension and this in mild compression. Again, this brings to these youngsters a certain kind of imagining that is good for them. They come up with a half dozen more notions like that. This has nothing to do with precise understanding of engineering but with understanding of carpentry.

We have lifted with this thing in Texas. I have been identified with it since its inception. I am called "Old Liftey." The
thing has served me quite well. I am indeed sorry that some
people in the eastern part of the United States know less about
concrete than the people do in Texas. It is not just concrete. In
Texas any carpenter can form concrete beautifully. They know
how to make it and handle it and they understand it precisely,
as we understand nothing whatever about steel. And we do not.

So this lifting business. Everything is lifted. And when I
think of the man-hours and the foot-pounds and the horsepower
that it takes to lift something, all of this stuff up in little pieces,
it is a shocking business. And the other day somebody tried to
figure the foot-pounds, man-hours, and horsepower and it ran
into the millions and millions of horsepower to put a little bit up.
Costs so much, so much gasoline, so much man-hour waste, all
of it. So this lifting thing is not a device, is not a slab, it is lifting
all of the building in a hunk. And I think it is the most significant attitude—I won't call it development—most significant
attitude that has come about in a long while. Strange, we have
lifted bridges, bascule bridges, all kinds of lifting, but never
lifted anything on a building except with a hod, crude gantry
crane, or elevator. That's where the architect comes in. You
can be damn well sure no engineer will ever move—they'll not
move away from the simple beam and the column and the simple systems of construction, complicated only by those things
the architect asks them to put together. I think of those great
artists, Mr. Severud, Mr. Nervi, and then I think of most of the
engineers I know, people who show me how to make it stick
together so it won't fall down. That's about it. They contribute
nothing almost to the creative process of architecture, and of
course, they are a part of architecture, these engineers.

So, in this lifting thing, it has occurred to us—a man
confronted by a lift-slab job, a big shower bathroom at a great
foundry in Alabama, the job fell through, was temporarily held
up, and he said, "We are going to have to take all of our money,

all of our resources, and build this steel barn where we will do the foundry work. We cannot build this magnificent shower-bath building." I said, "That lets me out, I am extremely sorry." I went down to the hotel and pondered and telephoned him, "Look, I want to see you again. I know how to build that thing vastly cheaper."

And it was a very scholarly process. All I did was put this rough truss on the ground. They have great welding facilities there. They weld this tubing together in a truss. So we welded it together, one truss right beside another, a man working in his habitat—and this is an important thing for the architect to know if he is interested in technological development. We put it together on the ground, the great venting hood, all the conduits, all the overhead piping, all made right there. Put one column in the middle, put the columns sixty feet apart. Then it's all set on this ground slab, and there is perhaps a beam there, may just be a pre-stressed slab fit into the columns, this simple jack, weld it at one and the same time, drawing great tension in the pieces of steel here which are four inches on centers. The building has figured 20 per cent cheaper.

It is not the first business of an architect always to make things cheaper. It is a rather delightful feeling that I can move ahead with engineering or with technology.

So it comes to mind again, these are simple exercises that we do. We need a dome. But I do not believe in building a beautiful wooden dome, a shining, fine piece of carpentry like that and making it tight to hold concrete and then pouring on the concrete. I don't believe it need be steel. I am not differing with Mr. Fuller, I'm not that presumptuous. They wonder through the years, what do you put on it, how do you cover it? I think it would be just as well to think of bones as bones and skin as skin and make them all of one piece and put them in the air. Very few of us know the process by which a building is put together. In pieces and parts, we know. But we don't know the process.

We studied the matter of moving earth. Now you can move earth in minutes, great masses of it. So let's put up a column here, like that [gesturing to a drawing or slide], let's put up a frame, something like this, and thereby light is trussed through here. Let's put the wheels here, like that. A little track here, a little track out here. Adjustment screws. Dome here and spilling the head here. Is that right? The earth is round. We will have previously put footings here, on the outside, like that, and we soon are introducing fill. So you start introducing a little shell. You have a few pipes in that, to keep the moisture content pretty even for four or five days, and adjust your screwers, and this form out here is the only form you have.

It can be done. We are making a model of it about ten feet across. It can span enormous distances, very little distance, top and bottom, beam steel, going over columns twenty feet apart on the outside, a form here and the steel is stubbed out. It's fine for us to think that the steel is stubbed out. It's good for us as architects, a way to create this design to know why we stubbed it out. Once this thing is poured, we are going to stretch wires around and around, side by side, to cover them up, we are going to pour concrete. Then we are going to lift this thing on jacks.

Will it work? Some engineers said it won't work. That doesn't mean a thing to me. Will an eggshell work? No engineer designed the eggshell, but it works. The thing will work.

I want to say this: all over the blackboard will be these things, and they will stay there for days and you come back, make notations, nothing happens, we leave the red and blue and yellow chalk, and I think we are going to have a wonderful time. I bawled them all out when I left and they bawled me out. We have an understanding. It is going to be interesting teaching for me because I know very little about teaching.

Now I am going to run off some of the slides. Unfortunately, I have not many pictures of the work of others. (Slides of Mr. Ford's lift-slab buildings at Trinity University were shown.)

1959

History and Development of La Villita Assembly Hall

In 1958 Ford returned to La Villita to design the 25,000-square-foot, circular La Villita Assembly Hall, which was needed for large meetings and events (figure 11). The building is most celebrated for its "bicycle-wheel" roof, which is an inverted dome hung by 200 steel strands strung between two rings 40 feet and 132 feet in diameter. It was the first such roof in Texas, and one of the first in the United States. Remarkably, Ford did not mention it in this statement. Instead he emphasized the ways the building harmonized with the much smaller buildings around it, and he drew attention to the fixtures and to the landscape, which was designed by Stewart King. He encouraged readers to understand the assembly hall not as a feat of engineering, but as a model of how to sensitively integrate new, very innovative buildings with old ones.

The Villita Assembly Building stands on the site of the first real power station in San Antonio. In its time the old yellow-brick building had seen many changes. Over the years its walls had been punched by openings in great variety—the underground powerhouse had been enlarged and changed, and new buildings had been added, some small brick ones on the east and a huge metal lean-to on the north.

And many changes were taking place in its surroundings: the San Antonio Library, immediately across the river to the

Architect's statement, unpublished, box 80, folder 12, O'Neil Ford: An Inventory of His Drawings, Papers, and Photographic Material, 1864–1983, Alexander Architectural Archives, University of Texas Libraries, University of Texas at Austin.

north; east of that, the Water Board spread out along the river, finally putting up a huge and brutal water-storage tank for a landmark. Directly opposite the old structure, La Villita was created. The restored Cos House and the Arneson River Theater became new neighbors, and further east on Villita Street, the San Antonio Conservation Society bought the house at 511 for its headquarters and the old O'Con saloon at the corner of Alamo for Conservation Corner.

As the old powerhouse gave way to new facilities, serving only the fewer and fewer users of direct current downtown, it came to be used more for warehouse and the storage of records. When the Public Service Board moved into its new, ample headquarters just a short block to the west, the records could be moved and the old buildings were finally available for other purposes.

There had been long felt the need for an assembly and meeting place for the board's employees, a place for home-service demonstrations and appliance shows. There had also been long under discussion the need of a large enclosed area to fill out the facilities of La Villita. The board then asked O'Neil Ford and his associates to make plans for the remodeling of the old structures. A long and careful study was made of the old buildings to see what could be created for usable space inside and what could be done to tie the odd group of structures into the character of its surroundings.

Inside, an attempt was made to create a large meeting space and auditorium. Outside, the attempt was made through overhanging balconies and patio arrangements to fit the scale of the little buildings in La Villita.

The very intense study showed that a large expenditure of money would be required to produce much less than what was needed and desired. The inside spaces could not be made large enough to provide for large assemblies for meeting and dining. The exterior forms of the buildings did not relate to the curving forms of land created by the river, conflicted with the huge drum of the water-storage tank on the east, and jarred the scale of La Villita and the rest of its surroundings. The old buildings interfered with the safe movement of traffic along Presa Street both as to view and space, and above all they were neither architecturally nor historically significant.

Faced with a great cost that would not be justified in the facilities to be obtained, it was decided to design a wholly new building, one that would provide the space and facilities needed and one that would fit its location, not by artificially and superficially [copying] old houses but by matching their quality in its own way, its form shaped by the uses and needs within, while fitting the movement and spaces of its location, its materials reflecting and repeating the spirit of its neighbors. It was to be a new building, individual yet harmonious.

GENERAL NOTES MATERIAL

The landscaping of the site was designed to relate the building and its setting to both the river on one side and La Villita on the other. A stone wall corresponding to the existing wall of La Villita encloses the large tiled patio that reaches to the river. The building opens on this patio through a large porch. The huge live oaks informally grouped in the patio and those more formally arranged on the outside provide shade to throw interesting patterns of shadow on the broad surfaces of the building. Around the trees and adjacent to the small meeting rooms are areas informally planted with shrubs and flowers. Along the street and among the trees in the patio, old gas streetlights have been placed to give a pleasant and friendly illumination that will fit in with the quality and play of light on and in the building. These lamps have been brought over from Copenhagen, Denmark, and date from the middle nineteenth century. Tile has been used externally for the terraces and patio consistent with the tradition and to take the heavy wear of many groups over the years.

FIGURE 11. O'Neil Ford; Stewart King, landscape architect, La Villita Assembly Hall for the City Public Service Board, San Antonio, 1958–1959.

As in all buildings done with great public concern, many people have taken part in the creation of this building. Acknowledgment must be made of the beautiful building work of the contractor, Mr. G. W. Mitchell, and his colleagues, his superintendent and the craftsmen and workers who put the building together. Throughout the entire course of design, planning, construction, outfitting, and finishing, all these people have been devoted to the creation of a building for civic use and satisfaction.

1960

Response to J. Robert Oppenheimer, American Institute of Architects Annual Convention

For its ninety-second annual convention in 1960, the American Institute of Architects met in San Francisco to discuss the topic "Expanding Horizons" and the role of architects in what was forecast to be unprecedented growth in the coming decades. Keynote speakers included an economist, a sociologist, a philosopher, and J. Robert Oppenheimer, the lead physicist in the development of the atomic bomb. In the 1950s Oppenheimer had come under intense scrutiny by Senator Joseph McCarthy and was stripped of his security clearance, in part, some believed, because he spoke forcefully about the dangers of the militarization of scientific knowledge. In 1960, along with Albert Einstein, Bertrand Russell, and others, he founded the World Academy of Art and Science. In his talk at the AIA convention Oppenheimer discussed the increasing pace of scientific discovery and, because of specialization, the widening gap in understanding between experts and the general public. This gulf was troubling, he said, because it made conveying the social and political implications of scientific discoveries increasingly difficult.

In his remarks Ford took up Oppenheimer's point and critiqued what he saw as a headlong embrace of technology without a full understanding of it. He condemned the failure to use science more effectively for humanitarian purposes. In an echo of his "Organic Building," the second section of "Toward a New Architecture," written with Thomas D. Broad, Ford linked the urge to build and an uncritical attitude toward technology to the destruction of the landscape and historic buildings. Ultimately,

Originally published as part of O'Neil Ford, Burnham Kelly, and George F. Keck, "Panel Discussion," *AIA Journal* 33.6 (June 1960): 65–72.

he pleaded for restraint and careful deliberation in science and in architecture.

Everyone has been so nice and so circumspect and the phraseology has been so lovely here in all of these speeches. I have never seen architects talk with each other in such courteous ways and with such lovely manners. Quite uncommon to you who are architects—I tell you that. You are putting on a good show. It has been marvelous.

May we compliment the people who arranged this series of lectures because all of us on the panel have thought that this is about the nicest thing and may very well have something to do with keeping this atmosphere of dignity. These are good things, done beautifully, and the people you have to speak are most outstanding. When I hear a lecture such as we heard from Dr. Oppenheimer and I see the ovation at the end, I know he is a beloved man. It makes all of us feel good that we are devoted to the ideals, to the things that he has done, to the history of his trials and tribulations; it makes us feel good about the intent and the attitude of architects to such men as he.

Now, I don't remember anything he said. It is something like a good symphony: if it is done well, you don't remember the phrases you may not know, and in this case I do not know enough to separate the phraseology in a great piece of music. I don't know enough to take his lecture and cut it apart. But I remember one important thing he said which fits precisely with what little I have to say. He said this great period of scientific growth has created new problems.

So I choose not to go along with all of the niceties, and I choose, rather, to try to be a little difficult. My partner, Sam Zisman, had a great old father who in Boston would come to every meeting, whatever it was. He would come there and usually participate in a violent manner, take some side or other side. One day he sat in the back and he didn't say anything. Not a word. So all the elders were quite disturbed that Mr. Zisman had nothing to contribute, nothing to hate, nothing to praise. Finally, they said, "Mr. Zisman, aren't we going to hear something from you?"

"Not just yet," he replied. "You will later, yes, and when I speak I shall be bitter."

In 1953 the president of the United States made a brilliant and one of the better speeches of his career. He said we should depart from this idea that atomic energy and all its developments and processes will be devoted entirely to the destruction of other people. We shall soon see—and I am not quoting, but this is the essence of it—great nuclear plants devised and designed so that life will become a much simpler, better thing for all of the free peoples of the earth. And so, since then nobody in America has built a nuclear-powered plant of any consequence at all.

This is the point. There have been three built in England, I believe—adequate ones, not just pilot plants—and I believe three more are under construction now big enough to do a job. What would happen if America had done what someone said it was to do? How would we face this revolution in the world, this revolution that is so far-reaching and such an upheaval that we can think of nothing like it at all, nor have we read of any revolution of such breadth and consequence? This is a time when America, with the precepts and the concepts that founded it, should be able to put these things into the hearts and the hands of the struggling people of the world, perhaps in the form of nuclear steam plants, electrical steam plants, because they need them and because they cannot buy oil.

The fact that every speaker has said something will double in ten years, something will happen in thirty which has not happened in all of history before—the fact that a few European countries have been able to double production of fossil fuels, one kind or another, coal or oil, does not mean they will be able to do it for very long.

As a matter of fact, all this building, all this production, all this snow-balling, this curve that goes up and up means however fast they produce from the bowels of the earth, they will be caught—and caught short. And what have we, as Americans, missed? The most marvelous opportunity.

Now, I am not surprised and I am not being critical of a certain political group, either, because our government is made up of all kinds of people. But I feel today that we must fight to save those things which are beautiful in our land, to save our parks, to crush the impending disaster of concrete and engineering—when I fight for those, I don't feel I have any representatives for sure to fight for what I believe.

I think that what Dr. Bell said yesterday is quite true. Some people not only do not understand the precepts of the Constitution and the Bill of Rights but some of the powers in the world which are represented eliminate my being represented. I don't have much representation.

May I make an example of this? We have not done what we might have done with atomic energy, but we have been sold bills of goods. We feel we have been sold the atomic age in beautiful phrases over and over again by speaker after speaker. Now, suppose that very soon somebody relents or somebody decides to wait for the leveling-off process in economics—which was the official reason, by the way, for the decision not to build nuclear steam plants—they will wait until things take their level and then we will see whether or not we need them. Dear me!

Well, Count Sforza didn't wait for Da Vinci to paint. He said, "You live in my house, get busy and paint." Of course, everybody remembers Da Vinci and they remember Count Sforza. Count Esterházy said to "Papa" Haydn, "You make music, make it now. You are almost a slave, almost a servant in my household"—and nobody remembers Esterházy very well. Nobody would remember him at all if it had not been for "Papa" Haydn.

What president, what great man will arise, what group of great men, what representatives of the free and wonderful people that we are, will stand up to this ridiculous thing, to the misplacement and to the misappliance of the energies of America, both physical and human?

My children, for instance—and I will make this pertinent with the things I have said as I go along—can draw the most extraordinary diagrams of elemental systems of atomic fission, and they know the words. When I told them I was coming here to be on a panel with Dr. Oppenheimer, they said, "Look, do you know about this, do you know about this, and so forth and so forth?" And they knew plenty. What are they? Twelve and nine. And so they went on talking and I was quite amazed and I said, "Look, where did you learn all of this?" And they said, "Oh, we learn it in school." They said, "We get this in the fourth grade. We get this right along." So I said, "This is astonishing." And as I packed to leave, I was disillusioned by all of this. You see, we are going to beat Russia by teaching all of this in the fourth grade. We are going to give them much more homework, too. We are going to give them calculus in the sixth and seventh grade. We're going to beat Russia, don't worry, we'll put it on them. As I turned to leave, the little boy said, "You know, I don't think he understood us." And the little girl said, "Neither do I. You know, I don't believe he ever saw an atom, I am sure he wouldn't know how to split one."

This is a father's position in the family—dreadfully sabotaged. But there are children who do know those things. I saw some of five and six when I baby-sat with some friends' children who worked an abacus so fast I couldn't follow it at all—little French children. I was astonished.

But my children, when they are taken from home to school, look upon the ugliest city, one of the ugliest cities in the ugliest country of all the earth, with the possible exception of eastern Canada and most of Australia. They look upon the dreadful sight, where the huckster is given every opportunity, every freedom to make for us this ugliness, and they don't understand precisely nor do they have any level of judgment to understand what we mean when we say we are being gobbled, completely gobbled and consumed by the unstudied, unneeded, ill-considered building of these gargantuan, foolish concrete structures called expressways which have become long and smelly parking lots.

These little children have been taught lots of wonderful things, but they cannot be sensitive to the things that I hate, which is the threat and destruction of the Commons in Boston. I hate the idea in my own town, San Antonio, Texas—some of you may have been there. We have a little more green than most other cities in Texas, we have a little water running through the town, we have a sort of civilized zoo and a park. How, I don't know. Foresighted citizens fought and bled for this, a lot of do-good women, old biddies saved it.

Now what happens? After two hundred years of trying to save what is charming and delightful, a town with a European background, a distinctive town, a town where I have taken friends of mine so many times to their delight to find that it was a subtle thing, with subtle architecture, subtle blending of Mexican and German.

Now here come a group of men who care not, who care not for this and who care not for those who would restore the steeple of the Old North Church when it was torn down in a hurricane, who care not about the destruction of the wilderness because soon we will have no wilderness—soon it will all mix into a messy nothing where there is neither urban nor suburban nor country civilization, and, dear me, if you come to Dallas and Fort Worth it is there. There is no edge of the land where the people farm, there is no edge at all to the city. It is not like Bath, in England, where the city ends and the country begins. You walk from one to the other. And you enjoy them.

I have talked very, very generally about the things that seem disastrous in America. I remember an artist in 1938, when Hitler first arose—I remember this artist and I wish I remembered his name, a rather famous name, who was on a radio program and they had a panel and they came up to him and said, "Sir, we should like to know very much if you had your choice what would you like to do? What most would you like to do?" So he said, "Well, I should like to be the Messiah with the courage and the means and the mind to destroy that thing which is about to destroy the world, that thing which is about to create hate and intolerance and thousands and thousands of deaths. If I just could somehow, maybe talk to those men, or maybe shoot them, or do something about this man Hitler, but since I cannot do that, would you permit me to play my piccolo on a coast-to-coast broadcast?" And he did!

Now I shall end. I shall end and try to put a little of this together. First, may we not feel indignation and hate for these tyrannical acts. Indignation for this callous destruction of our lovely land and our beauty is the first form of love—hate of these is love, hate of these is sympathy, hate of these is the daring to hope.

We have in San Antonio a city manager, and I would dwell on this as an example. This city manager is a member of a group of city managers, and it is a good form of government, I must assure you—although he is not elected in the strict sense by the people. But he goes from one city to another, from Toledo to San Antonio, which is a jump; from Hutchinson, Kansas, to San Antonio, Texas. He gets an increase in salary, he keeps in touch with his fellow associates, the other city managers. What happens? He makes a record. He goes to Cincinnati and gets $6,000 more a year, and he is not a part of things. He is a part of engineering or technology, perhaps, and he is something of a city planner, but he is not like an architect, sympathetic to all of the town, sympathetic to the people of the town who have made it, to the cultural background. He is a technocrat and must be treated as such.

So, if we have failed somewhat in the application and the use of these marvelous things, these marvelous things that this man knows so well, so intimately, and of which he says the discoveries will accelerate at a great rate, if men with brains and with education still are looked upon as eggheads, and if it becomes necessary in America—and I say this rather cautiously but with great respect for those who feel differently—if it becomes necessary in America that a man gather the courage to say we must take exception to this business of civil rights, somehow the real meaning of America is abdicated, is it not? I said if it becomes necessary that a man do this. And we are not attentive to those things Dr. Bell said yesterday—very few people feel deeply about the Constitution and the Bill of Rights and you would almost assume do not agree with their wonderful precepts.

I have talked a lot and round-about. I have tried to speak seriously about many things I do not know enough about. I will quote now a little something from one member who is present, a friend of mine, I hope, Paul Thiry, from this good *Journal of the American Institute of Architects*, which in the last several years has supported excellent discussion, documented in here, the writing so much better than what I have said this morning.

Paul says, "For the first time in the history of man we appear to be faced with the overwhelming urge to build everyplace and anywhere. This urge carries us far beyond recognition of existing values or correctness of what we propose to do. Because this urge is on an accelerating basis and relatively uncontrolled, it must be of concern to us. For as certainly as we cannot avoid building by building, what we do most inevitably has its effects. If we denude the country, it will be denuded, and if we build in the wilderness, we will not have a wilderness. As architects, we should know by now that all but the city dies with construction. We need open country and wilderness, both for our own use and for future generations. We are faced with the responsibility for the successful development of the community, the town, and the city. It is here where architecture provides the setting and the facility for man's activities. It is here where we depend entirely on architecture for the protection of our environment."

PART III

In and Against the World

1964

Texas Idyll

*While traveling in Europe in October 1964, Ford was tempo-
rarily separated from his luggage and, along with it, the draft
of a lecture on the history of architecture in San Antonio. Ford
rewrote the talk but turned it into a "letter" to his wife, Wanda.
He opened with deft, humorous, and vivid evocations of San
Antonio and Italy. The text reflects the architect's lifelong love
of the city and his particular capacity to identify continuities in
works of architecture from very different times and places. Ford
interpreted distinctive Texas buildings in terms of a wide and
ancient world beyond the state.*

*Ford urged his readers to convert their study of architectural
history into advocacy. He framed the cause of conservation and
the patronage of good new design in broad terms that conveyed
his deep sense of architecture's inseparability from social and
political life. The text was published in* Inland Architect *after his
death in 1982.*

Having spent this entire Sunday morning here in Naples trying to interest Alitalia Airlines in giving me assistance in the
search for my lost bag, I have wasted a day that should have
been spent refining the speech you have asked me to write
about the architectural history of our San Antonio area. I had
in fact written it all between New York and Lisbon, at odd
moments in Lausanne, between appointments in Zurich, and
had just about decided it must end.

What a sad flight from Rome to Naples (no landing), and
it was followed by a grim bus ride that finally put us here at

Originally published in *Inland Architect* 26 (September–December 1982):
32–35.

midnight. Now it is 8:00 p.m., and only minutes ago came a call from Alitalia's one really sympathetic person, a Mr. Cariolo, with the great news that my bag had been "safe and sound in Rome all the way." He thinks it—and thus my essay, neatly zipped in the side pocket—will come down Monday, but if this wild storm continues, I doubt they will fly (not even Italians would face this one).

So I am beginning to write it all over again as I smoke a dreadful Sumatra cigar and take a last look, from this eighteenth-floor room, at the bright lightning on Vesuvius and the houses bordering the bay. One flash beyond Capri just set up a sharp, clear silhouette of that jagged island. I should feel some measure of inspiration here above the Partenope, the beautiful Opera House, and its neighboring bright red Palace—but the urgency of this task blasts the romance.

It now seems sensible that I just make it all a letter to you, and I think that such a choice may have real advantages. Certainly it can't be one of those over-academic, over-researched things in many historical journals. I haven't any sources along for dates and places, so I must rely on memory, impressions, and strong feelings.

I can also make this one shorter than the one that lies in some storage room in the Eternal City. You will do well to read only bits and pieces of this, using them to make a plea for respect, responsibility, decency, and urgent needs—all of which relate to conserving those things in our town that are significant in keeping our interesting history and in making new things of beauty.

It does occur to me that it would be far easier to write about the history and architecture of the ancient Greek city of Paestum, just down the coast from here, than about San Antonio. Beautiful Paestum was contained so that what was inside its walls was Greece; outside, except for farms and simple shelters, was the unknown or the enemy. What can be seen in Paestum are the three wonderfully beautiful Temples, and the most casual look at them will establish the order in which they were built (which is also the order of their beauty). There are sufficient ruins to establish the location of streets, town gates, and irrigation ditches. Some good guessers have placed the shops and storehouses in its fine plan. Paestum is simple enough to understand. Its end was mysterious, and it is quite a dead thing. Its story has an end, a beginning, and dimensions.

San Antonio, over two thousand years younger, is quite alive. Its past is hours ago, measured by Paestum time. The peoples who made it, the places they came from, and the subtle mixing of many influencing cultures set the writer at a disadvantage. The result, these causes, and their manifestations make the city entirely fascinating. This unacademic history and character makes any kind of labeling next to impossible. Our pioneers were notoriously negligent about recording their activities, and even more sparse are the records of what was built and by whom.

Any historian proposing to write the whole story must sense that the inferences of the slogan "Six Flags Over Texas" would make his task formidable. The architectural historian would find his problems doubled, for the influences that shaped the character of San Antonio's buildings from 1730 on are vastly more numerous, mixed, and mutated than is indicated by the fact that six countries did claim this wide country.

It does seem rather remarkable that the earliest missionary padres and their slim little military escorts left a solid record of their comings and goings. Even the sad venture of the brave La Salle is a story with plausible continuity and sequence, the gaps being filled with reasonable legend. Only the strange and wandering Jean Henri [Jean Jarry], who survived to rule several Indian tribes, leaves us gaps that one yearns to see filled. Neither he nor La Salle left any buildings to mark certain places.

Yet La Salle's little fort on Matagorda Bay and Henri's camps around Carrizo Springs deterred Spanish colonization, while also keeping the padres alert to the need for pushing on.

Against great adversity of climate, hostile Indians, their own hesitancy, and the inconsistency of Spanish governmental bodies, who gave them only token protection, they made their thin paths deep into East Texas forests, setting up posts for their faith against the threatening French.

They built as well and as quickly as they could. With the meager skills of the native Indians, with their own knowledge and hands, they took any stones, logs, twigs, and grasses to hand and made their tiny mission buildings. Their retreat to the southwest, to San Antonio in particular, set them in a relatively safe area and afforded them soft limestone that could be quickly cut, fitted, and carved. In a few years there arose those buildings that were the strongest evidence that this had in fact become a part of New Spain.

These strong men built, much as they had in Mexico, by the style and systems they had known from Spain. There were architects among them, and sufficiently skilled masons and carvers, to make churches and chapels like the late Renaissance buildings that had been and were being built in the New World, above and below the equator, where conquest and conversion had spread at a great pace. This seems quite the wrong time to critically analyze any or all of the buildings and mission plans, but I wish to press one strong personal contention: Sentimental enthusiasts have fostered the naïve impression that these good padres themselves designed these fine buildings and provided the miracle that made them rise in their full beauty without benefit of design and technical knowledge. Any student of architecture recognizes that these relatively simple structures were reminders of a reasonably sound assemblage of foundation, walls, and roof. But something more was necessary, and this added thing was the important thing: Architects of some degree of professional ability had to be there—to draw plans, to direct the work, to make a new, beautiful thing in a particular place that was in the "style" they already knew.

The beautiful, rather Romanesque façade of Conception Mission is crowded with details that illustrate a primitive interpretation of a developed academic style. The oversteep pediment above the main door is hard pressed by the adjacent circular windows [he refers to the arched windows], and from above it is again weighed down by another too-close opening [figure 5]. Yet this fine front clearly shows how very good is the provincial interpretation of any style that has become too fixed to be vigorous.

The fine big plan and the beautiful church and granary at San José Mission need no word of explanation from me. It is secure as a national monument. Though its rather heavy elaboration in carving and molding makes it rather less strong and clear than Conception, it has the look of a whole thing.

There is no sufficient set of phrases or calculated praises for those who saved San José. When I first knew it, the dome was fallen and the quadrangle was no more than spotty bits of barely visible foundations. Again I saw it when the tower had been so neglected that it was split and half down. Then, still later, valiant efforts were needed and provided to prevent the cutting of the great green yard by a highway. Now it is one of America's great buildings.

The Alamo is "The Alamo," once the Mission San Antonio de Valero. Even the relatively recent profile of the reconstructed façade is made almost authentic by the honored place this little building holds in American history. It is pointless to bemoan the sorry early "restorations." There wasn't much to guide the rebuilders. It stands among hundreds of buildings of lesser distinction and it, along with the "new" river, sets San Antonio's identity most clearly. May the city fathers and the planners soon see fit to cut out the paved drive that slices across its front plaza so that grass and trees may extend to Alamo Street, thus providing a desired setting in a generous space. "The Alamo" should have no responsibility to anyone for the convenience of parking cars!

Down the river, on miserable road approaches, are the little Missions San Juan Capistrano and San Francisco de la Espada. They, like Conception, were founded in far east Texas but after a few years were reestablished here. Their walled yards have all but disappeared, and they have suffered innumerable alterations—having been the quarry for parishioners lining their water wells. But they are a surprise and joy as one comes upon them rather sidewise.

I clearly remember Espada when pretty little early nineteenth-century houses and pieces of older buildings almost surrounded the plaza. I remember when the newer, unrelated school building wasn't there at all: the old one could have been rebuilt, but "someone didn't bother" to look into that matter.

San Juan is barely there. The foundations of the original chapel across the plaza from the building now called the chapel (and used as a church) are much the most revealing detail of the whole group. It was ambitiously buttressed and ingeniously worked into a rather sophisticated plan, but it has long since gone to the spoilers. In the last fifteen years, the roof has fallen from the fine old hall adjacent to the present chapel, and the plaza, which I remember from my first visit in 1922 as a fine green place, now only shows neglect and dead trees. These two missions must be saved, and the time is short.

This little paper, much the sketchiest thing it had to be, is only fitting as an introduction to those who would plead for the preservation of our historic identity, which is best made clear by saving our fine old buildings and recording all possible truths about them, their builders, and those who lived in them.

The missions and the Governor's Palace were built and used, then abandoned, then intermittently used some more, and generally allowed to decay until recent times. In the hundred or so years between their building and the coming of organized, drifting groups of settlers, San Antonio was a lonely outpost that showed little sign that it would become a real, solid town. There were other Spanish buildings, and special sadness goes with their story. The Veramendi "Palace" was torn down a shockingly short time ago, and the Governor's Palace barely missed the same pointless end. The old, singularly beautiful San Fernando Cathedral is mostly there, where it always was, but is buried in the bigger late-nineteenth-century cathedral, which is made of excellent stone but quite undistinguished as architecture.

What is forgotten and lost that stood from 1750 to 1790? Little is known about the several houses and many mission dependency buildings. Someday some serious scholar may go to Spain and unearth pertinent plans and records. Few other buildings were built until after the Mexican and Texas Revolutions. After 1840 the move was on, and an incredible mixture of races and ethnic groups began to put together an entirely unique American town.

Except for the distinct Spanish character of the earliest buildings, San Antonio's significant historic character is nineteenth century. The whole flow of peoples of many states and lands took the problems (and blessings) of climate and materials and made a place of certain style, abandoning the rudimentary indigenous house-with-a-porch and adopting the styles of the grownup cities to the east and north.

The earlier houses, evincing personal resourcefulness or pure expedience, were of mud and sticks, vertical supports and clay, caliche blocks cut from the river banks, of the few precious [rocks] and stones they could quarry. When the first settlers from the young United States and Europe did begin to trickle in about 1840, there were the first slight signs of the Classic Revival. Such remembrances began to show in modest column capitals, now and then in a row of dentils, often in a simple pediment, more often in the replacement of a hewn door or window frame with laboriously planed classical moldings. One fine old house on Laredo Street had walls of cedar stakes driven in the ground—chinked with mud, and smeared with lime plaster—and a carefully carved row of dentils made of solid timber creased its narrow porch. Usually such economical pretentions were set on the old square-plan house, with its gabled or hipped roof of split cypress shingles, which soon gave way to the typical sheet-metal standing-seam roofs.

In the early 1850s, this period of copying stylistic affectations brought real architects to our frontier. John Fries from Germany did the Old Market House, the Old State Capitol, the Vance house, many storefronts on Dolorosa, and the Casino Club; Francois Giraud, born in Charleston of French immigrant parents, gave us fine buildings entirely comparable to any in the more developed East, including our finest group of buildings, the Ursuline Convent.

After the middle of the century, the Doric embellishment of the old square houses was showing in some new houses. Then the Victorian "lace" of jigsaws and lathes poured forth to express the exuberance of a growing, vigorous land, producing some of the most delightful "wedding cake" architecture in America. Its creators were Mexicans, Germans, Frenchmen, Irishmen, and the several traveled gentlemen who had seen this spirited style in St. Louis. They added their western variations and mixed the details they found in those close-at-hand plan books. Like the padres, and the precise classicists, they made the style more a local style. Perhaps the finest of these houses found in one area are on King William Street.

As I pause to ponder the impossible task of putting praise and bitterness to some purpose, the names and the looks of so many good buildings that are gone almost blanks my joy over the fair number that have been saved. How have I said so much but said nothing about the great good deed done by the Conservation Society when they purchased and restored the José Antonio Navarro house? Where is there space or time to say how grateful we are for the restoration of the German English School by the Hemisfair Committee? What can be said to make some way to save the Vollrath house on South Alamo? What is the future of the delightful Monier house, on Salinas, and the exquisite Santelben house, on Elmira and Flores, which once showed a fine old garden and great trees—now asphalt? Is there a way to save the Schultze store on Goliad? With genuine sadness I remember our losses, mostly absolutely useless destruction. I especially regret or resent, as the case fits, the destruction of the Vance house (by John Fries), which could have been avoided by a better use of the plot for the new building, the burning of the Schmeltzer house, and the unforgivable destruction of the Desmazieres house and store on South Alamo Street to make room for a tiny, ugly parking lot. It is reasonable that some fine buildings did stand in the way of logical change and progress, but hundreds were torn out for the most unacceptably foolish reasons, and casually, and on a few occasions with vindictive fervor and defiance. Almost every good building that stands today reflects our history and stands for beauty—indeed, for the good economics of beauty. How many foreigners and Americans (there are hundreds of thousands of visitors a year) would believe the shocking truth that the Alamo barely missed the adamant destroyers and that San José stands as "Queen of the Missions" because a lot of people spent a lot of time fighting to prevent a highway blasting through its grounds?

Here in Naples, just yesterday, an engineer from Turkey, upon learning that I live in San Antonio, grew enthusiastic in his praise of our little San Antonio River and was entirely happy to know that the plans to make it a more beautiful shopping and walking area are under way. He couldn't believe the story of its rescue from the sane, honorable, but unimaginative city fathers who almost covered it over to make a convenient rear-entrance service alley to get the trucks off the main streets. Now the river makes its especially strong point of character and delight for our town.

The departed buildings and special places, lovingly remembered, allow us a forcible reminder that we must now respect the works of our forebears, must solidly document our building history, and must press harder for the preservation, restoration, and proper use of good buildings from the past so that our descendants may know we were civilized to a considerable degree and so put in their share of effort to save something from a rather remarkable past.

Well, my dear, I got very sleepy and rather confused by the enormity of a decent freehand history. I do ask that you use only the readable paragraphs and do all the really significant explaining in your own earnest, exciting way. So it's now 2:00 a.m.—October 26, 1964—Naples. I am mailing this now—should be there in time.

1964

The Condition of Architecture

In 1964 Rice University celebrated its first fifty years with a lecture series titled "The People's Architects." Organized by Harry S. Ransom and published that year, the talks were delivered by some of the nation's preeminent architects, including I. M. Pei, Pietro Belluschi, Victor Gruen, and O'Neil Ford. This lecture was among the most important that Ford ever gave. In it he laid out his views on the state of the profession and architectural writing, and discussed his travels and study of history. Ford returned to the themes of sprawl and the treatment of the landscape that had animated earlier texts, spoke forcefully in favor of civil rights, and called on architects to "achieve the significant and larger purpose of serving all people."

I read much history, many technical articles, all possible literature about materials, systems, and devices, but I cannot bring myself to read the voluminous spewing of philosophy and esoteric writing that architects, editors, and critics are producing today. The adulation, deification, and omniscient postures of most architectural magazine writers seem to say little that is related to the man, the lines, the specifications, and the judgment—yes, judgment and discernment—that make good buildings. Nevertheless, my reaction to literary and conversational architecture is not so far from the center as my son's definition of architecture: "the stuff that is piled against the force of gravity and wind, and then leaks, cracks, and finally falls down." He may be as right as the glorifiers.

Reprinted from *The People's Architects*, ed. Harry S. Ransom (Chicago: University of Chicago Press for William Marsh Rice University, 1964), 31–50.

I am an avid listener, however, when sincerity and enthusiasm characterize an individual, a writer, or a group's search for answers. When a student, or, hopefully, an alive young architect, gathers to discuss architecture with his betters, his equals, or his professors, he finds causes, reasons, enthusiasm, moments of disgust, and some boasting expressed with refreshing earnestness. He answers, agrees, or stands his ground until the exchange is interrupted and the group is ejected by the bored proprietor. The talk continues under the lamps, and though nothing is resolved, the interchange is a creative exercise unhampered by time, economics, or any pragmatic demand. Recently, in Paris, I listened to such a colloquy that didn't gain momentum until midnight or resolve itself by dawn. As I drank the last of many strong coffees, I wondered how the adult architect—the hard-pressed practitioner—could ever find a similar stimulus in a group of his confreres, at a convention or in any of the journals that arrive on his desk every month. That experience in Paris was barely different from one in London where the students from the A.A. (Architectural Association School of Architecture) generated a violent roar, a fierce fight over the way things are taught in architectural schools, the way buildings are planned and built, and the way things are written about the way things are built. Watching these fine performances and proudly hearing the discourses of several American students in the groups, I was pleased to listen. I wondered when I had been to an A.I.A. meeting, a convention, or a public lecture where any strong or even weak sentiments were so fervently expressed about architecture. I have watched all of us become ethical professionals who scrupulously avoid and evade every subject or situation that might slightly imply our incompetence or the infrequence of any superior accomplishments.

A heavy cloud covers my thoughts as I ponder the gap between the freshness and idealism of these unusual students and the trivial and vulgar works of builders, architects, and developers that eventually appear and make up the negative nothingness of our streets and their positive ugliness. It is not just that contented egoism and adamant huckstering have made our country so irreparably ugly but that all the brackets of privileges and restraints that our great founders put on paper and so seriously and profoundly pledged seem so brutally abridged or selfishly interpreted by the "go-getters" and "not doers." These good founding precepts were not abstract prognostications but were the sharp, clear, and sensitively framed structure for the projection of an imaginative idea and a sensible civilization. The means and methods were clearly stated.

All physical ugliness and social ugliness have strong concomitants and roots. Incredibly, there is rampant today all manner of hate and fierce argument on the basic idea—of all things—of civil rights. Today our great privileges are so flaunted and license so condoned that in some of our cities 30 per cent of the citizens live in slums. Not just the physical man is crushed, but all rights, equalities, opportunities, and self-respect go down. It seems, therefore, not a crooked analogy to lock hand in hand the bitter disregard for the rights of others with the callous notion that a man may put up anything ugly, vulgar, or trivial he wishes so long as it is "big enough" and he has the money. Can you think how seriously tragic it is that any congressman or lawmaker, anywhere, can find a reason or the audacity to speak against the civil rights of any man or group of men? Isn't it indeed strange that in this land of billboards, ugly poles and wires, pop architecture and slums, we have as a complementary and parallel circumstance the monstrous idea that if a Samaritan loves his fellow man, fights for another's causes, simply does something for him, then he is a "bleeding heart"? Is it not incredible that if a man has intellectual attainments, or even intellectual curiosity, he may be labeled an egghead—this, in a country frantic to advance every curriculum to excellence, from the first grade to graduate study? Is the student who carries a stack of good phonograph records under his arm really a "longhair" or an "odd"? Is the young man who wears a beret more effeminate than the one who wears a Homburg? It is evident that the student or any man who cares more deeply about what he does than what he receives for it, architect included, must expect pointing fingers. An attack on personal rights, pursuits, and nonconformity of all kinds does seem like an attack on gravity, growth, and life itself.

This physical and social ugliness is producing a very real and shocking effect on the youth of our country. The usurpation and defamation of land by vulgarians and the construction of square miles of shacks have given us a generation of children with blinders built on both sides of their heads and minds. They move along our city streets, looking through a narrow slit, seeing nothing as they pass, and seeking only the decent places they know—their houses, their schoolrooms, their green playgrounds—where there is release and relief from the billboards, the dull architecture, and the flamboyant huckstering. Like sightless fish in deep ocean holes, they know not what they see or what they do not see. They have few discriminative powers; their standards *are* the billboards, the insistent neon signs, the black poles, transformers, and wires, the ugly lettering, the "misleading" advertising, the Perma-Stone houses. The wrong things men build cry out "impulse selling and buying." Last week, one of my children saw the point for a moment. As we drove along in our mental and visual parenthesis, we noticed a sign which read "Beware of Imitations—This Is a Genuine Perma-Stone Installation." We laughed, but not enough to shake the horrible house. So, we, and to a greater degree, our children, become unobservant as this ugliness creeps like a prairie fire, as towns lose their edges, as the separation of towns becomes more and more blurred by junk, by incomprehensible expressway intersections, by a system of speed roads that completely ties the man to strict observance and sharpened skill in a race through ugliness to his hut or to his castle.

In our marvelously engineered 300-horsepower steeds, in our bigger and longer compacts with appropriate chrome, stamped ridges, and bulges, we look over the extensive deck shining ahead of us, and without stretching our necks or moving ourselves at all, we see wonders of motels and restaurants and other sights of South Main in Houston. After we pass the big exclamation point, "The Shamrock," South Main becomes as noisy, brash, and vulgar as close-in Main Street was dull and decaying. As we progress northward on Preston Road in Dallas, the blaze of "selling pieces" is only momentarily interrupted by the chic of the Neiman-Marcus Store. A longer, more strident commercial effort vies for one's attention as one moves through the varied splendor of Colfax in Denver. Who has seen the sad things that Tucson and Phoenix have become? Have you seen the road to Alamogordo as it stretches through El Paso's own special neon slum? Who knows Ayres Street in Corpus Christi? Driving from the great prairies toward the corporate limits, the first establishments to greet the visitor are vast wrecked-car lots—acres of them, and growing. Then, through a fantastic variety of nasty architecture and nasty signboards, one makes his treeless way toward the bay, and not until he has reached the bluff is there any relief from the mess—the incredibly mediocre buildings. There is not time to recount the hideous accomplishments in Los Angeles, and we know they will become more numerous, but the city's sad influence on the surrounding desert towns is sickening. One expects little from Los Angeles, Reno, and Las Vegas, the latter two particularly having neither purpose nor direction, but it is jolting to see the environs of Palm Springs, Palm Desert, Indio, and a sad string of sloppy towns all the way to El Paso. This condition has spread where one scarcely expects it. The same disfigurement grows apace in Nashville and Charlotte, and the frilly grillwork of New Orleans seems a little silly in competition with the real gillifrass of the fringes. Finally, there is Oklahoma City! Its highways, leading from town into the Oklahoma prairie, may well exhibit the most miserable clutter of them all.

On the other end of the scale is the equally depressing variety and over-effort of Idlewild Airport, through which I have passed innumerable times. There are a few reasonably pleasant spots on the grounds, but there is almost no place for the traveler. Furthermore, he feels scaled to midget size while he is being pushed through the bewildering pattern of the dismal Big Plan of the place.

Do we condone this; do we really fight it? Do the Australians and people of Toronto know that they, too, are being swallowed by this appalling and ever-accelerating growth? Are we, as architects and planners, entirely impotent in the face of this irresponsible triumph of the vulgarians? How do we answer when we are confronted by a list of monstrous structures in Houston and discover that many of the buildings and the exotic signs were designed by architects? Many of the multicolored motels, capital eat places, and capital beer places came from the offices of honorable and upstanding citizen architects. They have chosen not to put themselves above the hucksters, or below them, but shoulder to shoulder. For example, there are the sure-footed supermarket designers who are quick to adopt any cliché, trick, or showy device that they see published in a magazine or that wins some institutional award, for they are set and ready for solid adoption or enlargement. I should not speak of the spread of Sheep Dog screens that are used across the fronts of so many buildings. I have never done one, and it seems that I am always late to see the value of such wildly accepted innovations. We are busy building just buildings, so we haven't time for serious thought about screens, glass blocks, corner windows, great sign pylons over rock, and cactus entrance gates until they are widely recognized as old hat. Every now and then one sees the ingenious perforated screens that seem to be the main purpose for building at all. They are, I believe, quite as solid a general panacea as Perma-Stone is at a lower level.

Just a month ago I heard an architect and an engineer heatedly debate whether a concrete-block wall costing $.80 a square foot would support a gorgeous concrete curtain costing $6.00 a square foot. I observed that the windows, vents, and walls were placed in disorder, befitting the disorderly plan, and that the shaggy screen would do wonders for this disorder of openings that were scattered vertically, horizontally, and differently on all façades. It seems proper, we observe, that Corbusier never seemed to worry about his disorder in the openings at Ronchamp as they pushed inward and outward [figure 14]. He knew precisely where he wanted them. It is refreshing to know that Corbusier's copycats soon find themselves on a dead limb. As soon as the derivers sense the freedom of his "disorder," they pounce upon it and vigorously apply it. The great man's sudden abandonment of a system or device must be bewildering. The copyists must come to quick stops and begin their adulation and rationalization all over again, as the master moves in his own creative sphere—rightly or wrongly, beautifully or sometimes clumsily.

All the boards in architectural schools now carry the burden of weighty and shaggy concrete blobs, and this, mixed with the Lincoln Log concrete style so affectionately fostered in several schools, may well produce a coarseness close to that period following the Columbian Exposition. What the early 1900s did to the classic orders will be and is being done to Ronchamp.

Just a few years ago the fad in hundreds of schools was the stiff and stringy drawings of the Followers of Mies. It was a hard and sharp contest with thin lines and sheer stretches of invisible walls—or no walls. They understood neither the weaknesses nor the strengths of Mies. Between these tiresome and extended rituals came thin shells. All the students, all the professors, all the competitors set them side by side by the thousands. This fashion in models and string flourished while Mr. Candela continued to build his inexpensive warehouses and factories in which he employed the blossom and tent shapes to cover big spaces with good design and interesting shapes, using cheap labor and materials. Soon the highways sported motels and filling stations with entrance features that were shells or nearly shells, and the superficial resemblance covered the timbers, wires, metal lath, and stucco. So quickly did the hucksters seize on the possibilities of this new and more exotic form that conscientious architects and enthusiastic students were forced to declare this feature passé even before they had learned the structural principles involved. The real, inherent advantages of the hyperbolic paraboloid were never fully understood.

I believe our office and our associates may very well have designed more buildings using these beautiful shells than any other in the country. We used it as a good principle should be used, aesthetically and structurally, as a beautiful and cheap way to make a big span-cover of concrete. We devised forms and erection systems that fitted the economics and techniques of the United States, and we tested and tested until we felt that we understood the limitations and the possibilities. Sometimes they stood for everyone to see; sometimes they did their job behind solid walls; but always they served a special purpose— structurally, aesthetically, and economically. It did not occur to us to give a name to this system any more than we felt the need to write poems for bar joists, wood studs, laminated beams, lamella frames, or post-and-beam deck systems. Years ago, when our office shared in the research and pioneering of the lift-slab system, we were amazed at the glossy stories and papers written about this obviously sensible way to build the conventional flat concrete floor or roof. We began by assuming that it would be faster and cheaper to lift all the ingredients at one time in one piece. Within the proper limits of span and height, this idea is quite as good today as it was on its "discovery" day in 1948. It is a carefully researched and gradually developed system of lifting. The objects lifted may be concrete slabs, grillage of beams, bridges, or concrete-and-steel space frames. This system has also been used to raise great domes and long trusses. It is simpler to pour concrete and place steel on the ground, simpler to fabricate trusses or frames at normal walking level, and simpler and quicker to lift them completely assembled and in one piece with machines. Just the other day I was asked, "Do you still jack up the old slabs?" Another person asked if I was still on the old shell jag. I could have answered "Yes, and I am still on the brick kick and the column-and-beam kick, and I shamelessly make big glass walls now and then." So goes the frittering and the quick abandonment of basic systems, basic ideas, useful developments—our "vocabulary" and our tools.

Who remembers the blare of triumph when curtain walls were discovered just a few years ago? There were many round-table discussions and workshop studies about these new walls. The magazines piled up pages of praise and appraisal on the subject. Now "curtain walls" is a nasty phrase—perhaps it always was a little silly—but this doesn't alter the fact that the prefabricated wooden walls of Gloucester are beautiful, that La Coruña in northern Spain shows whole streets of splendid squares of wood frames and glass, that Switzerland has whole fronts set up in one fine frame of wood panels and window panels. On a back street near New York's city hall is a Singer Building with beautifully constructed façades of iron frames and terra-cotta panels built long before the more recent and famous Singer Building. In their places, these early structures represented a builder's way of building and not another seller's fashion.

Just recently, the arch has been discovered. The bright Chicago architect Harry Weese has designed a brick school-house with Fall River Line, factory-style segmented windows. Now students who had believed that architecture began with the Lovell House are giving hours to discussion of this new frankness. The arch will soon be given much printed space, and it will be defended in strong philosophical terms as a fine, sound, new thing and a shaping force. Supporting evidence to this effect will be profusely provided. Examples will be shown of the Carmel and San José Missions, the Liverpool docks, and Richardson's big stone arches. Brunelleschi and Michelozzo will be given space and humble credit. Most important will be the gushy praise for the men or preferably the man who showed the courage, etc., etc. Precisely so have some architects discovered the Doge's Palace and Lincoln Logs.

When will some teacher in some school learn that he must teach the whole of architecture as it has grown, bloomed, and decayed, the results having been sometimes humble and beautiful, sometimes pompous and beautiful, sometimes brilliantly and even laboriously devised, or sometimes—in the indigenous vernacular—just grown? When will the extraordinary pleasure of learning about architecture be made more significant by presenting the subject not just in dull, contrived, academic chronology but in solid, analogous parallel to all history? There must be a way to discern the significance of all process and change instead of memorizing only the bold incidents and typical monuments.

On the occasion of the announcement of his retirement as dean at the University of California, William Wilson Wurster said,

Architecture is a corridor with many doors, opening into all aspects of human life. It unites many, many forces. I do not believe in embalming ideas. We, none of us, architects or others, have the privilege of building monuments to ourselves. Our work must be for people. I don't pretend to be a great teacher. I was a good administrator running fences for good teachers—my forte is in making it possible for things to happen. I do not teach facts, but teach as a process of arriving at facts.

It seems to me that this uncalculated statement is a well-rounded premise for good thinking and good architecture. The works of Mr. Wurster's office are wonderfully unalloyed and artlessly direct. Their influence has been good and lasting. I have heard the great Finn, Aalto, make a similar statement, and I have seen his factories, mills, and schools standing so forthright, so useful, so very beautiful. They were done with spirit and passion. The need for philosophy did not go into their making, nor is there a need for subtle explanations or clever labels for the finished product.

Is it not true that architecture is the enclosing of useful and beautiful space with sound and beautiful covering? It does not lessen the art that architecture has economic and structural limitations that prevent its being an abstraction in process or in the work itself. It seems right, however, to assume that these limitations should eliminate the arbitrariness of philosophical guessing and prognostication that is so prevalent today.

I have had occasion to see the work in many schools of architecture during the past twenty years. I feel that during ten years of this period these schools produced a kind of directionless wallowing between real creativity and the idolatrous rigidity of imitation of Mies, Wright, Gropius, Nervi, Candela, and others. Recently, at least three important schools have narrowed their casting to expert imitation—in words and in drawings—of the well-known precepts and works of their respective deans or directors. I do not presume to make judgment of the wearing quality of the works and words of the head men at Harvard, Yale, or the University of Pennsylvania, but I am well aware of the incredible inflexibility of the recent graduates who have studied at these and other schools where strong men reign. The formula is strongly circumscribed, and the explanation and rationalization is sophisticated and full of special phraseology. The men who emerge from these schools are well-finished products in a rather narrow area and attitude. I believe very few of Mr. Kahn's students understand that in his rich language, broad awareness, and personal capacity great things dwell. Instead, these students spread across the land with pat notions, a package of details, and a whole stock of thin analogies. Worse yet, they somehow manage to acquire the veil of cynicism that comes with the worship of a master. I can't imagine Mr. Kahn's wanting this.

Recently, I arrived at one of these citadels and observed the preliminaries to a jury session. When a half-dozen models, carried in by bleary-eyed students, were set in a row before the wise elders, I was astonished to see that they were as alike and as faithful to the dogma as the 1963 Chevrolets, Pontiacs, Fords, and Chryslers. The variations were superficial and arbitrary, and scale was uniformly disregarded. These products of weeks of deliberation, cutting, and gluing were devoid of any strong individuality. There was no indication that they were related to any material beyond cardboard and plastic. All were equally unfinished; all were essentially the same thing. The hairsplitting declamations and exclamations were tiresome and almost repetitive; the language was abstruse and the manner almost diffident. This is the essence of the brand of cynicism that pervades a lot of teaching and learning today.

Somehow the architect and the student of architecture have missed the pleasures of curiosity, study, and search for the meaning and significance of all building that has ever been done. The strong tendency to set patterns, programs, and overprecise prescriptions in the curriculum has resulted in a series of prolonged, but eventually abandoned, dogmas. The young man who is finally licensed between the ages of thirty and thirty-two has forgotten most of the mathematics and chemistry he didn't need in the first place. He has listened to the fancy language, has known the twenty or thirty men who teach, but has come out a well-squared expert in an overdeveloped, over-personal religion of style with sharp boundaries.

I have talked and worked with men who have come from the several "important" schools, and after a short time their work and their attitudes were no different, no better, no worse, on the whole than the same characteristics and accomplishments of men from schools less well known. I am repeatedly surprised that quite often the good but not outstanding schools produce men who have more curiosity about history, about the immediate environment, about the special indigenous character of local buildings and materials.

I have heard several of the big architects say that architecture is a business. No one can deny that busy offices must give certain attention to money and deadlines, but I believe the whole consideration of architecture as a "business," big or little, is wrong. The hundred biggest offices in this country seem to produce much undistinguished architecture. Worse yet is the architect who really believes that the most important thing is to "get the job." I cannot fully express my disgust with this attitude. Recently, I read only the title of an article by the editor of a "Home" or "Merchant Homes" magazine which stated, "Now in 1963—Selling IS MORE IMPORTANT THAN BUILDING!!"

For architects, all the education, research, study, design, analysis, drafting, specifying, and inspecting serves one purpose; that, of course, is building. I am often a little alarmed that our estimable and useful architectural society, the American Institute of Architects, puts too much emphasis on public relations. The temptation seems to be to follow the advertisers who oversimplify the process of creating and overemphasize the desirability of the product. What architect would want himself leveled to professional-society average so that he and all the others of better or worse qualifications could be packaged and sold to the public? I want no cellophane wrapper on a slick "how to hire an architect" kit or "how to hook a client" kit that fits me or anyone into a neat slot of conformity. I read our *Journal*, which is now certainly one of the best publications architects have ever had, and I am grateful for provocative articles, for good critical essays, for purely pragmatic information, for its attention to history and conservation; but now and then the huckstering creeps in.

I am amused that almost every regional convention of the A.I.A. makes adequate provision for a golf tournament; I am more amused when I see architect friends who are most anxious to display their skill on the fairway, as if it were a real tool of the trade. I went to one convention where there was, so help me, a bridge tournament on the program! At the same convention, much time was spent with a slick salesman who had been engaged, or was hoping to be hired, to write a series of booklets and brochures on "What the Architect Is and Does." The joke is that this would not be a description of what the best architects do but a recital of the procedure, fees, etc., common to all members.

We are at present planning a house for a Houston woman—a good, simple wooden house with no tricks and, so far, no excuses. I would be absolutely embarrassed to hand her a neat little booklet about our fees, our virtues, and the standards of nobility of *all* architects. She knows what an architect is, surely suspects the weaknesses, appreciates the effort toward excellence—the effort to solve her particular problems in her particular terms. I feel entirely confident that her house will be the best house we have ever done. I have felt this about every house we have ever designed, and no one seems to have been very disappointed.

Young men have frequently asked how they may get their work published, and, of course, one can't just rudely say that if it is good enough, or exotic enough, or sufficiently simple, or sufficiently complex, then there is no problem. For all the slick magazines' tendency to put out for public consumption only the more brash efforts, the more avant-garde articles, the magazines do exercise a reasonable discrimination about quality. They ride with each cliché and pot of cleverness, but they amend this just as adroitly by light criticism and the sudden elimination of that fashion from their pages. I care not what they publish so long as it represents the best work—the most imaginative, the most scholarly—or even just informative material, but I do resent all the mishmash of adulation and flattering language, the omniscient *pronunciamentos*, the wise words of these journalistic oracles. I do not want my parking garage, however romantic, likened to a "Roman Road" or my plain and simple factory to be called "Horizontal Gothic." The writer may do me justice by saying, "This is the house that Jack built—for Mr. Jones." The style of writing in architectural magazines has become quite as laboriously devious as the writings of art critics who bend hard to explain a painter's three swift strokes of green thrown across two brave blobs of red. Architecture is not something abstract; it is not nebulous; it is not tentative. It is accomplished by very much hard work.

Those who answered a checklist several years ago may well have felt pride in the importance of their checking "Play golf with prospective clients," "Regularly attend service club meetings," "Hold position on chamber of commerce committees," "Make lectures to service clubs, women's groups, etc.," "Know my local, state, and national representatives," etc.; but I prefer my own kind of checklist. I give many lectures, perhaps too many, for causes I believe in. I walk in the country and in every new town I visit in Europe, Mexico, and the United States. Mostly, I work—evenings and many holidays, as do my associates. When I am not working, I read. This reading is history of architecture and the other arts, history of religion and Western civilization, history of Texas and America. I have read every book on the architecture and art of Byzantium, on Moslem architecture, on the architecture of the Middle Ages, on the architecture of Latin America that I could get or crowd into air flights and the late hours of night. Two of my associates read more. One reads while he eats and one while he waits for trains or planes. We are excited—that's the only word that describes our feelings—about our discoveries in books. When I am in Europe (and I have been most fortunate to go there fourteen times in six years), I ride buses, planes, trains, and automobiles to see our wonderful discoveries. I have crisscrossed England, southern France, northern Spain, and northern Italy over and over again. I have also spent time in Holland, Belgium, and the Scandinavian countries. I have felt ecstasy over seeing the great cathedral at Albi [figure 12] because it was the subject of one of our serious studies. In its presence I felt quite humble. I have devoted hours to seeing Giselbertus's great sculpture at Autun. This could go on and on. I know the back streets of London better than the front streets of Houston because I had seen the beauty of the good Queen Anne and Georgian buildings in books before my firsthand visits. Twenty times I have seen Egyptian and Syrian sculpture in the British Museum, and I will see them again. Since 1926, I have traveled on side roads in Texas looking for the simple native houses—the log houses near Jasper, the Classic Revival houses from Austin eastward, the stone houses of the German towns in the hill country. I have been up and down the Rio Grande just looking and taking pictures. I have been to Victoria and Galveston to see the frilly houses of Saratoga Springs, the fine Victorian things in St. Louis and in Albany and in Augusta, Georgia. These and a thousand other towns I have seen and read about and loved. I do not know where this leads or whether it soaks into our work, but it is the essence of my pleasure and all of my recreation. I do not aspire to be a Kenneth Conant, who knows most of the medieval work by the square foot and how and when it was built. I feel no desire to be an expert on the late nineteenth century, but I cherish the vigor of its builders.

There is time for some of this, but much more time is required for just work; and I am not the least disturbed that I don't want to play golf or bridge, that I don't want to hunt or fish. I have not and will not make social functions, or rig a fishing trip, or play golf, or drink beer or even champagne with anyone just to put myself closer to a "prospect." I believe that an architect who knows how much he should know, how much work is required to cover his limitations of talent, what great happiness is on the inside of creativity, and what pleasures are in all the related spheres can do little more than work and study. I have a very good time at what I do and stay busy and not very businesslike. What we do is limited by the boundaries of our several and our whole abilities and time, but it is done with absolutely consuming enthusiasm. I hope this same enthusiasm goes to the people for whom we build. I do not want to know "how to have a satisfied client." I want an ecstatic one.

I do not want our group to become school experts, laboratory experts, hospital experts, or house experts. I hope we may learn to approach each problem and opportunity with the

FIGURE 12. Cathedral Basilica of Saint Cecilia, Albi, France, c. 1282–1400. Seeing it brought Ford "ecstasy."

resolve to put the client's needs first and to be ready to exert ourselves to meet any demand, so that we serve significantly and, as often as possible, design buildings of real beauty with a measure of originality that is purposeful and fitting. We strive scrupulously to avoid decorative fashions and to keep abreast of technical advancements and use them to the end that our work is entirely contemporary in engineering, erection, and material techniques. We study the construction of Romanesque, Gothic, Renaissance, and nineteenth-century buildings so that we may know better the sequence in the growth of systems and engineering that brings us to this day of great spans and heights, in order to make advantageous use of stressing, warping, precasting, and welding. With the knowledge and use of these techniques, we should be able to work in the real tradition of architecture and not find any necessity or desire to fling ourselves into the current parade of cleverness and playful, capital D Design.

I have no time to discuss the importance of the architect as the logical man in the logical profession to speak loudly and consistently against the brutal destruction of the good things our forebears gave us. Nothing has been said about tribute to those who have made themselves very unpopular by publicly standing against the gobbling of parks and green areas everywhere by casually designed expressways, canals, and parking lots. Only those architects who conduct their practice as a business—as a routine promotion and production activity—and carefully avoid controversy and debate can possibly remain entirely acceptable to everyone.

That I may proudly praise our city council (in San Antonio) for its attitude toward desegregation, its interest in the development and further beautification of our little downtown river, its growing interest in preservation of historic buildings, its vigorous program of urban renewal, and the support of fiestas and pageants is a strong source of satisfaction to me and my associates. When we must fight hard and spend money and endless days and weeks to oppose the cutting of trees, the destruction of a park or plaza for a parking lot, the expediency of "saving" land cost by setting an expressway through our great park and forested area, then the same men I previously praised for their better acts must look upon us as obstructionists and nonconformists. The Chamber of Commerce—of which I am a member—is pleased to have my support in their splendid plan to expand our downtown parks and widen and improve our river walk area, but when I protest their support of the expressway through a campus and parks, they must find me an annoyance. They must set me up as a belligerent and controversial reactionary when I cry, "Wait, study this carefully, take time to be sure there isn't another way through a slum. Take time to be sure the extra money for a better right-of-way isn't cheap compared with the irreparable destruction of open areas. Think, worthy councilmen, how we will need this 'unused' land when our population has doubled."

During the last several years the A.I.A. has begun to take a strong position against this new urge to rip apart our cities and remove all native identity and character. Yet, sadly, most of the fighting, the serious concern, the study of alternate solutions has been left to a few with courage and the willingness to be unpopular. The fight goes on around the world, from San Antonio to New York, London, Florence, and Milwaukee, and back again to Dallas. Architects must lead the fight and provide creative counsel and plans. May each of us with his particular ability join in the desperate fight to save our land from the reckless, the willful, the selfish, the unimaginative, and the just plain ignorant vulgarians. One important thing an association, with the help of its membership, can and must do is work to achieve the significant and larger purpose of serving all people.

My rambling remarks have been intended as a plea that may be summed up in a good scholarly way by a quotation from a little book by Ralph Tubbs called, modestly enough, *An Englishman Builds*:

I refer to contact of the mind of the builder directly through the form of the building itself, not by association; there is no intent to add "human interest." The knowledge that the name of the man who directed operations during the building of Lichfield Cathedral was William de Ramessey adds no more to our real appreciation of this cathedral than we are helped to understand Beethoven's Ninth Symphony by the knowledge that he dedicated it to the King of Prussia. The building alone and the music alone convey to us something which could not be conveyed to us by any other means than by the building or the music.

Buildings appeal to us in different ways; our eyes may be delighted by the color, texture or form; our intellect may be stimulated by the skillful use of materials or the brilliance of building techniques; or our sense of fitness may be impressed by the excellence of the building for its purpose. In each case, however, we see revealed to us something of the living man, for no architect can give his building a finer quality than exists in his own mind.

So may we look sharply to "quality," to the "joy of living," and to the fervent search for "knowledge."

1965

History and Development of the Spanish Missions in San Antonio

At a meeting of the Stained Glass Association of America held in San Antonio in 1965, Ford participated in a panel discussion with architect Brooks Martin moderated by writer and newscaster Henry Guerra about the city's colonial missions. For many years Ford and his colleagues, particularly Carolyn Peterson, worked on the stabilization and conservation of the missions. In his remarks at the meeting, he described the buildings, assessed their architectural significance, and even compared one to Le Corbusier's famous Notre Dame du Haut at Ronchamp, France, which was then about ten years old. Ford made plain his irreverence and irritation about the romanticization of the missions in the twentieth century when he drew attention to the inhumane conditions at the missions and the slaughter of Native Americans by Anglo settlers. He also stressed how far ahead architectural and cultural development was in Latin America by indigenous and Spanish groups relative to that in North America.

I apologize for first doing a little debunking. When I was walking about San José Mission several years ago with the archbishop, a most esteemed man, he said, "Here, of course, is where the Indians lived, in the quarters all around." I said, "Could you explain this iron ring in the wall?" He just passed it by, so I embarrassed him by asking, "Is this how they kept them converted?"

This town is really a part of the North because the Anglo-Americans came here and they predominate in the population.

Reprinted with permission of the Stained Glass Association of America from *Stained Glass* 60.4 (1965–1966): 28–34, 39–41.

They led the fight for independence and they prevail in the holding of money and properties. But here we are very close to Mexico and all the countries to the south and this points up the differences in our beginnings. When the first conquerors and explorers came to South America and North America, the group that came to South America arrived at least a hundred years before they moved up here. As a matter of fact, there were thriving cities, Spanish cities, in South America 125 years before they touched down at Plymouth Rock. It is interesting to me that the people who came to the northern part of the United States, the eastern seaboard, were a product of the Reformation. They were the dissenters. They came over to farm, to settle down, to build homes. Of course, they burned a few of their own citizens in the process, in their religious zeal to find freedom. They brought with them a pattern of European life growing out of the Reformation with a sense of independence.

The people who came to South America, very honestly, came to conquer and to get gold. To give you an idea of the empire which they completely destroyed—a great tragedy, and nobody regrets it more than the Spaniards of this day— when they found the Inca Empire, there were twenty-four million Indians living there. They had built absolutely exquisite, sophisticated cities, and no Inca had ever heard there was a Europe at all. They had systems of sewage disposal and all kinds of services that would be considered advanced indeed. But they were wiped out so the conquistadores could take the gold, go back to Spain, and enrich their homeland.

It took us in the North a great deal longer to win the land. We moved broadside across America, killing a few Indians a day. Being a descendant of the Cherokees, I feel this resentment more, I suppose, than some of you who don't have the blood. In East Texas, for instance, people who lived in wooden houses at the time of the revolution, the Texas Revolution against Mexico, were the Cherokee Indians, and they owned their land. The land was given to them, they had the properly documented title to it. Then one of our ancestors from Georgia came and saw to it that ole Chief Bowes and his tribe were all murdered and their land taken. So we too had a little bit of conquistador in us. We came along a lot later up here, but it is hard to say honestly whether the hostility of the Indians or the hostility between the padres, who were devoted men, and their own soldiers was greater. The Indians, in many cases, were very friendly and welcomed the padres, sought their help, and joined them, but their own soldiers were a real problem.

In 1725 missions were established southeast of here. Espada and San Juan were both founded up near San Augustine. Well, they couldn't be held as disease and hostile Indians came. Then, too, the threat of the French frightened them, and they pulled back to San Antonio. This leads to a very fascinating story.

After the padres left San Juan Bautista, a mission across the river below Piedras Negras, where they stopped on their way up from Querétaro and Saltillo, they crossed this river to a place near Carrizo Springs. There they found a Frenchman, one John Auriee [Jean Jarry], who was almost certainly one of the murderers of La Salle, who had worked his way westward. He had become the chief of twenty-three Indian tribes. When the padres came with their soldiers and their armor and their spears and all of the trappings that made them so decorative and so formidable, they saw he had the heads of five Apache chiefs hanging across the front of his tent. While he let them pass, he also made them believe that there was a great army of Frenchmen just east of San Antonio. John Auriee lived near San Antonio, had a great red beard and forty-five wives. He kept the Spaniards south of San Antonio away from San Pedro Springs, where a considerable settlement of Indians was located before 1700. But then, finally getting tired of forty-five wives, he joined the padres, became a very devout Catholic, and moved to Mexico City. There his story ends.

Another thing that astonishes me is the ignorance that prevails around here. How many times have you heard people say, "Well, those primitive padres and those primitive Indians." They think of them like you'd think of Norsemen who came to our northern shores in 750 or 800, and they say it's amazing that these unsophisticated people could ever build such buildings. Well, of course, they were really sophisticated people from Spain, wonderfully educated men. All the padres who came to Texas were purposely selected because they had excellent educations, were teachers and good farmers.

Another thing we had in common in North and South America was *independencia*, independence. Everywhere there were revolutions against the conqueror. I suspect that much of this came from the fact that our country as well as many countries in Latin America were settled by rather elite people.

One thing about the missions, physically, they are late Renaissance architecture. Interestingly enough, whenever these styles are built far away from their origins, the men who build them make them more vigorous and interesting than the originals. They take on a subtlety and originality that comes with the lack of certain materials and the absence of academic rigidity. Frontier ingenuity had to be used. Take the Mission Concepción, it is very much more a Romanesque church, and no such church had been built in Spain since 1500 or even earlier. It is not a sophisticated Renaissance church in the sense that San José is, with all the affectations of the Renaissance. The other two little churches down the river are even more primitive and show very little sophistication. But when you look at the façade of Concepción [figure 5], which is my favorite building in this hemisphere, you will see that everything done was wrong, academically. It has a little pediment which is way too steep and reminds you of Romanesque churches in Ireland, Southern France, Northern Spain, and the less populated parts of Italy, and can even be seen in the Byzantine architecture of Greece. The clumsy little gable is made too steep. It obviously doesn't look like anything you ever saw before. Then a window is placed right on top of the point, which no good designer would do, with two more below. All of this is quite wrong. If you drew one of these things, you'd fail sophomore architecture. This is the subtle thing that clearly illustrates the difference between [the mission and] the tiresome academic and rather hackneyed architecture of, say, the late eighteenth century in Italy. Well, in the middle eighteenth century, the Texas man was not a slave to academic process or to architectural conceits. He was an original person using old precepts and old notions.

In Mission Espada, a tiny jewel of a little building we all love very much, you will find another anachronism. In the arch over the door, which looks very Moorish, there is stone which I feel sure was brought from Saltillo or from Querétaro. As far as I can tell, it is lava, or from a lava source. It isn't native stone. The priest or the man who shipped it had not numbered the pieces right, so the stone at the bottom of the arch coming down at the pilaster was changed for another one, and the effect is beautiful. These are the subtle things that happened in the more primitive frontier—and the interesting things.

If you will go to the back side, the side that's in ruins, of Concepción [figure 13], you will see abstract aspects of architectural form, almost as if Le Corbusier had done it. It is like Ronchamp [figure 14], with wonderful gold shapes and forms.

When I was a little boy, in about 1921, I came down here. San José Mission was then just a cow pasture. The dome was all down and the thing was in a dreadful ruin. It's been a sad thing that the missions had been neglected so long, but when you reflect that after the fall of the Alamo and after the influx of Germans, Irish, and Polish people, there wasn't much interest for a long, long time. They were used for rock quarries, just as the Pantheon in Rome was used for rock quarries to build some horrible late Renaissance churches. The tragedy and neglect of them is understandable when you figure that in 1862

FIGURE 13. Mission Concepción, southeast façade. Photographed 1936.

FIGURE 14. Le Corbusier, Notre Dame du Haut, Ronchamp, France, 1950–1954. Ford said the building's "synthesis of shape and light and sound froze [him] still and silent."

San Antonio had 3,528 people. New Braunfels had 3,550 people more than San Antonio . . . Jefferson, in East Texas, probably 50,000 people. So San Antonio was forgotten for many years, which accounts for the fact that the missions were allowed to fall down. Actually, when I was a boy, there were buildings, mostly late nineteenth-century houses, all around the mission walls.

Perhaps you have gained some knowledge from my comment on the primitive aspect which I find the most charming quality of the missions. And I hope this will make them a little more pleasant and interesting to you.

1966

Mr. O'Neil Ford's Speech at the *Sculpture and Environment Symposium*

In the 1960s, as abstract sculpture and especially large-scale outdoor works were rising to prominence and architects and planners were debating the future of cities, the Art Department at the University of Texas at Austin organized a symposium on the broad topic "Sculpture and Environment." The event marked the beginning of the university's new Program in Creativity and included four speakers—two sculptors, James Rosati, who taught sculpture at Yale, and New York artist Herbert Ferber, as well as two architects, Ford and Louis Kahn, whom the Austin American-Statesman *described as "the most creative individual now practicing architecture in the United States." After their formal remarks the speakers participated in a panel discussion.*

Giving examples of art from Sumer, ancient Greece, and Mesoamerica, and discussing medieval and contemporary works, Ford outlined the qualities that distinguish great sculpture. While acknowledging that important differences separate architecture and sculpture, he said he admired most the works in which the two media were fully integrated, and in which the connections of buildings to the societies that created them were evident. Ford lamented the culture of celebrity in architecture that he saw emerging and spoke admiringly of Kahn's buildings.

Lecture at the *Sculpture and Environment Symposium,* University of Texas at Austin, November 19, 1966, transcript (unidentified transcriber), unpublished, box 61, folder 4, O'Neil Ford: An Inventory of His Drawings, Papers, and Photographic Material, 1864–1983, Alexander Architectural Archives, University of Texas Libraries, University of Texas at Austin.

I am in a spot today. Oh, what a picture. (Laughter.) There is nothing like what I hope was an unconscious gesture.

All the rest of these gentlemen will be gone in a few days, a few hours, back to where they work, where they live, to their own respective environments. And I will be right here. This doesn't move me, however, to be more circumspect or careful. As some of you know, almost nothing moves me to be careful. My wife says to me sometimes, "Why in the hell don't you apologize *before* you go to a party so that you won't have to send flowers and write letters the next day?" I am even going to read to you something that I have read to almost everyone here, I think a dozen times, and my wife again will tell me why I shouldn't have read it, but I think it pertinent.

Mr. Kahn, I want to say something to you. I have known Mr. Kahn many years and heard lots of his speeches, and this is the best one I have heard him make. I greatly appreciate the things that he has said and the way he has said them. I am a little annoyed with Mr. Ferber's worry and concern about the difference between an architect and a sculptor. I am sure he is not an architect, and I am sure I am not a sculptor.

I want to read you this little thing, this one tiny little booklet that a man in England named Ralph Tubbs made a few years ago, and I think it is pertinent. I didn't intend to read it because I read it at Rensselaer—in Dallas yesterday, and in Troy, New York, the day before. I am a-reading it again. None of you were there, were you? [Quoting from Tubbs:]

I refer to the contact of the mind of the builder directly to the form of the building itself. The knowledge that the name of the man who directed operations during the building of the Lichfield Cathedral was William de Ramessey adds no more to our real appreciation of this cathedral than we are helped to understand Beethoven's Ninth Symphony by the knowledge that he dedicated it to the King of Prussia. The building alone and the music alone convey to us something which could not be conveyed to us by any other means than by the music or the building, Mr. Kahn.

[Quoting Tubbs again:] "Buildings appeal to us in different ways"—and he is a little more naïve here than Mr. Kahn would be, maybe more than I would be—"our eyes may be delighted by color or texture or material or form. Our intellect may be stimulated by the skillful use of materials or the brilliance of building techniques, or our sense of fitness may be impressed by the excellence of the building for its purpose. In each case, however, we see revealed to us something of the living man. For no architect can give his building a finer quality than exists in his own mind." I would add that that is about what he ought to do. Now, the reason I read this, when I had no notion of doing it, is because I am more disturbed today with a sort of egoistic attitude that some architects have, and almost all sculptors and painters have.

And I am just as annoyed—and with apologies to you, Mr. Lou Kahn, I am almost as annoyed with this hierarchy of the people who have had—architects who have had their pictures on the front of *Time* magazine. Now, that is a very dangerous thing because some very good architects have their pictures on the front of *Time* magazine, but the people who decide [whose] to put [on the] magazine are not capable of picking the right ones every time. I talked to some of you students when Hugh Casson was here—whom I admire very greatly, by the way, because I knew him years ago when he was sort of an Edwardian exterior and interior decorator. He has now become an architect, and in a certain respect, an extraordinary sculptor. His Elephant House in London, I hope you all agree, is a great building, but he amused me no end when he said, "It would be shocking to have my picture on the front of *House and Home* magazine or on *Progressive Architecture*." Well, I have begun to feel the same way, particularly since the hope of my picture ever being on any of those is damned remote. Lou is the only one I know. But the interesting thing is that some of the lesser architects and those who are not in his camp at all have also had their pictures on *Time* magazine.

Now, I come to this because I am a prognostic and I am a kind of, oh, an adamant, excited, nervous historian, seeking, reading, jumping at any kind of thing I can learn, but I mostly find my pleasure if I am learning about the arts, in learning about things done a long time ago. I was just thinking, Mr. Kahn, I don't know why you said it, I don't know why you were so excited about something being on a wall. Now I don't think I know precisely what you meant. If Gaston Lachaise had a sculpture—a very good sculptor, by the way, I think—and it was stuck on a wall, I think it would tend to be less good and would become somewhat of a decoration and an adjunct to the building, and it would be necessary that it be on the wall, a full, rounded thing, it would be very good looking. But on the other hand, having seen some marvelous things that Egyptians did—which were really writing, but that doesn't make any difference—good-looking lettering, or glyphs, or hieroglyphics, or any sort of thing that a man wants to put down either as information or as decoration, I think, is a justifiable thing to do, I see no reason why you should get excited about things on a wall. I think they can go on a wall, and I don't think that they become subordinate to the building, either. They are concomitant to the building. They are part of the building.

This brings me to the other thing. Most of the sculpture done after the twelfth century seems to me to be less good than the sculpture done before the twelfth century. And most of the sculpture done *after* 1700 is nowhere near as good as sculpture done *before* 1700. Not as good as sculpture done before the twelfth century or even before 2000 B.C. Now, most of the sculpture done before 1895, that is, back to 1800, was pretty bad, and a lot of *marvelous* sculpture has been done lately. There is a wonderful understanding of what sculpture is, but it isn't all good, and I would be very hard-pressed to find eight pieces of sculpture in America as good as a lot of Cambodian sculpture I have seen, a lot of the sculpture on Poitiers Cathedral and Autun, that Giselbertus did. I would have a hard time finding a lot of sculpture, present-day sculpture, better than some of the sculpture at St. Mark's, and I am talking about [it] in the same way, I am not talking about a thing that's just vernacular carving. I am not talking about Oceanic art. I am not talking about Primitive art. I am talking about sculpture done by people who intended to do sculpture, a long time ago.

So what is bothering me, and I am getting to the point, I feel that Lou Kahn's statement that when the Fourth Symphony is played, an old friend walks in the room—but the important thing is that I do not think it made any difference whether Joe Smith composed this symphony or John Brown, or whether I do a house that nobody ever recognizes that I am the architect. I would be just as pleased, as I have said many times before, [to hear,] "This is the house that Jack built for Mr. Jones." I think we keep forgetting that architecture is the important thing. I think that maybe Mr. Ferber has forgotten that architecture is not always building. You can have an architecture that is un-building, or non-building, or not-building, and it can be a marvelous thing.

I saw a sculpture up in Finland one time, and it was done—it wasn't just in the woods, there was some consciousness of making a place for it, which I think was proper because it was a good sculpture. But it was in some trees, the trees were in a great circle, but the trees there were to me precisely the same feeling when I went in there that I get when I go into an English cathedral, with all the branches above and all the tracery. And there are some great sarcophagi, which are in themselves marvelous sculpture. I think that some of the great sculpture in the world is the early English sarcophagi, carved on the tombs.

Well, what I am trying to say is that I should like us all to be more anonymous. We can't be anonymous as Mr. Kahn or Mr. Ferber or Mr. Rosati, nor can I be fully anonymous, I am a man working, but I'd rather there would be something of *me* in it without my name having a thing to do with it at all. I would like all architecture to be an expression of the whole of a building, and I think I get very tired sometimes of listening to students nowadays talking about how they have "*discovered space.*" Well, what in the world were people doing when they did Durham? What were they doing when they did the Pantheon? What were they doing when they did anything *but* space? They were doing space all these times.

People are always discovering something new. I have discovered the arch, about five years ago. Lou Kahn has discovered the column, and, you know, light and dark. Well, that's all right. I am all for a re-understanding, a re-understanding like the column is light and creates light and there is something that's not light between. This makes you think, it makes me think, and doesn't make me treat a column as "that stupid piece of sculpture" at the Erex—how do you pronounce it?—at the Erechtheum in Greece. The earliest vulgarity, I suppose, in sculpture were these caryatids, holding up the temple.

This, of course, is doing sculpture the great disservice that some architects do it today. Some architects think that the sculptor is to come in and make their building decent and presentable, make their space sing. Well, I know a lot of sculpture that I would like to steal and just put anywhere and go see it— in a building, out of a building, in a garden, in the trees, in the woods, it makes no difference. A lot of sculpture is beautiful anywhere, anywhere, and very few architects have buildings worthy of truly great sculpture.

And now I am to another point. There have been very few good buildings done since the eleventh century. . . . And again, one of the reasons is this egocentric notion from the time of, well, let us just take a time, just take Inigo Jones, you know. Because, actually, Michelangelo was a pretty good architect.

He was a sculptor and a painter and all of these things. He was all of these things. But when you take the beginning of the professional architect, Inigo Jones, and then one of the really great ones was Sir Christopher Wren. Well, somehow or other it became more profession, and more organization, and more annual conventions, and more things for ladies to do at conventions than it was architecture. Now, I really believe this. So I am saying the same thing about architecture, I suppose, that I am about sculpture.

I think that Lou's definitions are valid. I have heard lesser men make very valid definitions of what architecture is, but I sort of wish we would quit defining it and *do* it, and do it with love and subordinating ourselves, and if you don't mind, I wouldn't mind subordinating our buildings to some of the natural surroundings, where they would be more befitting.

I brought along a lot of slides which I am *not* going to show. The same ones I showed yesterday and the day before. In one of them there is a circular building, a kiva, and next to that a square box, and that's at San Ildefonso out in New Mexico, the Indian reservation. And I know some architects who could make a two-hour speech on that. The juxtaposition. The counterpoint. How these geniuses did it, you see. I could show you some slides of Uxmal and Chichén Itzá and Tulum, where I have been twice this year, and I will tell you that if you can tell me whether this is sculpture, Greek sculpture, two to three hundred feet square, great temples two hundred feet high, or whether it is architecture, you will do something I can't do. I don't know which it is, nor do I care. I don't feel that there has to be this hair-splitting line about what you do or I do, although I would rather do the architecture for you sculptors than do what you do, I can tell you that right now. Or I'd rather Lou would do it.

But I think that we keep forgetting, we keep thinking of ourselves as having been here a long time, and we have only been here a little while. And as professional, personal, easel artists with studios and ateliers, we have only been here a day. And this [forgetfulness], of course, is the same way in architecture and sculpture; [it is how the arts started their] slide down the inevitable hill of egocentric thinking, of self-expression, of expressionistic notions about how I shall do it. Bellini and Filippo Lippi did pretty good paintings on altars and they worked for a dollar and a half an hour or something, and the great sculptors of the Maya cities were really writing and recording. They were the victims of a civilization, at least particularly with the Aztecs, where art served war—art served the priesthood, the priesthood served war, and the capture and the sacrifice to the gods of all of the people they *could* capture served agriculture in bringing rain. Agriculture served the arts, and there was no separation whatever in the whole Aztec and even Mayan setup. There was no separation between what is art and what is architecture. It all was to the worship of something, something pretty hierarchical, something pretty brutal, but these people had no notion, they didn't know Greece existed or that Cambodia existed. They didn't know that any other art in the *world* existed, and they created things that are so subtle, so beautiful, so very, very good as architecture, so fine as exterior space, they didn't build any interior spaces—and here I would say that everyone thinks architecture must have spaces. It doesn't have to have any at all. Sculpture can have spaces in it, just as well as architecture, holes in it, voids in it. And I think when people get to worrying about architecture as decoration, Mr. Kahn, I mean sculpture as decoration, I always think of those roof combs which many of you know, at Uxmal, down in Chiapas, which are just the most superb sculpture, with holes, and they are decorative like Grandma's lace collar, and yet they are *absolutely* essential to the architecture.

Well, I will stop now. The fingermarks—by the way, I like that, what you said about fingermarks, but I think I am trying to say the same thing. I want the fingermarks. They are the great forebears left to us. I would like to see the Sumerian people and their sculpture better understood by modern sculptors.

I would like to see the Mayas and Olmecs and Totonacs and the Huastecans and some of the people even in Ireland and England who did rather remarkable and wonderful things on one of the early Christian churches, which were, I do not know, decoration, sculpture, or architecture. Nor do I care. They were all of one composition. Precisely as music is made up of many, many phrases, and they are pretty different sometimes from front to back, and I'm not talking about vulgar things like Richard Strauss, which are *over*-variety.

Well, I think that is quite enough right now. I always enjoy hearing myself talk, and feel ashamed if I am with my betters, but I do like to think that I am not an idiot for being completely thrilled, and just about orbited oft times, when I look at pictures of the Great Mosque at Samarra, which is a building like a ziggurat—near Baghdad?—and wonder if anybody will do a thing any better really, and I don't know whether it is sculpture or architecture. I wonder when I look at Modena, a cathedral down in Italy, I don't care whether it's sculpture or architecture. It has a void in it, but it is full of great surface, great color, marvelous configurations, in stone, in arches and vaults, and I don't know which it is, nor do I care, but I am really given some kind of thing which I can't translate into the practical business of being an architect, and do not care. It makes *me* a different thing. So I suppose what I am saying is I am a product of all of this and delighted and very glad that I don't even know enough to talk about it very articulately. Thank you.

REBUTTAL: O'NEIL FORD

I don't know just what anybody will think of this, but I think one of the blessings of architecture is its limitation, and in the effort and process to *do* what is *good* architecture, we can be grateful that architecture has this limitation. In a way. Now, it is not only a limitation for the truly imaginative person, but it is thought of as being limited by size, span, cost, its purpose;

and I think Mr. Kahn made a very important point when he said that it doesn't make any difference, it will grow into a thing immeasurable, it will grow into a thing useful, and it must be. But you don't *set out* hard and fast toward this purpose.

I like the idea, though, that architecture ought to be really a marvelously vital and vigorous expression these days, right now. It ought to be more now than ever before, actually, with all the tools and so forth and so forth. I don't think it is. I think one of the reasons is that architects generally are not *willing* to accept the limitations as a blessing. Too much of resources, too much of variety, too much of hucksterism is in the marketplace of architecture today and the business of building. And I think architects, as a big group, as a whole profession, forget that simplicity, the *lack* of too much variety, the *limitations* of size, money, span, and so forth, all really are a great, great friend to this building a thing measurable and useful but extremely beautiful.

I would like to ask Mr. Kahn to tell me in a few minutes of his new building in India [figure 15], the big brick buildings which are to me something very important in architecture at this time; they are the first really inspiring thing I have seen

FIGURE 15. Louis Kahn, Indian Institute of Management, Ahmedabad, India, 1962–1974. Ford considered the project the "first really inspiring thing I have seen in several years."

in several years. They don't seem to fit into any tight hierarchy or anybody's tight philosophy of what architecture is, but I look upon them and wonder why should anybody *ever* think they are or are not sculpture, or are or are not architecture, or are or are not more beautiful or less beautiful than trees.

1967

The End of a Beginning

As the second major phase of construction at Trinity University was concluding, the university invited its architect to deliver the commencement address and awarded him an honorary doctorate of fine arts. In his speech, which took the form of a letter, Ford summarized the history of the "Skyline Campus," to which Trinity had moved in 1952, and emphasized the intimate relationship between the design of the campus and the character of the institution as it was reshaped at midcentury. The coeval development of the buildings, landscape, and institution had created, Ford said, a place that was unusual and very special, a place of "positive, progressive protest." Ford admired Trinity's leaders for their willingness to take risks on a new construction method, to build in a modern rather than a historicist idiom, and to support architecture scaled to people. Having heeded the advice of William Wurster to fit the buildings to the rocky, rugged, irregular site instead of onto a formal plan on flattened ground, and having hired Arthur Berger and Marie Berger to design a modern landscape using native and drought-tolerant plants, Trinity's leaders and its architects created one of the most distinctive campuses in the United States.

President Laurie, members of the Faculty, Distinguished Trustees, Friends of Trinity University, and members of the Class of 1967:

Never before have I struggled so long and with such serious deliberation in an effort to say "thank you" in such a way

---

Commencement address, Trinity University, 1967, published in *A Trilogy 1967* (San Antonio: Trinity University, 1967), 21–32.

that this simple phrase would fully convey the real depths of my feelings about this great honor that you are giving me.

As I write, I sit close by the case that holds the drawings and building specifications and letters written by the entirely remarkable Mr. Jefferson—a master of expression. I have read his beautiful words that gave direction to the shaping of a different kind of nation, and I have imagined what impact they had on those fortunate men who first heard them spoken. All the beauty of that simple and entirely comprehensible document, the Declaration of Independence, the hard sense of the Virginia Statutes, and his essays and pronouncements concerning public education are so uncommonly wise and so remarkably expressed that it is doubtful that there are any other official papers so inspiring.

Not long since, I was privileged to hold in my hand his equally remarkable letters. Whether Mr. Jefferson was writing about seed or soil, or brickmaking or food, or just relating an interesting and provocative experience, he set down his fine words with a freedom of expression and with an enthusiasm that is entirely lucid, fresh, and stimulating.

This very special experience with Jefferson's letters did teach me that I might, at last, have found a way to speak to you.

I am an architect—a builder—and not an orator or philosopher. To address you in the pompous phrases of an oracle or elder statesman would be both presumptuous and impossible for me. On the other hand, if I could sit down and freely write a letter from me to you—simply, directly, and without any effort to be impressive—I might convey at least a measure of what I feel so deeply on this occasion.

And so I begin this, a letter to you, "Dear Good Friends of Trinity University, 715 Stadium Drive, San Antonio, Texas, May 29, 1967." But since this is the new, conservative me, maybe just to be safe, I had better add: zip code 78212!

At the outset I wish to make some resolutions. These are: Number 1. That on this occasion I will make every effort to thwart those here who have sometimes referred to me as a

"Hot Gospeller"! I will do my best to demonstrate that I have no desire to appear before graduates and genuine doctors and tell them about the enormous challenges of this dynamic age. Neither will I challenge you graduates, as you stand on some vast threshold, with admonitions about the harder, rocky road and urge the choice of sweat and sacrifice and self-denial as you seek to attain the great heights, etc., etc., etc.

Number 2. I resolve that I will hold in check my rather over-developed sense of humor—something I greatly admire in your president, and have scrupulously tolerated in your public relations director. I will, instead, try to make a proper response to the wonderful things you have done to make my sixteen years with you the best possible experience for an architect in his effort to serve and be freely creative. I confess I would prefer to sing or dance in order to let you better understand the joy and exuberance of my mood tonight. But I have, for the first time, received some real restraining directions and warnings from those responsible for my being here, and so I must repress those natural impulses at least for the moment. What happens later on remains to be seen.

Nor will I go into detail about the warning, though premature, reaction of my students at the University of Virginia, where I have just completed a term as Thomas Jefferson Memorial Professor of Architecture, when news of my intended "elevation" reached there, except to say that I was greeted by a loud "Hail Herr Doctor Architect Tex" and the sign on my office door was changed from "Tex" to "DR. TEX." At the Colonnade Club—the faculty club, several regulars arose from their naps and softly said, "Good morning," which, according to my friend the dean of Architecture, is tantamount to shouted approval or praise.

I do feel that I should explain that my beginning work with Trinity just sixteen years ago was not my first association, nor is this the first time I have made an effort to fill a speaking assignment at Trinity. Just thirty-six years ago, in the month of May, 1931, I journeyed from Dallas to Waxahachie with some lovely young Trinity student, and there I made a great oration on the subject of etchings, aquatints, and lithographs, and how to make them, to a whole dining room full of eager young ladies. It was my first appearance before a learned body, and on the return bus trip, I, for the first time, experienced the elation and complete relief when such a performance is over and the polite ovation is just a memory. Furthermore, they paid my bus fare and gave me cookies and tea. I believe I have almost broken my second resolution.

In my search for a fitting subject for this letter to my Trinity friends, I sat and stared at the whole panorama of my years with you. As the sequence of association and events marched steadily by, there were hundreds of strong points of punctuation and many pictures called up which were sources of wonder to me. Soon I realized that the pace of the times and the intensity with which we all plunged through those astonishing and demanding years had given me but little time to stop and ponder and to observe that here, on this hill above and below our good rock bluff, I had been a part of something quite uncommon, even in a world full of unusual and revolutionary happenings.

It is about this unique quality at Trinity—this uncommonness—that I would speak to you today. I want to make an effort to tell you what I know about those things that make this place, with its people, a university that is much unlike any other I know.

I will quickly say that I expect to speak of this, your university, as a place of consistent protest. I would also like to make clear that there is an important difference between protest and reckless revolt. For protest, as applied at Trinity, far from being negative in character, is in fact daringly affirmative, and here has led to a completely positive and objective series of decisions and events.

I am deeply convinced that a university or any place of learning that swims against the tide of the commonplace, the perfunctory, the banal or "fully accepted practice"—in protest!—is doing precisely what a modern university should do. That is precisely what all great universities have done. And that is precisely what Trinity University is doing—and doubtless will continue to do. Out of this spirit of positive, progressive protest—with its strong admixture of common sense and devotion, of generosity and courage, of remarkable and ordinary events—Trinity University has grown. The tangible evidences of that growth are things which we could not, in the beginning, quite imagine.

Though the broad campus plan and building character were strong in our consciousness from the first, we who have seen every yard of rock cut away, every brick put in its purposeful place, probably feel an elation and something akin to surprise that isn't equally shared by you who have only recently come here as students to an almost completed living and learning center. And while the faculty, the board, and even my fellow architects still share in your bewilderment as you awaken to the crunch of bulldozers and rattle of jackhammers, we are also sadly aware of an impending, lonely silence and the years when we, the planners, mix yarns about our exploits with the conscience that tells us we might have done better. For in a very real sense, we are approaching the End of a Beginning.

My own participation in Trinity's modern growth began with a trip to M.I.T. with friend and Trinity board member Frank Murchison to ask William Wilson Wurster, dean of Architecture and Planning at that institution, if he would serve as consulting architect to the Trinity Building Program. The shortest possible version of this memorable visit with this great man is best expressed in his response—a kind of surging, poetic verbal shorthand: "YES—if you expect to dream beyond ordinary accomplishment; NO—if you want just buildings; YES—if you have a place for Ford in the design side of the work; NO—if you expect miracles and instant shelter; YES—I will be there next Monday."

Architects Bartlett Cocke and Harvey Smith had already been engaged, and I was pleased that they most graciously took

FIGURE 16. Trinity University, San Antonio. Northrup Hall is in the middle distance, Murchison Tower is in the center, and the George Storch Memorial Library is in the foreground. Photographed c. 1966.

me on the team and even more pleased that they were happy to work with Mr. Wurster as consultant. We plunged immediately into making a huge, very rough, and, I believed then, very brave site plan. All of us agreed that we had struck a first blow for "freedom from artificial axes and academic and superficial monumentalism." We used such words in those days.

One cold, wet, and windy day this big man, William Wurster, came for a look at Trinity's future campus—an abandoned rock quarry strewn with many years' accumulation of battered battery boxes, broken glass, twisted wire, and chunks of asphalt, and spotted with cactus, catclaw, and piles of tree trimmings—a dismal and antagonistic jungle. The great man strode heedlessly through the refuse, twenty feet ahead of a struggling Dr. Everett, who was the president then—that was seventeen years ago, and a line of equally struggling board members and architects. Stopping where Bushnell Avenue then crossed the land and where the library, the new Paseo (or Esplanade), and the Student Union now stand, he said, "What a truly beautiful piece of land. How wise you are and how great the promise with such a piece of earth to shape our work. When can we get this silly road removed?"

And, marvel of marvels, next day three stalwart board members came back from city hall with word that Bushnell Avenue, long a point of contention, was to be cut off at our west line. And so, inspired by Bill Wurster's vision, this was the first stroke of protest and we were started on our long swim upstream.

I wish I had more time to acknowledge Mr. Wurster's gift to Trinity, but that would take the full evening. I must be content to say all too inadequately that what is good about this campus is due almost entirely to his sharp admonitions, his stubborn resistance to half-measures, his great power of visualization, his high purpose, and his even higher spirit. Permit me to take just a moment to give you a glimpse into the mind of this great artist. On the occasion of the announcement of his retirement as dean at the University of California, William Wilson Wurster said,

Architecture is a corridor with many doors, opening into all aspects of human life. It unites many, many forces. I do not believe in embalming ideas. We, none of us, architects or others, have the privilege of building monuments to ourselves. Our work must be for people. I don't pretend to be a great teacher. I was a good administrator running fences for good teachers—my forte is in making it possible for things to happen. I do not teach facts, but teach as a process of arriving at facts.

And so, after the planners had drawn building plans even while the fund-raisers were still trying to raise funds to pay for it all, in a simultaneous action of questionless good faith—for that is the way uncommon men do uncommon things, when purpose is stronger than doubt—the long, plain administration building, set in a sea of cactus and exposed rock outcroppings, rose and stretched, lonely and stark, and we rejoiced that there was a university on Trinity Hill. It was surely the cheapest building ever built as well as the most expensive we could afford. It stood for everything and sheltered everything, and all the offices and laboratories and the auditorium and the registrar's and business offices were compressed along two sides of its long corridor.

I well remember when the youthful and resourceful public relations director called to joyfully announce that Sears, Roebuck had given some great kerosene heaters for that first building, and how I arrived to see sheet-iron flues straggling crookedly from the window sash up and above the wide overhangs in a classic pattern of black metal columns. And inside there was warmth—all kinds of warmth—and pride for the resourceful provider.

At this point I have a consuming desire to tell you about some significant happenings I have witnessed on this hill—happenings which singly, and by cumulative weight, have made this university a place of freedom. For as the physical campus grew, with building added to building as the years sped by, there was an accompanying growth here of a spirit of enlightenment and respect for man. I do know many things about the many judgments of your president, your faculty, and your board which have quietly but inexorably obliterated the barriers of bigotry and intolerance. Someday I wish someone might detail and document them all. But for now, please simply believe me when I tell you that there have been numerous incidents of defense of the unorthodox and in support of the man and the idea. These are events that have truly shaped the style and character of this university of positive protest, its atmosphere, and its spirit. And they have made their solid imprint without fanfare or the usual accompanying self-righteousness of official bodies.

My concern with this growth of freedom is not so far removed from my concern with building as one might suppose.

For the Trinity Treatment of things and men that makes this a place for the different and differing drummer touches the intellectual and the builder alike. Thus the freedom to be different and have different thoughts extends to planning and building differently and without the fetters of rigid restrictions or preconceived notions.

And—while I am always left with the nagging belief that any job on which I have worked could have been done better—I believe the results of the Trinity Treatment are commendable.

You, of course, have had, are having, and will have an opportunity to judge for yourself—for believe me, an architect has very little opportunity to bury his mistakes. But while you look and judge, allow me to point out a few of many considerations which guided the planners and builders.

The buildings on this beautiful ex–dump heap are ranged above and below the rock-quarry bluff with enough ease and order and interrelation to make them relevant to each other and to teaching and learning and sleeping and eating and play and worship. This has resulted from a determination to put things where they logically belonged rather than setting them in some prescribed monumental or geometrical pattern.

The location of each building, walk, or road was determined only after a careful and exhaustive study of the site and its topography, relationships to other buildings and trees and all-important open spaces, and only after it was clearly demonstrated that each served learning and the right to know.

At no time has any board member or giver asked that we design or place a building so that it is dominant or imposing.

The Ruth Taylor Fine Arts group is near our eastern entrance because it belongs there.

The Chapman Graduate Center is back on the grounds at the head of a permanently established green valley because it should be a little apart—a community of scholars.

Some memorable honest differences arose over locating Sams Memorial Center and the Margarite B. Parker Chapel, but in both cases solid planning principles prevailed.

Sams Center, in its low setting, is in proper scale relation to the great parking areas which couldn't be anywhere else, and the chapel is in the campus, with surrounding trees and plaza fitting to its height and very nature as a place apart.

And I cannot possibly pass this opportunity to call your attention to the most wonderfully civilized and sensible item in our storehouse of things we were allowed to do. I hope you haven't noticed it, for this would be the perfect tribute, but has it ever occurred to you that nowhere on this campus does one encounter the all but universal banality of a capital E Entrance or a capital B Building? Nowhere does a building shout authoritatively, "Look at ME! I am the house that Jack built for the Uptiology Department!" I proudly submit that I am deeply grateful for this devastating departure from the prevalent.

And are you aware of the friendly nature of exits and entrances that demand no salutes or obeisance but are just comfortable and pleasant ways into and out of, and through and between?

The administration building is entered through a high-ceilinged, skylighted corridor garden, and one may go into either the theater or the art building under the same simple canopy.

The music building and the east end of the art building are entered through a gallery that is barely an interruption of the landscape, and one walks through the library, not at and into it through formidable bronze doors.

Please join me in my continuing joy that this one important accomplishment has been my privilege.

Just as the Trinity Treatment—the spirit of positive protest—has freed the planners to ignore the conventional banalities of italicized entrances and exits, so also has it fostered tolerance for change and creativeness and inventiveness in the best possible sense. So has it given us the freedom to do serious work with new tools.

To best illustrate, I must once more go back to beginnings—to the "old" administration building, and to that first flat slab of concrete forming the east-most roof section between Northrup Hall and the new administration office section. In 1949–1950, I had been excitingly engaged in a research project seeking to establish that money and time could be saved if floors and roofs of buildings—particularly multistory buildings—could be poured at ground level and then mechanically lifted into place. The inventor and backer of this widely suspect idea was the late Tom Slick, a remarkably imaginative young man and a member of Trinity's board. We had spent hundreds of thousands of Tom's dollars to perfect the system and tools, and our research projects had been entirely successful—though not to the satisfaction of many doubting engineers, architects, and builders in an industry that continues to build wooden buildings, fill them with magic liquid stone, and then throw away the wooden buildings.

We were convinced of the soundness and practicality of our system, but we needed a customer. Not surprisingly, we chose poor, penniless, Presbyterian Trinity University, with its first new building on the drafting boards, as our prospect. Without dwelling on the painstaking preparation of our sales pitch to the Trinity board, I will only say that after a few sentences of its delivery, we were sharply interrupted by someone who said, "Yes, gentlemen, if you know you are right and you can employ this system safely and economically, then go ahead. And now, can we take up this vexing problem of the girls' washing machines?" or something equally weighty.

Thus the first lift slab of a real building—the Trinity administration building [later Northrup Hall; figure 16]—was poured at ground level, and on a cold winter's night a number of us, including Tom Slick and Dr. Everett, then president, worked stealthily all night long to set up the powerful jacks and rigging which would lift it. We nervously warmed our hands over fires lit where Dr. Bruce Thomas's office now is, aware that a multitude of doubters would come with the dawn to jeer us into permanent exile if our absolutely perfect system failed to work. At 4 a.m. we stood prayerfully mute as the valve to the hydraulic lines was opened. There was first a deathly silence, then a solid sucking sound as the 150,000-pound sheet of concrete came free and quivered an inch above its earthly base. The first lift slab in history had been lifted, and some devout little man whispered, for all of us, "Gracias a Dios."

When 1,500 doubters and 10 well-wishers appeared later that morning, and when we had hoisted the slab to an incredible altitude of forty inches, there were a few handshakes around. And then dear Dr. Everett turned to me and said, "Now let's crawl under it, open a blueprint, and studiously study it. Because," he continued in response to our incredulous stares, "if that thing falls, that's where we'd better be!"

Far from falling, this Trinity first became an international sensation in the construction industry and the subject of discussion and lectures and articles in both lay and professional publications everywhere. Today it is a recognized and universally employed method of doing something unusual and useful—and a glowing tribute both to Tom Slick's and Trinity's protest against the common practice, the accepted, and the perfunctory.

And there is yet more, for at Trinity we have been allowed to build a tower which for all its simplicity and good old familiar brick is also a radically revolutionary structure. Paradoxically, it was built about the same way the Romans built their aqueducts and heavy walls. Here again, we were able to use concrete as our structural material and yet eliminate the costly wood forming. Instead, we just used brick forming inside and out, filling the enclosed cavity with concrete and steel every day as the tower grew upward. The bricks remained bound to the concrete structure as handsome walls inside and out—bricklaying is a skill in which San Antonio craftsmen definitely excel. When the tower was as high as we wanted it, we simply put a lid on it, installed Mr. and Mrs. James Calvert's beautiful bells, and had ourselves a beautiful dedication. By the way, don't you agree with me that Trinity does excel in style of groundbreakings and dedications?

The Ruth Taylor Theater is a veritable showcase of innovations put together under Paul Baker's expert guidance and the wonderfully sympathetic eyes of Vernon and Ruth Taylor. I can take little credit for the array of better and more exciting devices and places and elements of plan and structure that make this building so essentially right for its purpose, but I can take all the pleasure I can hold from the fact that some bravo men—some positive protestors—brought Paul Baker and his great staff to Trinity University—and to a grateful San Antonio.

In the big flowing plan of the whole campus that becomes three dimensional as buildings split and stairs climb from one level to another, we have allowed nature and our own determinations to make some places—plazas—piazzas. These are the greeting grounds and the areas for respite and relaxation and mixing of faculty and students. You will probably remember these big and little places longer than you will remember the more typical functional places, like classrooms and laboratories. At the entrance the happy fountain seems far more fitting than some great columns and obvious lettered sign such as grace most entrances to colleges, hospitals, and cemeteries. The fountain is the right thing for the right place—something alive and dancing.

In front of the chapel and from the old classroom building to the sinuous crosswalk is a green place that will be there forever. The little triangular-roofed space at the east end of the bookstore is another hello place—someone told me you call it "rally alley" . . . and the plaza below the art building that makes a front for the theater to flow into . . . and there is the big rallying square in the ell of the Sams Center. These are the less planned, in-between places that will grow in beauty and use.

The Promenade itself, with its water garden, street lamps, and benches, is just a long, thin plaza walk. Except for those that had to go when buildings were built, the campus has many more trees than it had before we started, and now that the prevalence of bulldozers and concrete trucks is subsiding, we are seeing new gardens come into being. A big, new greenhouse will further support this most important flower and plant project. Please come back to look at these places that are just as important as buildings . . . as often as you can. It may be another miracle for you.

I cannot end the list of out-of-the-ordinary things without making a short comment on some of the things we have that far richer universities have not. Your chapel organ is a great instrument, not matched in Texas, and in the chapel are the bright banners by Martha Mood and my brother's glittering lighting fixtures and carved screens. There are colored-glass windows in the chapel that are a far cry from the standard kind. The theater and the Chapman Center have lighting fixtures that did not come from any catalog, but were made for the place. These things are everywhere, are things entirely useful but, we believe, things of beauty and special character.

And now I come to that writer's wall where, as he finds his heart grow fuller and his subject endless, his dilemma is insoluble. As we approach this end of the beginning, how can I ever find means to say how deeply grateful I am for the simple kindnesses, the strong support, and the evident forgiveness for leaks and cracks and broken pipes that are inevitable attendants to my art? How can I convey to you the poignant sense of sad relief I find in the unrewarding knowledge that James W. Laurie soon will call no more to say, "There is a strong possibility that we will break ground for another new building by July 1st. Can we expect to go out for bids by June 1st?"

We have yet to build the badly needed auditorium and communications center, but it will come—we still have faith. Never have I walked across the parking lot east of Northrup Hall—usually in search of free coffee—that Mrs. Hyman or "that man" hasn't knocked on the window to beckon me to the warm presence where I heard of dreams and goals and jolting schedules. I can only hope that my own contributions to Trinity reflect in some measure the generous and civilized treatment I have received here among you.

Never have I been asked to do one single thing that was not honest as structure, as decoration, or in any way contrary to integrity of purpose.

Here I have never been told I must seek to make a building impressive or sumptuous or imposing—or one that would awe or evoke critical praise.

As an architect and builder, I could ask for no greater gift.

And so it is with humble heart that I give thanks for the honor you do me on this occasion, but even more for the great privilege of participating in the inexpressibly happy and rewarding growth of this place of learning—this great university of protest—this University in the Sun. And now I will end this letter, which I have written and rewritten many times, by saying: I will remain always your grateful, admiring, and devoted friend.

Sincerely yours,
O'Neil Ford

Culture—Who Needs It?

In 1968 President Johnson appointed Ford to serve on the National Council on the Arts, which was created in 1964 and advises the chair of the National Endowment for the Arts. Shortly after his appointment Ford gave this irreverently titled lecture, the text of which was found among the architect's papers but without information about the venue in which he delivered it. Ford spoke using slides, to which he frequently referred by saying "this." Some of the slides are identified on the Alexander manuscript, and those are noted here in parentheses. The explicit references to slides make it possible to imagine particularly clearly being in the audience during one of his lectures.

Ford spoke at length in this lecture about education and history, outlining more completely than he had theretofore a vision of how to teach ordinary people to see the world around them and to think about the past. He more fully embraced his position as a public authority on architecture than he had in other talks and offered a vision of the role of the National Council on the Arts. His comments on buildings by other prominent architects are notable as well. Returning to themes that appeared in his writings in the 1930s, he spoke again of organicism in architecture and linked disrespect for people not only with a disregard for the landscape but also with a failure to appreciate the character of building materials.

The National Endowment for the Arts named Ford a National Historic Landmark in 1974. The designation was somewhat tongue in cheek because landmarks are nearly always buildings,

---

Lecture, unpublished, box 81, folder 01001, O'Neil Ford: An Inventory of His Drawings, Papers, and Photographic Material, 1864–1983, Alexander Architectural Archives, University of Texas Libraries, University of Texas at Austin.

works of art, archaeological sites, or districts, but it also was a tribute to his architecture and public service. The opening lines of the citation capture the spirit of Ford's public service, driven as it was by the entwining of love and fury: "Whereas the Alamo has not been torn down to park four Buicks, and whereas the freeway across Brackenridge Park stands like an embarrassed dinosaur at the gates of San Antonio, and whereas many great buildings exist across the land with architectural quality, human scale and compassion, and respect for natural materials, and whereas all these things and more can be in part attributed to the imagination, perseverance, and genius of one O'Neil Ford . . ." The landmark designation made Ford's position as a major US architect official.

What I want to talk about today is of such concern to me that I often find myself expressing my convictions at the National Council meetings, and Clark Mitze will verify that. As a member of the National Council on the Arts, I don't pretend to know how to solve all of the problems—especially in those subjects involving statistics. I am aware, however, and I think the National Council—and each of you—should become aware of what is happening to our children today. It saddens me.

I have four children, and the oldest, I guess, is twenty-two or twenty-three, because I am forty years older than she. The other two of them are teenagers, and one is just over the line. The shocking thing to me is these people are bright, they're studious, they're serious—dead serious. They are serious about some of their protests, some of which is partly valid, indeed. I know this because all of the brilliant people in Texas are in this room and all of the idiots are outside. This is a little bit the way they feel. They also feel that some of you are untouchables and that some of you are in ivory towers, and it is quite true. It's absolutely true. You know, what Mr. Hicks says is of no concern whatever to my son, who is a Romanesque Byzantine expert. He wants to know what a happening is like. He's right. He's quite right—that is, to him.

When you think what the children's standards are today, it is a thing to shock you beyond belief. I grew up in Denton County and maybe the standards of beauty were low, but the standards of ugliness weren't high either. The standards of ugliness nowadays, which are the standards of children, are represented in the billboards, and the hamburger joints, these vulgarizations forced on the people by somebody who wants to make a dollar. That is an impasse. There is no responsibility on the part of a person who will not hire an artist to do a beautiful sign. Some of the buildings are rather all right, pretty good, but then they have to do an ugly symbol, a projection of their trade, which is huckstering—and the wrong kind. Well, these are my children's standards and they are your children's standards. It is tragic.

With this regard to standards, however, someone mentioned earlier the guitar player and singer Elvis Presley. Actually, I think he is a pretty good musician. And my children the other day explained to me why he is a good musician, and why Louis Armstrong is a good musician, and so forth. So whereas their standards are confused, they understand a great many fundamentals, and they do not quite deal in the superficialities that we do—that is, all of us sophisticated persons. We do deal in some superficialities, there is no doubt about that.

So, as a member of the National Council on the Arts, I want to propose some things: that we get down to a different level, accepting what is good, along with keeping the wonderful high level that we've got. What I would like to see is more touch with the people and the minds of these children. This can be done by all the councils on art, the commissions on art, the societies of art, leagues of arts in all the states—and the national one, which, by the way, is a miracle of the last thirty years. The fact that we have a National Council on the Arts, which has accomplished so much in such a short time, is beyond belief.

In talking today, I am going to tell you exactly what I have been telling high school kids. Mostly in private secondary schools—and in some public schools. And I have been talking in many places. I have been talking in some states where the higher education is about like the secondary education in some other states that I know of. But all of these groups of people want to hear something about who they are, what they feel, what they see, what they can become, how they can develop an awareness—discrimination, how they can develop a reasonable and sensible outrage at ugliness. What do they do about these children?

The other day I was talking to some little girls—ninth graders, I guess. And they were listening. I was trying to tell them something that they would understand. Incidentally, this is the effort I'd like to see made on a different scale and vastly expanded so that it reaches all of the people. I hope it reaches the thirty thousand people who go to see the starving artists show on the river, downtown at La Villita in San Antonio. Twenty thousand—about twenty thousand go to see the River Arts Show, or maybe even more than that. Then we have an Art Jamboree with attendance at six thousand. Why do all of these people go to these? They go, but they don't necessarily go to the McNay Gallery. They go to this because they feel that it's a place they can go and participate. Why do all of these people paint those paintings, put them along the river? I would stop anybody who would try to set standards on that. That's the way to do it. Let them paint anything they are big enough to paint or carry—and some of them are pretty hard to carry. Hard to look at, too. Why do these people who have evidenced an extraordinary interest in something go to a heck of a lot of trouble to go there to stand all day? They walk along the river, and they get so excited, then they fall in the river! How do we find these people? How do we find these people! How do we find the sixty thousand people who go to hear Louis Armstrong? How do we get these people who go to see the Fiesta, and the parades, and the Fat Stock Show, to our theaters, and how do they get interested in art?

Well, I was talking to these little girls the other day and I said, "You know how to have fun and how to sense something about your surroundings, your earth, your land, your sky, and all of that? I've got a hunch that if you sit down on the beach, a perfectly barren beach, or sit down in your mother's garden, or if you are an Aztec, sit down near a ruin, or a Mayan, sit down at the place that your forebears built, and if you reach out as far as you can, making a circle—just stay there for two hours looking at it and you will be absolutely astonished at the beauty of little things. Nearly nothings. Bits and pieces of shell, strange little things, and a plant so small you didn't know it grew. This is an experience. Or if you pick up a board or see a board on the steps in your home and you look at the grain, you might say, 'Let's start here with the sinking of the *Maine*,' or, 'Let's start here with the beginning of the First World War and let's count back.' Those grains are very close together in the dry season. They were all grown slowly above six or eight thousand feet. And they get farther apart and that's where Lincoln was assassinated. This very board was alive. Here is the day George Washington died, and at this time, Thomas Jefferson presented his paper, the Declaration of Independence. It's all in the board, it's in my house, it's in San Antonio. The whole thing." What does this do to the child? It gives him another dimension in orientation, in history, in land, in lumber, in wood, and the respect for what that is, a piece of dirt, a piece of wood, growing out of the earth.

These things, it seems to me, need to be told to children in books, in slides, in films. I can think of fifty stimulants, and the people in the room can think of five thousand. They should be written. They should be like Bernard Rudofsky's book *Architecture without Architects*. How many people have read that book? It's just one of the extraordinary books of the world, because he points out this very thing, that man keeps dealing in academic history taught chronologically, which is the silliest way to teach history I can possibly imagine. You have to teach history for what history is. Teach it backwards and you'll find the reasons for things and you will go back to beauty invariably—almost invariably.

Well, at the dedication of St. Mary's Hall in San Antonio, the children were all there. What can you tell these children about the building? I don't know whether the architecture is any good or not. Somebody will know someday. It's a little building instead of a monstrous box of a thing. It's got warmth because of the brick and the wood and so forth. What else can I tell children about it? They are not terribly concerned about that, and they are not discriminative, having billboards as their standard. Well, what I tell them is: Did it ever occur to you that in this building, in the brass, in the plumbing fixtures, in the air-conditioning and so forth, that all of these things come out of the earth? The most sophisticated piece of glass, the control instrument in a thermostat, was a piece of dirt. By man's ingenuity it was processed; it was beaten; it was stamped; it was melted; it was poured; it was cast; it was ground; it was polished; and it was made into this thing.

Now let's get back down to the earth and think about the earth. I'm going to use these color slides to illustrate my thoughts for you.

Once upon a time there was no problem of understanding, on the part of an Indian—whether he was from New Mexico or Peru or Yucatán or Tehuantepec, it made no difference at all— he understood his technology all the way through. Precisely as our children cannot possibly understand anything at all about finality in technology. These men knew finality. They knew beauty without calling it beauty, and it fit the earth and was of the earth. And they knew precisely what to do with it. It could not but be beautiful.

This I ran upon in Peru not long ago. I asked once, "Who do you think designed that?" Someone said, "Was it Lou Kahn?" Another one asked, "Philip Johnson?" You know these are the only names they knew, the ones that have been on the front page of *Time* magazine. They say, "No, Le Corbusier." Well, of course, it was built in 1750 [1766–1768] out of mud. An humble material, a simple material. Technically a good material. But this was the Plaza de Acho in Lima, Peru, which is a bull ring.

They didn't even care whether the arches were round because they corbeled them and it worked just as well, it's made of mud. It's essentially mud, as is this church in Mikonos. I think one does not judge beauty by what it is made of at all. They made it of what they had. The dovecotes here are of mud, and the building is of mud. That doesn't show at the top. It is a marvelous dome anyway. All made of mud and dirt. Cool and proper. My children understand this by seeing these slides. Incidentally, what I am doing now is a condensation of what I should like to see done by the National Council on the Arts, preferably. It is a marvelous, wonderful series of slides that will inevitably teach a child the fundamental processes by which we have come to what we are and what architecture is and what related arts are.

This wonderful church—out in Arizona—looks like Petra. It, of course, is dirt, again. It is just wonderfully restored. And by the way, all power to the National Park Service. That's as far as they are going, there is no point in doing any more. It is good enough.

The Maya house. This is as understandable as anything ever. But if you spent time talking about a Maya house and looking at a Maya house and analyzing a Maya house, you would know that there is scarcely any other kind of house at all as good as this for the climate in Yucatán. Just almost none. They started out building modernistic schools down there. Very clever, indeed. And they got back to schools exactly like this, just as good as the original—a thousand years ago.

So it's a fundamental thing. Just as we must remember our past and respect it and know, for instance, that San Antonio got its architecture from Portugal, from Spain, and Italy, and so forth. This is the kind of history to know, and this is the kind of history I think that a child will relate to, precisely as the Peruvians do nowadays. The children in school there will learn to relate to what the pre-Incas did. It is theirs.

This is Machu Picchu, high in the mountains, and an extraordinary thing in every way. And terribly sophisticated in the terms of living. Rather crude in terms of the later buildings on top, when they got in a hurry. (The Spanish were lurking along the coast.) However, it is absolutely exquisite. Technically, well, it is the best stonework in the world. Nobody has touched it at all, and nobody has the foggiest idea how they did it.

This is related to us; this is related to Mexico; this is related to our children today. It's something that they can read and understand, as is this building at Chichén Itzá in Mexico. Incidentally, these were the first people (and I can teach this to a boy, twelve) who knew anything at all about prefabrication. The Egyptians didn't; the Greeks didn't; and, of course, this was built about 700 A.D. It didn't matter when it was because it had no relation to the rest of the world. There was no time relation to this civilization. All these little bits and pieces of decorative things were made by four thousand people who were a mile and a half away. We went there and looked at a number of the places where they had chipped—thousands of people making bits. The architect did as he does today. He picked out things—units, bricks, moldings, columns, tubes, extrusions, and he put it together the same way. I could teach a boy that. And by teaching him that, he would learn, anyone could, that it could get a little more complex. He could also learn something that colleges and schools seem never to teach, and that is how to plan something on the ground. Instead of building a lot of pseudo-Georgian things, like chicken houses, all over Texas with a lot of anonymous prairie in between them, it's integrated and it's as good as the Simon Fraser University in Vancouver. I hope someone's seen that. It gave me such an inferiority complex I had to leave. This was done because thought was given in terms of how the people lived and not where the donor wanted it built, although we need donors, all right. The slightest glance by twelve-year-old children will enable them to understand, with no explanation, the juxtaposition of things and how in the flat land you can create changes in level in a beautiful way. (Slide: The sculptured stone, Machu Picchu.)

It's easy to teach a child something about sculpture—space, sculpture, and art—if you show him things as simple as this instead of something esoteric. San José Mission—shadow and light, and juxtaposition of pieces and bits and shapes and sizes. It's easy to know. No trouble at all. Well, we feel that these things are a marvelous lesson, not just in Baroque architecture, for heaven's sake. They're not the best, you know, but they're good buildings—in San Antonio. How much you could learn about processes; how much you could learn about the easy way it was started and also the tribulations and the trials they had in continuing after the Indians were converted. They had to be locked up every night because they got out and ran away. Then it was necessary to go get some more.

This is San Juan Mission. I have a great pride in it, and this is my story. Do you know that at the San Juan Mission, the archbishop wanted us to do some restoration? It will remain a ruin, as it properly should. They have a parish church and they want to go to church there, and they want a little meeting hall, and so we go that far with the restoration. We also made a boundary wall. You'd think, well, this is simple enough, too—cut out of the river bottom—which was the way it was done because the builders couldn't get away. They would have been killed by other Indians. So what we did here was look for stonemasons. And we found stonemasons. Good stonemasons who do peanut-brittle rock work in Olmos Park. But the stonemasons now have learned how to work too artfully and with too much deception. They couldn't lay it. So what did we do? We had to go get boys from SANYO, San Antonio Youth Organization, which is a relief-work organization, and they could do it because they were ethnically like the Indians. And this is what we did. They put the thatch on the roofs; they built these walls up from down very low. And these boys learned something because the problem was not calculus; it was not chemistry; it was not complex history; it was not remembering a date. It was remembering the impact of these missions on civilization, aesthetically and theologically. They remembered all of this, and I got to talk with them about how they were built. I think they now know something about it. I told them why you put buttresses on a mission. Some of the purists down there had a dying fit when we started putting buttresses on it. The reason we put buttresses on it was so it wouldn't fall down. Well, the boys understood that.

Continuing with dirt buildings, if these were drawn today and presented to a building and loan association, they would say, "We can't allow none of them modern buildings. Those one-sloped roof buildings. We can't allow none of them." The F.H.A. and any bank would not make a loan on this or this—because that roof is "modern." Well, of course, they date from 1750 down on the border in Nuevo Santander [modern Tamaulipas and South Texas]. I should like to see us get some vernacular architecture that is not just the Neill-Cochran House in Austin. Not "just" this house or that house, although those are beautiful houses—well-documented, beautiful architecture. (Slide: Quihi, Texas.) But I would like to find those things that are off to the side; that were contributors like the buildings in Quihi and those out from Castroville and along the border, that almost nobody has said a word about. I would like to get those in the picture as a part of history. Because they make architecture more easily understood. They make technology more easily understood, if you start with this. Well, that's Quihi.

Torn down to park four Buicks. These are some things our children would understand and know nothing about at all.

In San Antonio, someone from the Carpenter's Union came to me one day and said, "Mr. Ford, the house on the corner down there, I understand that you have been fighting to keep it from being torn down." I said, "I sure have. That's a marvelous house, a beautiful house. It's a sort of Italianate Victorian house. We haven't many left." He said, "Would you advise that we buy it and make it our headquarters?" Well, I sat down.

This pioneer thing that we have is beautiful. The classic things came. Now, I am talking to children and not to you. But they will understand it better when I show them the one in Waco, which is Victorian and attenuated. Long, skinny classic. They will understand that. They will understand this more academic Neill-Cochran House, and they will understand and identify this with the Greek Temple instantly without studying Greek or Roman architecture. They will understand the beauty that the Victorian jigsaw brought, attaching itself to classicism. This was really the end of the Renaissance. I do not agree with anyone, yet, that the Renaissance ended way back in the eighteenth century with Sir Christopher Wren. It ended about 1890, I think. The real Renaissance kept right on going one way or another, because the Renaissance and the Industrial Revolution were actually one thing. It was business, technology, advancement, the arts—the exuberance of the people and government. People were beginning to govern themselves, humanism entered into literature, and so forth.

After that comes this mechanization thing and this absolutely confusing age of technology, which, I think, we don't quite understand and isn't at all identifiable with the cruder means of the Industrial Revolution of the nineteenth century. I think that was very crude and much more related to the Renaissance. So here is the last in San Antonio. That one house. And then, of course, it moves into the romantic Victorian concept and this beautiful Steves house—the other one was in Austin; another one, Grandmother's Hat, in San Antonio; and Kaiser Wilhelmstrasse; add another one, Mr. Groos's house in San Antonio: are all great art. They really are great art, any way you take it. You don't have to take the standard from classicism or from Gothicism, but you take it from what it is and teach the children how it evolved; from the ability to cast things, the ability to saw things; the ability to machine stone and how this whole exuberant business like Maple Avenue used to be here. It was marvelous, had great houses on it. Now look at it. Or don't.

This is Fredericksburg. It's easy to show a child how this relates to Romanesque architecture and how this structure is about as real as a building can be. There is hardly any way that you can improve on it. If you took anything away from it, it would fall down.

You are also teaching a child what's under his eye, what's in his own hometown. You are not teaching him things that he isn't willing to digest. Even if he is willing to digest it, he may not be able to, but seeing architecture or seeing a building, seeing sculpture is an altogether different matter. You can talk about shelter and show him in Brownsville what shelter means. You can talk about a ranch house and show him how good and simple and real it can be, and it ain't nothing like a subdivision ranch house at all in, let's say, Westchester. (Slide: River Oaks, Houston.) And then you can show him the world he lives in pretty soon. He will know the differences pretty soon—he'll know all about it. He'll become dreadfully articulate, even profane, about this kind of thing.

This is the stereotyped world we all live in. This is where Colonel Borden lives, on the front porch drinking his mint julep, but the milk processing is in the back. Nothing is so absurd as that or so funny.

You must be respectable with a shopping center. You can see in this shopping center, that although this is modern over here and therefore efficient, you must get a bit of old America in it so that it has respectability. Now, it is air-conditioned, too, see? There is the air-conditioning, right there.

And this is the entrance to the beautiful City of Missions, San Antonio: trees and a little river along the north. And this is the entrance to San Antonio from the south. You will see there the beautiful Mission San José, Queen of the Missions, right there in a marvelous pile surrounding of litter and junk. It can, of course, be more marvelous in no time at all. Now, who fights this? Has the arts council said much about this? Not very much. This is where we have a gap. This is where the children must react and feel outraged. (Slide: Ugly alleys—vacant lots downtown.)

These are our courtyards in America. Looking down from this luxurious apartment in a major hotel, you can see the "between" places—a parking lot, half a tooth, a whole tooth, and no tooth, and it was all snaggletoothed because everybody is so busy tearing down buildings to make parking so that they'll have business. It never occurs to anybody—businessmen, anybody—that if you have just got parking lots, you haven't got many places to shop. It's a dead end. It's a dead end there, it's a dead end in San Antonio, Dallas, Fort Worth, and everywhere. It's poor planning. These are the American courtyards. They are everywhere.

Now, this, I'd like our children to know about. This is their place to play, and, by contrast, this programmed play yard is about as bad because the frigidity of it is almost more forbidding than the warm friendly brick in these. And this, of course, is esoteric, and I've got a worse word for it, and patented. Fearful stuff as opposed to America. To be understood by the people and understood by anyone looking at it.

This is Paley Park in New York [figure 17]. One of the most astonishing things I have ever seen is this tiny little place. It is beloved. Thank heaven for the man who designed it. It is done so well. But this one thing in this great city probably has as much impact as, well, almost any other thing that has happened in New York in a long time. We need it.

(Slide: Underground houses, Morocco.) These people live in a hole in the ground in mud. And that's a courtyard. Inside there are pianos. One of them had a grand piano. They have good rugs—better oriental rugs than we can afford. In Morocco there are sophisticated people, but they think that this is a good place to live in their climate, and it is. Well, you can teach a child the difference between these in a very short time indeed. You can inspire him for what his world is today, show him a courtyard in Denver that is good looking. (Slide: Pan Am Building, New York City.) You can show him that some people are such absolutely gross and greedy things that they build a building where there is not room for a building. From this elevation they

FIGURE 17. Robert Zion, Paley Park, New York City, 1967. Ford said it was "one of the most astonishing things I have ever seen. . . . Thank heaven for the man who designed it."

ruin a street. There is not room for it. There is not room for the building anywhere. There is not room for the people in the building. It makes no sense. It can't be sane. It is not difficult to show children that this garage built right on the San Antonio River, removing a lovely parking lot which was marked with live oak trees, is an intrusion in his interest, in my interest, and in your interest. And I think it should be shown as such.

Then there is what is known as "perfunctory architecture," adequate architecture done by adequate architects. The ugliness of this is that nobody cares and the ugliness of this is that the man was too exuberant and he wanted to impress himself and everybody else that it was designed by an architect. (Slide: A hospital in Denver.) This was done by a man who hates bricks. He hates people, too, because this is a hospital.

My children have learned to look for these incongruities, and they have turned them into something of a game. They have fits about seeing some of these things and go find them themselves. Then they remember Chichén Itzá, Uxmal, Teotihuacan Oaxaca, Monte Albán, and then they see this. What a sad, sad thing this is. What a dreadful thing has happened to Mexico, where they have copied some of the worst of the things we do and they have forgotten about much of the tradition. Not that they should copy the tradition, but they have forgotten the influx that has made the tradition a great thing. Then there's a kind of school building that isn't offensive but it is sexless, in every way. It has no heart, it has nothing to say. Well, it says, "I am aluminum." That is what is called conservative.

And then there are the things like this, where the girls who stand up and sleep have rooms, and the girls who lie down and sleep have rooms. (Slide: Hill College House dormitory, University of Pennsylvania.)

Then, of course, this dreadful thing has happened. All these cheap, gift-wrapped fronts on stores in downtown Austin. Congress Avenue once looked like this with some regard to taste and consistent style. I ask you, is there one [that is] more scholarly, more architecturally significant than the cheapest gift wrapping you ever saw from a basement of certain stores we know? That's what America turns out to be. No regard.

And then you find a man who hates paintings. He builds a building and he makes it impossible to see more than half of one. (Slide: Guggenheim Museum, New York City.) I've never understood what was wrong with a square room for paintings or a hall. I've never understood that. Of all of the devious things people do to make galleries tricky, when what people come there for is to see the paintings, not the architecture. People are square—not triangular.

Sometimes one is allowed to do something organically, and this is where the young people really begin to sound off. They really understand. They dig this all the way. We take a piece of concrete like that, and you take a piece like this and put the one over the other. We roll it to a place with holes in the floor and little things to weld to, and the next thing that happens is it becomes quite creative indeed. The architect has oriented the young man to metals and materials. He sees this coming together. He reacts the same way that he reacts to an architect's or a teacher's description of how Gothic cathedrals are built. Of course, he derives the same good sense of differentiation and awareness and discernment. So then you build a building. You build the paraboloids up above and all of a sudden you've got this wonderful chance, and you explain to him, if you can, why they are so strong, only two and a half inches thick and sixty-three feet square. (Slide: Texas Instruments Semiconductor Components Division Building, Dallas.) You explain why you did them on a factory building of a million feet or so instead of designing a flat ceiling. It's because it would be dull, it would be tiresome, there'd be no variety. You explain this to him, how these floors were made and how this building has a certain kind of beauty, whereas the one that had to have baby-blue spangles painted on it and do a lot of ingenious and arbitrary things to make it palatable usually failed. But this one didn't have to fail. It didn't have any wall. It intrigues my youngest boy that somebody built a stadium that had no folderol to it, the same as the column that held it up. Now, that's as simple as a Mayan house. There's no difference at all, and it's as modern as ten years from now. You can explain Félix Candela's beautiful paraboloids, and you can explain that some people hate concrete, too. And they build houses like this with concrete because it *can* be done. The sorriest reason to use a material is just because you've got it. You just might as well use another, if the only reason you are using it is because you've got it or that it is the new fashion. (Slide: Concrete house, Kingston, Jamaica.) That's a concrete house in, of all places, Kingston, Jamaica.

This, of course, you would expect to be in Los Angeles because it has little wires to hold it together, in case there's an earthquake. Stainless steel. (Slide: Spanish car over Niagara Falls.)

So, this is a tour de force—ridiculous, making no sense at all. Somebody understood steel here, just the framing. He respected steel. He made a thing of absolute beauty out of a pragmatic thing. Touched it ever so subtly, gently, with a little discriminative hand, not much, but it is a thing of beauty. We've built things like this, which are exciting. It is especially exciting to the people who are asking what is coming up technically. Well, what is coming up is about what it's always been, done with a little different tools. There are not many really new things invented in the world. New in every sense. Chemically, at least.

So, here is a steel frame on the ground. In an hour and a half it is lifted up in place, ducts and everything. It is an interesting process. Heaven knows, I wish architecture could look like this. I wish architecture could be like this before they put the architecture on it and ruin it. (Slide: Trinity University gymnasium.)

These are cables. It is an exciting, cheap way to build a building. Well, the response to this by all of you is strong, is favorable. People like this. It's something great to see. Of course, we got thinner the next time and used very thin steel cables for the roof of the building. Had it ever occurred to you that it is unlimited in span? You can span the Golden Gate Bridge. This is what you tell the boys. You get a bridge, a crude bridge, and then you turn it. And what have you made? You have made a marvelous building. A great, wonderful inverted dome that spans, what, five miles? two miles? How long can tension go? I don't know. Forever, almost.

Then there are those people who didn't want their building to fall down. (Slide: Cain Sloan Store, Nashville.) It's the only steel building frame that I ever saw that you couldn't see through. This is one of those disparities. Well, it's so vulgar that it makes a point to anybody, anywhere.

Now and then we [allow] ourselves [to show our own buildings]—and this is the only time, I don't ever like to show our own things, except in gratitude to the people who have a few times allowed us to do some fundamental things. (Slides:

Braniff Tower, University of Dallas; Murchison Tower, Trinity University [figure 16].) We built these towers. This tower is built of brick. No apology. It is fine Sumerian material. They built upward three feet a day and poured it full of concrete as they went. Just the way the Romans did. They built a veneer and poured it full of concrete all the way. Then we went all of the way to the top putting in our steel. One hundred eighty-five feet high. With one-by-two pieces of lumber, we wrapped them and wrapped them, nailed them and glued them and made the lid. They weighed nearly nothing. And I'm very sad they didn't put it up [on top of the] tower with a helicopter. It's all great. It's "essential" great. It's "respectful" great. And this respect for materials is best taught by a simple thing like this.

This is another we did. About the same height. At Trinity University, with much more subtle engineering to keep it from bursting and tearing itself apart, as all towers do, which, by the way, is something interesting in physics. In the sunshine during the morning, it leans westward about two inches. When it shines on the tower in the afternoon, it leans about two and a half inches to the east. When the sun is in the south, it just stands there and grinds. If you look at the obelisk in a New York park, or any of the obelisks in the world, you see the bottom is rounded off from just that reason. It is spalling.

Now, how to tell the boys and girls of the significance. Well, what I tell them, we build five or six of these towers and we hook cables between them and we have a building which covers all. All climate is out. We've got it all climated. We don't have to have walls and rooms and bricks and dormer windows and chimneys or false chimneys or fake dormer windows or anything. We don't have to have any columns. We have people living in a universal, university atmosphere underneath many extruded concrete columns that go very high up. Well, if you talk about the simplicity of things—shapes and form of lines and bricks—a brick structure can be built today like that and be beautifully built. We don't mind reaching back, and we don't mind showing people that certain fundamental things cannot possibly be improved. (Slide: *Bovedas* [vaults of brick].) I worked with an engineer, Mr. Candela, one of the great engineers of the world. He worked a day trying to figure out what made the structure stand up. It cannot be improved. It's like a flower that grows; it's like a cloud. There's no better way to make a better cloud or better flower.

If you were teaching children you might show this—the fishes and flowers that are sold in the morning in front of the opera house where the patrons go in tuxedos in the evening in Helsinki. You're able to show them what sculpture is even if it's old or new. You are able to relate this marvelous sculpture, architecture, mud-building process, elementary things, and vernacular architecture in this little Mexican graveyard almost better than any place in the world. You are able to tell them how beautiful this is, and it's not a bit difficult to talk about.

If you explain this cypress tree as sculpture and these trees as sculpture—columns, as lines like columns—if you explain that, they better understand the earth as sculpture. The University of Virginia lawn, this wonderful thing that Mr. Jefferson did that hardly any architects have ever been able to do since [figure 4]. I doubt that anyone has so beautifully respected the land and made sculpture of the whole composition as Félix Candela did with his little chapel at Cuernavaca, which included parking—beautifully [figure 18]. I don't know that I've seen the earth more beautifully sculptured than this slag heap at Canterbury in England. It's an old slag heap, and a man had an idea and that's what he did.

These are some of the things that stimulate children, and stimulate me and probably stimulate you. This is a beautiful sculpture which is as good as anything I've seen done in a studio. It's the cage of the little car that goes across Niagara Falls. I looked at it and looked at it. Has anybody built anything more beautiful than this? It is a wonderful thing, agile, light, and strongly engineered.

FIGURE 18. Félix Candela, Chapel Lomas de Cuernavaca, Cuernavaca, Mexico, 1958. Of the work Ford observed, "I doubt that anyone has so beautifully respected the land and made sculpture of the whole composition as Félix Candela did with his little chapel at Cuernavaca."

What is beautiful is understood if it is put in terms that people know are real and not phony. There is no problem at all when you are perfectly honest with yourself about what it is and what it is not. This is what we can teach our children.

1968

Physical Planning versus or for the Individual

As the populations of downtowns across the country shrank and were shaken by riots, as freeways sliced through cities and across landscapes, and as suburbs swelled, faculty at the Austin and Arlington campuses of the University of Texas convened an enormous conference on planning. Like their colleagues throughout the United States, the participants were interested in how planners and architects should respond to rapidly changing social, political, and economic conditions. Conveners sought a dialogue about planning in humanistic terms that would also focus on the challenges and opportunities presented by new technologies. The conference took place over two days, beginning the day after Martin Luther King Jr. was assassinated.

Forty-eight speakers, respondents, and discussants came chiefly from academic institutions in Texas and Louisiana. Ford spoke and served as a discussant on the panel concerned with "physical" planning. In his remarks he repeated some ideas on landscape and civil rights that he had introduced in his 1964 lecture at Rice University, "The Condition of Architecture," and he quoted from his 1932 article with Thomas D. Broad, "Toward a New Architecture." Ford opened by summarizing ideas that had emerged at the meeting of the American Institute of Planners in 1966 in Portland, Oregon, and mused on the role of the planner. Most significant were his exchanges with panel respondent Reynell Parkins, pastor of St. Martin's Church in Corpus Christi and professor of architecture and planning at the University of

Remarks at the Planning versus or for the Individual Conference, University of Texas at Arlington. Originally published in *Planning versus or for the Individual: A Regional Consultation at the University of Texas at Arlington, April 5–6, 1968* (Arlington: University of Texas at Arlington, 1968), 106–110, 127–128.

*Texas at Austin School of Architecture from 1968 to 1970, and
discussant L. S. Turner Jr., president of the Dallas Power and
Light Company.*

*Parkins spoke of the need "to teach people to live in . . . pro-
ductive, creative tension" and argued that planners and "all
Americans" failed to understand the value of it. He critiqued
Ford's implication that racism lay somewhere else—in the minds
of some politicians and their supporters who fought against civil
rights. Parkins urged his listeners to identify the prejudices they
carried, and, as enslaved people had had to, to find beauty and
self-worth within in order to persevere and do good in the world.
The minister concluded by saying, "Planning need not separate
human beings; planning needs to bring together people of all
races, all cultures, all creeds in their common finiteness to sit
together so that human beings can be taught to have the courage
to be human."*

The Portland conference proceedings include the following:

We desire to a) encourage more citizen participation in
community affairs, b) enhance the individual sense of
political efficiency, c) genuinely disburse power widely
through American society, d) increase the variety and
accessibility of options available to society, e) economize
rigorously on the use of compulsion, and f) more generally, minimize the need for citizens to think consciously
about governmental restraints on their behavior.

The tentative plan until now has been to favor the
proliferation and centralization of bureaucracy. Traditionally,
the main function of planning has been to conceive of ways to
offset the dysfunctional by-products of the free market. The
collective impact of these factors is not expected to decline
rapidly, but can the planner implement collective goals in non-
bureaucratic ways while including them in the policy-making
process? My point is that technology does not change society,
it destroys it. And yet, we hear a lot about technology—how it

will no doubt correct, cure, and satisfy all the needs of man in the next thirty-two years until the year 2000. Well, I remember very well thirty-two years ago, and it's not very different now than it was then—except it's a bigger mess now in the world. In all sincerity, I must say that a lot I read is pertinent to the subject discussed in Portland, but not very pertinent to things in general. I was born in Texas, and I have lived in Texas all my life—Denton, Dallas, until I moved to San Antonio in 1939, and what I see happening in the country between Fort Worth and Dallas is a shocking sight. Take, for example, the drive out to the University at Arlington. The street is an ugly street. Shall we face it? It wasn't planned, and it might not have been any better if it had been planned. Access to the highway would first have been settled. Then it would have been uglified—uglified because there's no bureaucracy with the guts or the power or the inclination to stop this dreadful uglification of America.

My thought for the future is that if America is not going to change the direction in which it is going in the next thirty-two years, then I'd just as soon live somewhere else—even on the moon. On the other hand, however, I believe that America will change for the better. The holocaust is upon us, we have no choice but to start behaving like civilized people; none of us must want to live in a totally ugly world which cannot produce civilized children or civilized adults. On the chance that it will change the right way, I will gladly live the next thirty-two years in a country with an even chance of turning out to be the most monstrous place on earth or a very beautiful country.

An article I wrote in the *Southwest Review* in 1932 says precisely what I now think, if in different, more naïve words:

Historians have described vividly the dauntless courage of the pioneers, and there can be no doubt that this bloody ground of the frontier required and produced men of more than ordinary stamina and enterprise. When it was a question of struggle of bare existence against a hostile environment a certain allowance is necessary in describing the word "individualism," which seems to be no more than a polite understatement. But as the frontier passes and the cities grow up from the prairies, the traits that were necessary for the conquest of the continent survive as a cultural lag in the new environment, which requires a considerable degree of group-consciousness if life is to be tolerable at all. And as this growth of cities becomes the dominant factor in our new civilization, the negative aspect of pioneering becomes quite evident indeed. For the pioneers, while they have founded an empire, have also stripped our land. But you've heard all this a thousand times. You've heard about East Texas and the coal fields in Kentucky. You've heard about the gravel pits, and you've heard about what we are leaving behind. But the thing hasn't changed. It's our real concern. And we talk about so many other things when the concern is the defamation. When the concern is the replacement of defamed areas, ruined areas with something just as bad. Shopping centers that shouldn't exist. Strips of street that shouldn't exist.

An American house must express its owners' personalities and must never agree with the one next door. The banker's house is Spanish; the next one is funny; the bootlegger's house is Italian; and the dry goods merchant's is an English cottage of twenty-two rooms. The banker and the bootlegger and the dry goods merchant are the sons of the pioneers; and like their grandfathers, they still find a terrible challenge in their environment to their respective identities and to the need for stimulating self-assertion. All physical ugliness and all social ugliness have strong connections and roots. Today there is all manner of hate and fierce argument on the basic issue of civil rights. Our great privileges are so flaunted and license is so condoned that in some of our cities 30 per cent of the people live in slums, so that not just physical man is ruined, but all rights, opportunities, and self-respect go down the drain. The bitter disregard for the rights of others goes together with the callous notion that a man may build anything he wishes—ugly, vulgar, trivial; big or little—if he can pay for it. Can you think how serious or tragic it is that any congressman, or any lawyer, anywhere, can find a reason or the audacity to speak against the civil rights of any man or group of men?

Isn't it strange, in this land of billboards and poles and wires and pop architecture and slums, that we have a complementary and parallel circumstance? If a conservation society lady fights city hall, if I as an architect fight the building of a garage on the river in San Antonio (this poor little river carries a terrible responsibility), this is important because it is visible evidence of what a planner has done.

What is happening is that the physical ugliness around us is producing a generation that doesn't know what ugliness is. My children don't know what ugliness is. In San Antonio, they're not alarmed at driving to Austin and seeing one long slum called U.S. 81. They're not disturbed when they come from the Chapman Ranch into Corpus Christi, this "Queen of the Bay," this lovely town in many respects, and are greeted by four wrecked-car lots on Ayers; they continue right on to the beach in Corpus Christi. And it's ugliness, ugliness, ugliness. And it's everywhere. Have you been to Albuquerque lately? Have you been to Midland? Have you been to Denton, Texas? Have I been there? Yes. This is the world my children know about. And the only one they know about. It's all they react to.

People say, "Let's build everything in America, including school buildings, on a temporary basis, or for a twenty-year life, because things are going to change, such as education, through the technology of teaching." However, the atom was split in a very old building in Oxford; similar progress was made in Chicago in some rather antiquated places. A man who assumes that we can tear everything down in twenty years is simply making an excuse for building a worse slum than he built before. And the bonded indebtedness of schools in America and the increase in population will not allow us to build some ridiculous building out of sheet metal that can be torn down right away. Buildings ought to last sixty years, seventy years, eighty years, but will they make sense eighty years from now? Harvard makes pretty good sense. So does Oxford. So does Cambridge. S.M.U. doesn't make much sense. Nor does T.C.U.

The wrong things men build cry out. Impulse selling, impulse buying. Recently, one of my children saw the point for a moment. As we drove along in our mental and visual parenthesis, we noticed a sign which read "Beware of Imitations. This Is a Genuine Perma-Stone Installation." I have no contempt at all for this esoteric rationalization of the phenomenon of growth and change and the staggering problems created by—*what*? No planner has told me what created this stuff, nor why it's allowed to go on, nor why it's profitable for it to go on, nor when it's to end. Planners mark on a map: Recreation; Dense; Less Dense; Commercial; Industrial; Educational. These are on a map and they make sense. Intrinsically they're sensible, but all around them a fire is burning. The fire is growing, and while all this is happening to us, nobody in city hall is powerful enough or has enough courage or enough education to do anything about it.

What I wish the planners could do, and all of you in business, and particularly all of you who teach, is to work out some way to do something about it, so that we planners, architects, and artists can learn how. We are the conscience in America that's needed. We are like the men who made Florence, and worked for the Medici. Business furnished the money, but the artist made it beautiful. Yet the artist keeps taking third place, backing off to the statistician and the sociologist and so forth. But the artist is what we need.

Then what has the artist got to have? He's got to have a client, and he's got to have a client different from the clients in city hall. This cannot be a client who assumes that the city manager and all the city managers in America are going to decide what this country is going to be. The city managers' job is not to decide what this country is going to be, it's to manage the cities. Were city managers not cut out of a pretty strong piece of goods, they would know they need the artist.

Who doesn't know the story of San Antonio? Who doesn't know the story of Dallas, where something sensible has happened in regard to this city manager, artist, and client concept? I'm pleading for the use of the artist and the client who has sense enough to use the artist in the statehouse, in the city hall, or on the school board. In Dallas are some of the most generous people I've ever known in my life. Much money is given away, and given for good purposes in Dallas. Thirty years ago, at the Kessler Plan meetings in Dallas, I heard about the Central Expressway. It took perhaps twenty-five years of talking, conferences, and meetings to get it built, but it was finally finished and it destroyed nothing. It went where the railroad tracks were; it's pretty good. But then, what else is happening in Dallas? Cotton Belt tracks are made into a toll road. Well, how sensible can you get? Of course, Dallas hasn't a lot of historical things to fall under the bulldozer. It never did have. When I lived there, there wasn't much that you couldn't part with. But, even so, these two expressways don't plunge in like bulls in the Garden of Eden.

I would like to finish on a note of despair. In San Antonio we've had the City in court for nine years. What for? Not because the men in city hall are evil; and not because the men in city hall, the council, are going to make any money out of this, although it often is rather amazing who gives money to carry on the fight against bond issues. Expediency in every city hall in America, expediency in the planning profession, expediency everywhere is the disease. Nobody has a goal. Dallas has some goals. Some will be implemented. Some places have goals. I have goals. Some of you have goals. But expediency makes the City of San Antonio rush out, find a way to run an expressway northward; keep it in public lands; scrupulously keep it in public parks—in Brackenridge Park, over the old sunken gardens in Brackenridge Park, an old quarry there that's kind of a strange, interesting sunken garden; straight through Incarnate Word College, splitting it in half, five hundred feet—in places—wide; great interchanges; out through twenty-seven acres of Franklin Field. Did any planners come to help us? One. Did any architects speak up at the hearing? Two. Did anybody from the University of Texas come down and say, "Look, this is a civilized fight, and we'll help you"? No. Nobody.

So this is what I would like to say to planners: For heaven's sake, get your feet muddy. For heaven's sake, all of us, get out with the architects. For heaven's sake, raise a little hell. There's something worse than losing a job. After all, not too many of you are going to live beyond 2000 A.D.

And, if any of you can stand to look at it, all right. Go with the establishment.

Buckminster Fuller said the following: "First, what could society, backing up into its future, with its eyes fixed only on the ever receding and less adequate securities of yesterday, do to make this evolutionary process a gratifying rather than a painful experience? Second, what could the average intelligent and healthy, moneyless individual best contribute, singlehandedly, toward bringing the earliest and happiest realization of advantage for society in general through taking and maintaining the comprehensive, anticipatory design—science initiative—in the face of the formidable axiomatic errors and inertias of academic authority as well as the formidable economic advantage of the massive corporations and their governments and mutually shortsighted foci of resource and capabilities exploitation?" Buckminster Fuller is an entirely remarkable man. Although he may be considered a little old fashioned right now, he taught us a lot. Bucky is an old man. And he has had to wait until somebody would buy something from him, would buy an idea from him. I'm perfectly willing to wait. I'm perfectly willing to fight. I'm perfectly willing to cross swords with people like the man in San Antonio who built a garage on our river. It's a monstrous thing, on city property. No one knows now who owns it; nobody knows what it cost; nobody knows who will buy the revenue bonds. It was built in a hurry—the fire was coming.

FORD'S RESPONSE TO REMARKS BY
L. S. TURNER JR. AND REYNELL PARKINS

People think the business community is different from anything else. Planners often think that businessmen are different from others. I am the director of a bank. I'm a businessman. I find that businessmen like to think of themselves as being altogether different because they're in production, manufacturing, commerce, or distribution. But a businessman must be all things. He is a generous man. He is the head of a foundation, on the school board. And being in business is not very important, really. In business you are close to money. You are close to public affairs.

When you say, Mr. Turner, that beauty is in the eye of the beholder, I'd say you know very little about what you're talking about, because just the other day I talked to the man who builds the Ramada Inns. He put up a great and spirited speech about how they spent all the money designing these beautiful buildings. Well, think about the beholder a little. The Ramada Inns are not beautiful; a lot of other signs are not beautiful, but you talk to the man who makes neons and he gives you a pretty esoteric story about how beautiful they are.

Of course, the hero of this whole evening is Rev. Parkins. I really think he took a few things out of context, but his way is obviously a better way. Progress takes time. It takes fighting. It takes patience. I say this to him personally, to all Negroes, to all people who want to join and have joined the fight for Negroes in every sense of the word, and for all people in America. Abraham lived in a land where his father was a stranger. This is a very significant thing, because Abraham was not a stranger in this land, but his father was a stranger. And this is the best thing happening to us today. We live in a land where planning is not a stranger, nor is the planner, nor is the man who says that the nature of evil and the nature of ugliness are much alike. The protective, productive, creative tension is what we need.

PART IV

Looking Back,
Looking Forward

1978

Foreword to *Lynn Ford: Texas Architect and Craftsman*

Throughout his life, Ford worked closely with his extraordinarily talented younger brother, Lynn. Best known for his exquisite wood carvings, Lynn also worked in metal, and he created many of the works of craft that enriched his brother's buildings. Their collaborations, some of which were enhanced further by the works of ceramicists Mary Vance Green, Beaumont Mood, and Martha Mood (who also designed textiles), mosaic artist and painter Tom Stell, and glass artist Ruth Dunn, embodied both the continuation of the principles of the Arts and Crafts movement that helped define architectural modernism and architects' renewed interest in integrating the other arts into their buildings at mid-century. Ford's foreword to Mary Lance's book dwelled mostly on his brother's work rather than on their relationship.

During all the months before and after my brother's death, I have watched the patient and thoughtful searching for and finding of Lynn's work carried out by his friend and good neighbor Mary Lance. All of us in the Ford family and so many of Lynn's friends are deeply impressed and grateful. As she began to draw information from Lynn, from me, from my sister, and many others, I became increasingly aware of the great amount of work that had come from the various barns, sheds, and backrooms that had served as working places for some fifty years of Lynn's life. More recently the work done by the staff of the Trinity Press and the photographs by Michael J. Smith have shown me another great measure of devotion to the gathering

---

Reprinted from *Lynn Ford: Texas Architect and Craftsman*, by Mary Lance (San Antonio: Trinity University Press, 1978), ix–xi.

211

and sorting of a vast amount of material that would or might adequately document all that a very hardworking craftsman had done throughout his adult life. I believe all of us have come to realize there is no real end to the search, as something we did not know about, some project Lynn never mentioned, is one more of the discoveries.

We did learn that he did the work with pride and devotion, shipped it or installed it himself, and went straight to the bench to start another job. Much of his work was done for buildings that our office had designed, but the search has revealed other items commissioned independently. He finished a work when he felt it was complete and right and almost never gave any thought to making a photograph or keeping the beautiful sketches he had prepared. I often urged him to tell me when I might make photographs, and fortunately I did drop in at a few completions and made quick shots. He and I often mentioned taking a great trip to dozens of towns to see the people and the works. He kept the "customers" for good friends but never was able to spare the time for the tour.

I cannot remember once in his life when he had any time just to rest—just to be free of the pressure of getting something done and delivered. He never asked for a commission, never sought a better-paying project, and just worked at carving wood, hammering copper and lead, casting and modeling clay, and making all the pieces of any project, no matter what materials were involved. His skills and capabilities came from an almost intuitive sense of the proper limitations of the material with which he worked. He required no long practice period when he used a new material or new technique but, instead, thought through the inherent nature of the wood or clay or metal and the capacity of the tools he had on hand—and he had very few good ones. He often remarked that an over-full chest of tools or a shop with every needed machine made many craftsmen believe their own resourcefulness and serious purpose were not really very important. I believe his old drill press was bought, secondhand, in 1932, his jointer in 1935. Many of the old carving chisels had been ground down from six inches to two inches. These old chisels were something he loved and understood. I well remember his joy when I brought several from London in 1951. I believe I must have brought twenty or thirty more when I made other trips to England. They were the best birthday presents and Christmas presents. The chisels and hammers and mallets were the hard extension of his own strong, ambidextrous hands.

As I write, the whole half century, with the dozens of places where he lived, the many makeshift shops, and the extraordinary array of strange old cars he coaxed all over the country, becomes a story of a man who worked more hours than any person I have ever known. I am sure he must have spent fully half of every hour of his life—awake and asleep—doing hard work on beautiful things.

I do remember some little times when he and I went to horse races. And I remember the late-night coffee, the friends, and the outrageous storytelling sessions. He collected the most amazingly talented, most imaginative, and most devoted long list of friends one can imagine. He saw the special character of each of them as actors, workers, and unordinary men and women.

Now the impossible task of telling the whole story shows me the sharper pieces of his life, and it all seems to make one picture of beautiful things and another of long days and nights of work when he added tired to tired. The many persons who own the things he made are so proud of their treasures and grateful to the maker, but I remember how weary he was most of the time. I cannot guess how many nights he never stopped the mallet and chisel, how the chips piled deep around his feet, just because he felt the compelling duty to have it done when he had promised it would be done. I knew that he should not have set deadlines at all and that the finished product should justify any delay. One could not expect the purchaser to understand how slowly a hard piece of oak is cut and shaped. It is impossible for anyone except the craftsman himself to understand how long it takes to shape a three-foot-diameter piece of heavy copper into a half sphere just by hammering.

His quiet pleasure in his quick look at the finished article was just a brief time in the same hour that he started another work. The process was as much his art as were the products.

As we discover more of his works, learn more about his disappointments and pleasures, I am amazed at the prodigious amount of work he did, but I am not the least surprised that not one single thing, part or whole, was expediently conceived or executed. I believe Lynn was incapable of doing anything ugly or expedient. It was all a matter of the honest way to use materials he loved and understood—there were no shortcuts, tired or not tired.

FIGURE 19. O'Neil Ford, Howard Wong, Nic Salas, Mike Lance, and Alfred Carvajal, Margarite B. Parker Chapel, nave, Trinity University, San Antonio, 1963–1966. Doors, chandeliers, and screens by Lynn Ford.

1981

Lessons in Looking

*Near the end of his life Ford collaborated with the nonprofit orga-
nization Learning About Learning Educational Foundation,
which was based at Trinity University, to record conversations
with children about architecture that could be shown on television. The architect's brief lectures and exchanges with the seven
children were published as a slim, illustrated book,* Lessons in
Looking, *portions of which are included here. The book has pictures of many of the things Ford illustrated in slides and sketches,
as well as photographs of the architect and members of his young
audience. The children were students at public schools in San
Antonio and at St. Mary's Hall, a private school there, the new
campus of which Ford had designed.*

*In addition to its holdings on architectural history, Ford's
personal library contained numerous books on children, child-
hood, and education. The* Lessons in Looking *project was in
many ways the culmination of the architect's lifelong interest in
education, and in it he laid out more clearly than in any other
text his views on materials and the process of developing a discerning eye and critical understanding of architecture.*

*Characteristically, Ford made his points using examples
drawn from a wide and deep history of architecture. The children heard about things as varied as vernacular Texas buildings,
Maya temples, factories, bicycles, and modern sculpture, which
Ford showed in slides. He encouraged them to read, write, draw,
touch, look, and ask questions.*

Excerpted from *Lessons in Looking: Dialogues with O'Neil Ford, Architect* (San
Antonio: Learning About Learning Educational Foundation, 1981).

LOOKING

How do you learn to look? Learning to look means learning to notice the shapes, the forms, the sculptural qualities of whatever you're seeing.

Learning to look is making comparisons and analyzing what you see, forming opinions about what's good and what's bad. Learning to look is a lifelong process, a lifetime adventure, a lifetime journey.

Looking is not the same as seeing. We see the road we are traveling, familiar or unfamiliar, in order to get where we are going, but we don't train ourselves to look at the environment around us, which may be full of surprises. We rarely make ourselves really look at what's beautiful, what's ugly, what's ingenious, what's abusive.

Now I'm going to give you some problems to help you think about what you notice.

First, I want each of you to think of a building or a structure that you like, just because of the look of it. Maybe you like the shape, or the material, or the color; maybe the way the building or object stands against the sky or in relationship to the other buildings around it.

Next, I want you to test yourself. How many of you here have ever really *looked* at power lines all over town? How many of you know from your own observation how they are made, why they appear so carelessly strung up? Can you remember what's on the first busy street near your house? How many of the buildings, signs, shapes that you see every day can you really remember?

I've brought for you a crazy collection of things to look at today. I want you to jot down notes and ideas you may have, ask questions. Some of this may seem a little vague, so I might just ask *you* what you're learning! I hope that each of you will get a feel for the differences in looking and seeing in your own mind.

Learning to Look Means Educating
Your Eyes and Your Hands

Hands are remarkable tools. We should study what man has made with his hands. In a huge sculpture, in a building, or in a little piece of clay, we can see the imagination and the feeling for materials that the creator had, through the work of his hands. A knowledge of what hands create influences how you look at what's around you and what you see.

Before I became a really discriminating person, I might have made a funny remark about Henry Moore and his blob sculpture. That's because I didn't know better. But recently, when I was in England, we came upon this sculpture in the park. I saw where Henry Moore pulled the clay out a little, pushed the clay in a little; when he finally got the clay the way he wanted, he made the molds, and cast it in bronze. His hands showed all over—the marks of his hands were all over.

The magic of the hands is often just overlooked. Hands are the most remarkable of all the tools that have ever been invented in the world. (Hands make tools work—what is a screwdriver without hands? or a saw? or a violin?) I want all of you to get to know the joy of working with your hands.

If you take clay in your hands, and you do things with it for fun or to make a present, I suppose it's sculpture. But what it mostly is . . . is your experience with clay. Your hands and this wonderful clay. Now, if you were able to carve in wood, as a lot of primitive people did, why, you experience wood and you get to liking it very, very much. You understand all about wood. Likewise, stone. Anything that you cut, carve, whittle, or model becomes a wonderful experience in your life.

Most sad people have never made anything with their hands. Most people are deprived of making anything with their hands . . . so keep your hands busy. Do things with your hands. Make things. But don't worry about whether they impress anyone or not. They're your happiness and you're doing it.

Only by making things with your hands can you get to know the tremendous possibilities of materials. So begin to educate your hands. You can start very simply.

Spend time pushing, pulling, and shaping clay. Find out how you like to work with the clay—how does the clay feel in your hands? Don't try to make anything—just experiment with the shapes and forms you enjoy from the feel of your hands working with clay.

SCULPTURE

Where do you see sculpture? There are sculptures in your town—in parks, museums, galleries. Those are the sculptures people call sculptures. There are also unintentional sculptures. These are buildings or structures in our everyday environment that have sculptural qualities. By looking at real sculptures and then at buildings and streets and objects, you start to educate your eyes about the sculptural qualities of the environment.

As you look, you should remember sculpture doesn't have to tell a story. A sculpture should be seen as an interesting shape, form, a special use of materials. That is what you should learn to see in sculpture.

This is my favorite sculpture, in Peru. [The Intihuatana stone, sometimes called the Hitching Post of the Sun.] Stone cut with obsidian—a beautiful monument at Machu Picchu.

This is in Temple, Texas, by Richard Hunt—a friend of mine. It's a beautiful, exquisite use of brass. It soars like a bird, yet stands still, and makes itself and its place an important part of the land.

If you go to Grand Rapids, Michigan, you'll see a sculpture by Sandy Calder, which he painted red because he likes red. And it's made of steel—it looks like steel. It doesn't look like clay or wood or marble or anything else. It's just plates of steel. And it's very successful. In this rather plain town with a plain plaza, when you see it every day, and walk under it and see children play around it, you know it's a good thing for the town.

The people love this sculpture in Lisbon, Portugal, though they probably don't know who he is—he's actually St. George. He's sort of like a buddy to everybody in town, you know. "Our buddy and our pal." I believe he's made of lead. The lead takes on a wonderful old patina. As it gets older, it gets better—like copper. I like St. George. He's just standing there. He's not striking the serpent or the devil. He's just standing there—proud. And that's the way I think it should be.

This one's done by Sir Jacob Epstein, on Cavendish Square in London. I doubt whether anybody will ever see a better Madonna and child. It's just wonderful—standing still, with the little boy's arms out. He's not doing anything—this just made the art. If he'd had his hands down, he would have repeated the folds in the Madonna's skirt. It would not have been so interesting.

Some Sculptures I Dislike

All of you have seen soap sculptures. But have you ever seen anything look so much like soap as this? They're all white—very white. It's about thirty feet high, in Lisbon. The great dictator, Salazar, had these made in his honor, just before he was exiled. They are probably the dumbest of all sculptures made in the world. Certainly the most expensive.

This man aspires to jump through a wedding ring. He's made of brass and gold-leafed. He's in New York. It's pretty dull, because you don't expect or want to see brass figures jumping through wedding rings. You want them to stand still. And that's the only reason I show that.

In Washington, this is Justice, who looks like Moses, in front of the Rayburn Building. You walk by fifteen times a day and never see it at all. It's just something expensive.

Now! What do you think you are learning from all this? I wish each of you would spend time looking at sculptures, to get a feel for the nature of the materials from which each sculpture was made. I want you to learn to appreciate what wonderful things hands can do in different materials.

Next I'm going to be showing you some structures you might think of as pretty far from sculpture in a museum, but we are going to consider them as if they were sculptures—as shapes, forms, inventions with material that dwell in their place and either enhance or detract.

- Questions from Eddy, age fourteen: "Does the sculpture say mud or clay? Wood or brass? Can you see the creator's hands at work in the materials? Does it make its place somehow more special, more important for everyone to enjoy? Or is it *just something expensive?*"

It's dangerous to answer your question because there's a danger in being a little bit snide about an answer. At the same time, there are vulgar things and there are beautiful things. Now, you and I don't like the same things—precisely. Nor would anyone else here agree with me—all the way. And that's fine. Otherwise it would all get pretty dull—there would be just two sculptors doing all the sculpture, probably. I think the thing to do is fill your head with all the knowledge you can— read the books, go to the library, and just look at pictures all day. Go back and look at books again that you once looked at that didn't make much impression on you. They will make more impression now, as you get older.

My belief is that a person develops sensitivity and doesn't have to go around discriminating between good and bad. Knowledge is the only thing that prepares a person to sense the little differences and the big differences in good and bad. So have a good, tolerant attitude toward all things you see, and don't try to develop a terribly discerning taste for good and bad, too soon. Don't do it too soon. Keep looking. Keep reading. I've had myself turned around many a time. All the way around.

Things I thought I liked when I was younger were pretty bad. For instance, I liked the fireman's monument at the

County Courthouse and thought it was a marvelous piece of sculpture. I later on realized how absolutely ordinary it was. But that wasn't true when I was fourteen. So you do change, and you should change all your life. You should know things when you're eighty that you didn't know when you were sixty, that you didn't know when you were twelve. And you should have this wonderful experience of learning, all your life.

LOOKING AT STRUCTURES

We can learn to look at structures as though they were sculptures in the landscape. All around the world there are remarkable sculptures that people have built to live and work in. I am going to show you some things which are pretty far from sculpture but involve an understanding of beautiful form in materials.

Then I am going to show some real ugly stuff, which you encounter every day on the streets. As I show you these things, I want you to make comparisons in what you see—still noticing shapes, forms, uses of materials.

This is a little church on the Greek Island of Mikonos.

This is in Washington, D.C. This is a fine way to turn a corner. The man put a sculpture on the end of his building and people can walk in it and look over the city.

And this city, high on a cliff, is itself a marvelous stacking of sculpture where thousands of people live.

In Weatherford, Texas, this man has a mobile that pumps his water and a sculpture that he can sit out on and look at the countryside—in many ways he's got Calder beat.

This is a serious chimney on a laundry in Nice, France. This man put a sculpture on his laundry. He wanted to give some beauty and still have a good smokestack.

But we go down the highways of America and this is what we see—these are our sculptures. We go by these every day, but they are so commonplace we never really stop to look at them, to evaluate what's interesting and what's ugly. To me, they are intruders on our beautiful land.

These, I Suppose, Are Ultimates in Good and Bad
This is a building in San Francisco—theoretically. It's not really a building—or is, incidentally, a building. It's really an ad for an insurance company. They've built a building like this so they could make stationery and ads that showed this building and nobody would ever miss the name of that insurance company. So it's an imposition on the landscape of San Francisco, which is beautiful. It's an ego trip by someone, a wrong idea.

And this is Monte Albán, done a long, long time ago near Oaxaca in Mexico. You never hear an architect compare himself to the men who built this structure. They just stand there all day with their mouths open. And architects who go there come back with far less ego!

STICKS, MUD, AND ROCKS

In this lesson, we are going to focus on what man has created with the first materials on the earth he had at hand—mud, sticks, stone. What man has done and does do with these materials is remarkable and sometimes amazing. We're going to be looking at some ways of building that are several thousand years old.

In our discussions, I want you to remember that we are learning to look at the relationships of three things:

First, we are learning to look at the remarkable earth that we walk on, dig in, abuse, or care for, without really stopping to think what we are doing.

Secondly, we are learning to look at the amazing and beautiful things, the ugly and useless things that man has done on the face of the earth.

Finally, we are learning to look at the materials from the earth man has used to build things.

You should remember that everything you see here in this room came out of the earth. There's no such thing as a synthetic. All things are combinations and amalgamations of materials from nature, either grown or mined, hammered, sawed, melted, fired, polished, or pressed. In a thousand ways, the genius of man has done this.

Imagine you're a person living on the earth long before cities, long before concrete highways, long before steel and brick buildings. Or imagine you've left the cities to pioneer a land without lumber mills or brick plants. What materials would you use to build a shelter? What are the simplest, most ordinary materials that you would find almost anywhere on dry land?

When you go to the country or to a sandy beach or to a river bank, look for the natural building materials that are around you. Look for shelters, caves, or rock overhangs that occur naturally. Write and draw about the kinds of structures you might build in the different environments.

Think about these questions:

What happens to a mud house in the rain?

How would you cut large trees without a saw?

How could you protect a dirt house from bad weather?

Over the world men have used the earth's resources in ingenious ways to build what they needed for the climate they lived in.

In Tunisia . . . a Desert Land

In Tunisia, mostly a desert land in the northern part of Africa, great holes are dug in the ground, as big as several tennis courts.

Then holes are dug back into the sides of the great holes with steps and a door. The person who lives there has a good house down below the earth, where the heat of the sun never gets to him. He's cool. He's cool the way you're cool in the cellar of your house.

In the Yucatán

These extraordinary houses are built now precisely like they were 1,400 years before Christ. They're beautiful and absolutely perfect for Yucatán. They built a modern school down here in the jungle, but the children didn't like it; the teachers didn't like it; so they went back to the old mud school. They have television in it and all of the projectors and things that you have in your school. But they gave up the modern school because it was hot.

Right Here in Texas . . .

In San Antonio and nearby old towns, the native material is stone. It is soft rock, easily cut, easily taken out of the ground. Early settlers built almost all their houses of stone because they had very little timber. They had mesquite trees, but one couldn't get a very long log out of an old mesquite tree, could he? So they had to cut short logs. So a house could only be as big as one log joined to another log to make a roof, with a stone wall under it. So around San Antonio, Castroville, Bergheim, Quihi, Fredericksburg, and other little towns, a very distinct and unusual kind of architecture grew up, almost as natural as the trees, as natural as the flowers, and very good-looking just for that reason.

Here are more remarkable ways of building in Texas.

In Brackettville, Texas, there were little trees; a few sticks helped men enormously. They made a ditch, drove the sticks in the ground, and then plastered in between them with mud. So they had a mud-and-stick house, called a stockade house.

The first houses in Texas, when the people moved out here from the East, were inspired by Swedish and Danish log cabins. The logs were short, so the rooms were small. It was difficult to fit logs together, so they filled the big cracks with mud.

This was interesting to me—again, vertical poles, which you can barely see, then thin sticks nailed to them (that had been split off with an axe). Then they filled in between the two walls with dirt and stones, which made a stockade wall. But also these little sticks made a nice, rough surface that could hold the plaster. So they used a combination of ingenious things.

Here we are with dirt, wood, stone—simple, elemental materials you find anywhere and everywhere. Dirt, wood, stone—that's the whole palette of these artists.

Mud Structures
On a Greek Island . . .

Buildings made of mud have very interesting sculptural qualities because of the shapes, the forms, the shadows, the angles and curves that happen when you use this simple material. The material gives the building a beautiful character.

This is a great example of the sculptural quality of all buildings built with mud in Greece, on the island of Mikonos. It is a very good example of the beautiful quality you get because you don't have half a dozen materials, you have one simple material. So the beauty of the buildings depends on the form, the sunlight, the shadow, and in this case, the wonderful curves.

And in New Mexico . . .

This is the back of a church in New Mexico. And it's just a marvelous thing piled up almost like a small child piles up clay in a very crude way. It's a good building, and it's been there a long time.

Here's the front of a church in Santa Fe, which is very, very simple, right out of the earth. Only timbers to span the top are introduced as something besides dirt. Everything else is dirt.

These weren't designed by an architect. They were made by the people, out of the materials available.

I think these are better than most buildings designed by architects. They make sense because what they built was the best that they could build for the weather, with what they had to work with.

All of architecture ought to be like this, and it generally was until, oh, the last three hundred years.

I live in a stone and brick house, sort of crude, but it's a good house, and looking at brick and stone is a good deal more pleasant than looking at asbestos shingles and some of the more plastic-looking houses that are built everywhere now. But in general, stone and adobe and earth houses are used less today because of the economic factors.

In the United States, where wages are pretty high, and in France, in Germany, in England, and in Italy, mud is just about abandoned as a material. Now, a rancher who has three or four cowboys working for him could make adobe while his hands are not doing anything else. I think nowadays this is the way you do earth buildings or adobe buildings; you do it in odd times or odd seasons. The main reason it isn't done more is that it's slow and therefore labor-consuming and expensive.

There is a great deal of interest in earth houses now, or houses that are underground, or partly underground, because of the high cost of heating and cooling. Underground they're cool, like the ones I showed you in Tunisia. I think that it's probable that there will be more dirt houses built in the most favorable places, where there's the proper soil and less expensive labor.

STONE

Stone is one thing nature produced that has been man's real standby all along. He lived in stone caves; he built with stone; he fought with stone hammers; he cut with stone chisels; he did amazing things with stone.

Men have built the most extraordinary structures with rocks and stone. We, nowadays, with building technology what it is, have a hard time understanding how they did it, and that's all right; that's one good mystery left in the world.

There Is a Mystery in Peru . . .

This is a fort up above Cuzco in Peru, at about 13,000 feet. These stones were laid and dragged great distances, way before the Incas came in about 1350 A.D., maybe a thousand years before. This is pre-Inca. These stones are joined so you cannot put a razor blade between them. They have no mortar, nothing to stick them together. Not only are they joined without mortar but the joining surfaces between them are curved, each stone fitting the other—precisely. It keys together so it can't fall down. One can't move because the other holds it. No engineer, no architect, no scientist in the world has any idea how they did it; and many, many, many people have spent lots of time on expeditions studying it.

. . . A Marvel in England

This is Stonehenge, in England. Now, to move these stones took hundreds and hundreds of men. They moved them a great distance, and the way they put them up (if you'll see me privately, I'll tell you how they did it, but I don't want to tell you publicly because I'll be told off by somebody who says that I'm not right), they dug a hole in the ground, they skidded a great stone up to the hole, pushed the back side up and it fell in the hole. So they didn't have to lift the whole thing, it sort of fell in. About half of it—almost half of it—fell in the hole, and they didn't have so much to lift.

. . . A Sculpture in the Jungle in Tikal

This is another building in Guatemala, Tikal. It's the most terrifying thing to climb because it is *steep*. When you sit in the door at the top, you can't see the steps below you. This structure is a strong and awe-inspiring sculpture as it soars above tall jungle trees.

Mass and Weight Are Principles That Give Stone and Mud Structures Their Strength

Everything in stone and mud must have real weight because
th⸢⸣   u've got. These materials don't have much tensile
            ⸢ely any properties of tension at all, like steel. The
            ⸢ to weigh something, one part has to lean against

This is a splendid example. This is a drawing of a place on the border that Eugene George made, which shows the ingenuity with which people used mud and stone. They make a strong corner. They put up a chimney. One thing braces another.

This is the Tachs house, and I love that chimney. I remember it from the time I was about your age, when I went there, to Fredericksburg. It's as strong as it can be. It's heavy; it's massive. It's essentially stone, carefully fitted together—lovingly, proudly—by a good mason.

Here Are Some More Uses of Stone—Far Away and Nearby

All over the world there are more sophisticated kinds of things that can be done with stone. These are the things that people did when they understood the sculpting of stone and had the will and the money to spend. There's a sculptural quality to the details. When they understood how to cut stone, they began to express themselves in a truly artistic manner. They could think about other things than just a matter of getting housed.

This is the ultimate of what people did with stone, and it hasn't much to do with what we were talking about earlier, because we were talking about primitive people and beautiful, simple things. It's interesting that man can move from dirt to this building at Pisa, where the Leaning Tower is, in Italy.

The German stonemasons built this beautiful St. Joseph's Church right here in San Antonio in 1868, I believe. I believe this may be the best nineteenth-century spire in the United States, or anyplace else for that period. The stonework is marvelous.

Our missions in San Antonio are very particular stone structures. They are all built of little stones. That's all they could find. You see, they couldn't get to Bergheim or Boerne or out in the country to get great big stones. They were down below town, where there was no stone except for some fossiliferous stone in the riverbed. So they built all these missions out of whatever they could get, pretty ingenious but not lasting too well. We have to take care of them very carefully.

This is our wonderful baroque Mission San José. In the old days, the cowboys pulled the heads off the figures with their ropes and nobody cared. Now everybody cares.

These are houses at San Juan Mission, and they are very much like a lot of houses around this part of Texas used to be. They have grass roofs and are made with any kind of stone people could find.

This is Concepción, my favorite of all the missions because it's the simplest, the most straightforward.

That's why we study the past. It's always helpful to know about how man used the earth, how he treated its resources, and how the earth, in return, treated him.

You see, an architect has got to fill his head with all the knowledge he can . . . he's got to educate himself and build inside himself an inner resource for thinking and working.

Let's say you've studied architecture, and let's narrow it down: you've studied old architecture of Texas. Well, you're not going around copying that architecture—it'd be a little bit absurd. All your houses would look like Fredericksburg or Castroville. But in your head is the knowledge of these houses that were built for this climate. It becomes part of you. And it's evidenced in the work you do.

Architecture changes as new materials, systems, techniques come along. Now I can transport, on trains or in planes or trucks, material to build a house from Colorado to California or New York. So I don't have to depend on what is just here in San Antonio, as did the people in the last century. Now it's a troublesome and complicated thing to be an architect. You want your house to look like your own part of the world, don't you? You don't want it to look like it came from Boston or England or even Houston. There's no point in a house in Texas looking like it was shipped to Texas. I hate to see a house here that doesn't fit our land and climate and our living habits.

So, remember to have respect for the materials and feelings

of your part of the world. I think a building should help make its place in the world somehow special and important.

METAL

Metal has changed the way men live in so many ways that we never think about! For instance, can you imagine your town without cars?

I want to talk about something we see every day but think very little about, and that's the magic of metal. The metal we want to talk about is steel because the invention of steel, the development of steel, has changed all of civilization in thousands of ways. From tools to implements to airplanes to automobiles, everything has changed because of steel. I suppose, of all the metals, it has had the greatest effect on the economy and life in general. It's made miserable things happen, as in England, where the great steel mills were places labor was exploited; but at the same time it's given us great and wonderful things, which are rather magic, when you think about it.

I want you all to think about how metal makes magic in your world. What can you see on the street and in your house that wouldn't be here if it weren't for metal? Make a list of all the metal structures and objects you know of. When you are finished, look out the window or take a walking tour down the street. Add to your list—how many things made of metal did you forget?

Cars were wagons and some brilliant man named Baines invented a little engine that he could put in a car and make it move—ah!—at twelve miles an hour! And so we were launched into an amazing culture completely guided by automobiles: what they do to us, where they take us, what they say to us, what they look like, everything. When I was young, cars were skinny. You could not wear one out; I don't believe that anyone ever wore one out. They got disgusted with them and threw them away because they were kidney-breakers; you know, the roads were kidney-breakers.

This is a 1938 MG TB Tickford. To me, this car is more honest than what we have now. Nothing sticks out in front of the axles or behind the axles. When you sit in it, the wind blows in your face, and you have a good time driving. It isn't just transportation, it's great fun to drive. And of course this has beautiful wire wheels instead of the dreadful mag wheels that cars have now.

What has happened to cars? Cars have become a marketable item. They have nothing to do with the running and nothing to do with the beauty and nothing to do with anything except selling them, making them almost alike, and describing them as being greatly different, each one. And where do they go? They all go to the car graveyard. Beautiful metal, wonderfully formed, wonderfully shaped, totally useless, of no value except scrap. And, of course, they enhance the landscape!!!

Cast Iron

The magic of metal, especially when you think of architecture, really began with the development of cast iron. Iron, forged from ore and made liquid with heat, was poured into molds, hardened, and then pieced together into all manner of buildings, furniture, and machines.

About 3000 B.C. somebody discovered iron. Now, we don't know exactly how, but I suspect and a lot of people suspect that some great fires, forest fires or fires that people were using to keep warm, were against a red rock cliff, with the wind blowing, providing a lot of oxygen, and the fire caused something to drip out of the cliff. And right away it was magic to them. It was iron. Just rough, rough iron. After many years, maybe two thousand years, people were able to forge that and make things of it.

When the Civil War came to the United States, there were huge cannon factories that produced enormous amounts of cast iron. Now, these cannons ended up, most of them, on the fronts of buildings like this one in Savannah, Georgia, or down on Alamo Plaza or someplace like that. When the war was over, there were all these huge factories in New York, New Jersey, Pennsylvania, and even in Atlanta, in the South; they were out of business. Nobody was buying cannons.

So right away they started making other things. They made benches and tables and all manner of little things, and these things were strong and they lasted very well because cast iron doesn't rust as fast as refined steel. Then they began making buildings of cast iron—lots of buildings. New York was full of them, and a lot of architects became quite famous because of their knowledge of cast iron and how to use it.

Here's a beautiful little building in St. Louis, which, alas, was destroyed to put up a rather tacky building, probably made of mirrored glass. That's just an opinion: that this was beautiful, but what's there now is bad. This is cast iron—every bit of it; with columns, little arches, everything. Actually, it's a kind of imitation of other things, like stone. But it was very handsome, and at that time, a very valid way of building.

Here Are Some Cast Iron Structures
I Love In Savannah, Georgia . . .
Probably my favorite house anywhere, with cast iron balconies. They were made in England, then shipped to America.

The Blum Building in Galveston . . .
They put iron on the first floor because iron is very, very strong, and if a flood came, it wouldn't wash away.

In the Old Capitol of
Louisiana, at Baton Rouge
All of the ribs curving up in this dome are cast iron.

Back in England . . .
This is a gassorium, with great tanks that floated up and down where artificial gas was stored. To keep it from being

an ordinary old thing you'd find in an industrial district, they built this wonderful piece of architecture, which is rather amusing in a way, and yet very beautiful, an exquisite use of cast iron.

On Johnson Street in San Antonio . . .

There was a bridge that was moved from Commerce Street to Johnson Street—a thing of great beauty. Later, some ill-advised people from the city hall—that's the kindest word I know—tore it down and threw it away. Now the parts can't be found. We have found a few pieces and cast some more at a wonderful casting place right here in San Antonio. There are plans afoot to rebuild this bridge very soon.

STEEL

The magic of steel is that it is strong and can be used as a very thin, light structure to hold up great weight. Like cast iron, it is strong and can be shaped, but it can also be stretched and made into thin cables. With the invention of steel, our lives, our tools, our machines, and our architecture all changed again.

This is a good example of the beauty of steel. This is in Baton Rouge, and made out of steel reinforcing bars. A man built this structure between two buildings that he owned, put plastic on the top of it, and he now has a garden shelter.

Now, steel is iron much refined. I have a little piece of paper that describes it which I'll read to you because no one would believe how you make steel of iron—cast iron or pig iron: "Steel may be prepared by passing hydrogen and pure refined iron compounds"—the oxides, for example—"at high temperatures by electrodeposition from solutions of iron salts." Well, there you are—that's simple. All of you understand that? And that's how you make iron into steel. Seriously, you should all find out more about the process of making steel. You should find out where the steel for buildings in your town comes from.

Structures That Show the Beauty of Steel

Before aluminum, early airplanes employed all of the qualities of steel exquisitely. The material couldn't weigh too much. The maker could not use a great column, or beams. He had to use thin wires.

This is a prize! It's called the Spanish car—it goes over Niagara Falls. And twenty or thirty people still get in it today. It rides on thin little cables, sagging right across the falls. It's a machine, and this is what holds it up. All is done with the most exquisite attention to the thinness. They didn't want a heavy cage—and they had a lot of fat people. They wanted to take care of lifting the people, not the cage.

This was done by Mr. Buckminster Fuller, a great American engineer, architect, and philosopher. This structure was built for the Montreal Fair. It's all little pieces of metal—aluminum, actually, and so thin and so strong and involves such great understanding of mathematics and nature that it's really a revolutionary thing. You've seen geodesic domes and that's what this is, but this is a pretty complicated one.

See this? This is light, thin, airy!

Now, this is the first use of steel in a building, that I know of. This building is the museum at Oxford University, and it's all steel. And it's an extraordinary experience to walk in there. You can hardly believe the thing! Now, they were a little embarrassed about any mundane or ordinary thing like steel in a museum, which would ordinarily be stone or marble, so they painted it. You can't quite see it, but they painted it all kinds of colors and then beat out metal leaves to go at the tops of the columns. That made it proper, for the times.

But sometimes people abuse steel. In 1955 in Nashville, Tennessee, somebody had more steel than he had ingenuity, and he wasn't going to let his building fall down. Of course, you can't even see through it. So that's a wasteful, foolish use of steel.

I think all architects and all engineers ought to be very, very serious about not wasting things—not wasting money, not wasting resources. After all, everything we have is limited.

We all must learn to have respect for metal—that fabulous material we see every day. Every day we see steel misused, we see steel frames probably four or five times as big as they need be. That's what I'm talking about when I talk about economy— not in dollars, but economize on the idea, economize and use a material as it ought to be used. And don't treat it casually.

This is something exciting man has made, using steel. This is steel in compression and in tension.

But here is something more amazing! Man has made nothing like this—this is one of the extraordinary things in nature. Have you seen a spider web that has had dew or rain upon it? It's unbelievable. The blobs of water on that fine, fine little fabric weigh 1,500 times as much as the thing holding them up. That's what an engineer at a university told me, after figuring a while. That means that this little fabric that the spider has woven is vastly stronger than steel, per inch or per millimeter, in thickness. If you had a spider web an inch square and an inch round, it would hold up a million pounds, whereas steel would pull only sixty to seventy thousand pounds before it yields.

What do spider webs and trees have to do with buildings? All the same principles are at work—it's just that some of nature's materials are more magical than anything man has been able to invent.

Nature has some peculiar secrets that are just incredible. That's the reason we look at nature with a different eye.

We look at a tree, still standing in a strong wind, even when all the houses blow down. There are some lessons for all of us, and for architects especially.

This is the old aviary at the zoo in Washington, D.C. Each cage is made of one center column pushing up, supporting the roof. Thin wires were strung tightly from the edge of the roof to the ground, to make a frame for the wire screen. So they had tension "walls" and one compression column.

This new aviary is probably one of the most beautiful structures in America. It is very advanced in design and engineering. I don't know that I ever saw anything I like better. It just soars and winds and is graceful. Every good word that you could say about architecture, you could say about this. Here's the top of it. That's where the cables come together. Then they spread out and do a lot of different things: they hold up the arches, the arches hold up more wires, more wires hold up more arches. Everything is working in a wonderful combination, like an organism. Like your own body. Everything is in tune with every other thing.

BRIDGES

Bridges are especially interesting because they're almost all structure. The push and pull of the structure is right out there to see.

Modern bridges are using the same simple engineering principles that were used hundreds of years ago. For example, in Peru, they built stone columns and they put ropes across them and made bridges across the Urubamba River, which has a very deep chasm. And every year they would put in a new rope, or if it fell with a few people, they would put in one quicker than that, because rope, of course, doesn't have the strength of steel.

These are two of my favorite bridges.

This bridge, the Albert Bridge, is in England, across the Thames. The columns are, again, cast iron. It's heavy and strong and fitted together in pieces and bolted. This one is unusual because all of the cables that hold up the bridge come off at beautiful angles. So you have thin cables coming down from the heavy cables. That was an early bridge—actually, fairly crude, but extremely beautiful. The man planning this bridge thought an awful lot about aesthetics and beauty, but not a lot about engineering.

Here is an amazing bridge. This is the Brooklyn Bridge, in New York City—once called the eighth wonder of the world. When it was built, nothing like it had ever been constructed. Few people believed it could be done, and they did everything to hurt the man that designed it, and to make it politically and physically impossible to do it. But he did it! Those cables were invented by Mr. Roebling. They are made of many, many wires twisted together. The Roeblings built bridges everywhere, but this was the most astonishing of all of them—just like walking through Star Wars except better, lots better.

I'd like to say a word about engineering. Of course, all engineering is first imagination. An engineer's got to imagine the job and imagine it pretty accurately, then go to the computer to work with the numbers to confirm what's imagined. Bad engineers design everything with the computer. They start with a computer. Good engineers first imagine the whole structure, and then consult the computer to confirm or deny their visualizations.

BICYCLES

Push and Pull at Work

Here is a magic thing that man has made. A two-hundred-pound man can sit on it, on the top of this thin little thing. He could pick it up in his hand and toss it in his car. He could take it in the house and up the stairs. An absolutely marvelous piece of engineering that sort of grew. Nobody engineered the first one—he just made it. Then it was refined and refined, made lighter, and made out of tubes, very thin wire tubes for spokes.

The top few spokes—let us say, the top third—are doing all the work. The weight is coming down and pulling them. If you pluck them, they will make music because they are in tension—pulling—holding up the sides. The bottom spokes—what are they doing? Well, nothing, except keeping the wheel from collapsing under the load. If you pluck them, they will go boom—because there is no tension. All the spokes are very close together so the thin sheet metal on the outer rim won't bend.

Using the Strength of the
Bicycle Wheel Another Way

Try this experiment. Take three bricks and balance a bicycle wheel on the edges. Stretch across the center a long board—strong enough to hold four, six, or even eight people. One by one, get these people to stand on the board. Pluck the spokes. Find which ones are in tension and holding up the load. Find out which spokes are not pulling at all. This is an amazing amount of weight for one little wheel and a few little wires to be holding up!

Building Buildings Using the
Principles of the Bicycle Wheel

This is a building downtown at La Villita in San Antonio, a building built something like a bicycle wheel [figure 11]. Here's the inside of it before they put the architecture on it.

Here is a better one we built. This is the City "Whoopee Room" in Denton, Texas. Again, this is a bicycle wheel. The water would run off of a bicycle wheel because it's sloped, and the water runs off of this because it's sloped. The tension is in the bottom ring; the others sag a little, though they still slope away. I think the building is about two hundred feet across.

But how big can you make something like a bicycle wheel? Can it be five hundred feet? Can it be two thousand feet? How far can you stretch a wire? What are the possibilities?

You might put a whole university inside one wheel. You might put a whole shopping center inside it. I don't know why people haven't copied this; I haven't had a chance. I'll copy it again and again, of course.

A Building Invention

Now I'm going to try to draw for you a building that is just a piece of wild imagination, but I think it's a wonderful building idea that will work. Suppose we've got to design this structure to contain a whole university.

First, we've got a great column like that. Here's two, three, four floors of parking below ground, where you can't see it, which is where parking should be. We've got the footings going down to hard rock, of course, to hold it up.

The first thing we do is we put a truss at the bottom. A truss is heavy steel, very heavy, with big members that hold up a lot of things. With jacks, we lift the truss to the top of the column. Now, this truss is very strong, maybe fifteen feet high and steel, as you know. It's a very big, gruff thing.

Then we make a very light steel floor and another and another and another and we stack them up, as many as we like, and we lift each of them up to its proper place. These are all floors. Now, after we've got them up, wires are fitted to them. You haven't any columns on the outside of your building, you just have rods holding up all the floors from this giant truss at the top. Now, this is where the people live, and let's say there are fifteen floors of dormitories.

So we stretch cables way out to either side. But we put a roof on it—part of it is plastic so we can get the sun in and light. Part of it is another metal or polyester, or anything you can find that will make a proper roof.

The roof's high enough so you can grow trees, real trees, in here. It's high enough and big enough that you can have a football game inside the place. The next thing you do is tie other cables to the roof to keep it from fluttering in a high wind.

Then you've got to have administrative offices and you've got to have a cafeteria—let's put the cafeteria up on top, where you can see everything. Then you've got to have in here the air-conditioning equipment, and so you lift up a space for that above the offices.

At the edge of the roof the wires are fifteen feet off the ground. That's where you have classrooms, all around, clear around. Between the classrooms and the column are the playing fields and the trees and the fun places.

Now, how do you hold down the outside? Here's the column, pushing up; here's the guywires that make the roof slope out from the column toward the ground. So you extend the guywires past the places for classrooms, and take them on down to a concrete blob in the ground. The whole thing's held up by one giant column. This structure is a great, wonderful tent. That's about all it is.

But how big can you make a tent? I don't know. I'd like to make one like this about a thousand feet across. I'd like to make one that would cover half of Brackenridge Park. So you could have all manner of things inside of it.

Ideas for buildings come together from a lot of different places—from the experiences and the knowledge inside you. If you have a lot of poor experiences and very little knowledge, you're probably going to have a very poor building.

Ideas come from building things. Maybe at first it's a playhouse for your brother, or a doghouse for your pets, or a henhouse for the chickens—if you have chickens. And then you've got to evaluate what you have built. Does it work for the job it needs to do with the materials you have available? How could you build a better one? Imagine the possibilities. Then build again!

You've got to have inside you a knowledge of the possibilities of materials. And that knowledge comes from making things with your own hands. Architecture is using the materials the best way you can, wherever you are, theoretically. That's the best way to make a good building.

Architecture is the thoughtful condensing of the right materials, the reusable systems, the making of space and shape for shedding rain, keeping out cold, holding in heat or cool. Also, it's knowing what is strong, what is weak, what's too costly, what's inexpensive, and where to get it, putting it together, writing it down, making drawings, trying to find somebody to build it.

This is what you should be learning.

KEEPING A JOURNAL

I think everyone who is learning to look should keep a personal record book. Your book can contain words, phrases, names and places, thoughts to remember, drawings, research notes, poems—whatever comes out of you, or is interesting for you to put down.

I've kept a daily journal for the past thirty years. It's an exciting way to save your thoughts and notions of people, places, the world around you. It's a good thing to look back over the years to see how you are growing and changing, what you are learning.

To get you started, we've listed some places you might go, some books you might look at, some questions and problems you might consider. These are meant to help you fill yourself with all the knowledge you can—you can start very simply by observing and thinking about the structures and objects in your neighborhood, your town.

I hope you will follow up on your special interests and curiosities. Treat yourself to a day of looking in the library every now and then. You should find your own personal ways to consider and use what you are seeing, reading, thinking. Learn to ask yourself questions. Every now and then put your ideas together and share them—as a poem, a set of drawings, a letter, photographs.

These are all important for developing your inner resources for thinking and working.

Eulogy for Tom Stell

When Ford remembered his longtime friend and collaborator Thomas M. Stell, a multitalented artist who was best known for his mosaics, he returned to the earliest days of his career in Dallas, when he had met Stell at David Williams's salon, The Studio. Along with Jerry Bywaters, Harry P. Carnohan, Otis M. Dozier, Alexandre Hogue, William Lester, Everett Spruce, John Douglass, and Perry Nichols, Stell formed part of the "Dallas Nine," a group of painters, printmakers, and sculptors who were active in Dallas in the 1930s and 1940s. They were the first important group of modern artists to work in Texas. Known as regionalists, the artists participated in the multifaceted, international practice of integrating recognizable elements of local culture, tradition, and landscape into works of modern art. Ford particularly remembered Stell for his expansive, inclusive view of history and credited the artist with helping inspire his interest in Byzantine, medieval, and Victorian architecture.

Those of us who are gathered here have something to remember that is precious and unique and entirely lasting. None of us will forget how Tom Stell changed much of our thinking and perceptions concerning beauty and those persons and things that have made beauty. We will remember the sharp lectures, the admonitions, and the incomparable recitations of history of all the arts—music, automobiles, paintings, mosaics,

---

Eulogy for Tom Stell, delivered at Stell's funeral on April 2, 1981, handwritten text, unpublished, box 81, folder 8, O'Neil Ford: An Inventory of His Drawings, Papers, and Photographic Material, 1864–1983, Alexander Architectural Archives, University of Texas Libraries, University of Texas at Austin.

sculpture, and even shoes and shirts—and all of architecture. Every person with whom he talked was a learner, whether or not he knew it. Every question I have ever heard put to Tom got a serious and studied answer.

When he first arrived in our poor studio-office in 1929, an entirely new and challenging world was opened to me and to so many young artists—I well remember William Lester, Everett Spruce, Otis Dozier, and dozens of others who got articulate and meaningful explanations that they had never got before. All his instruction as a teacher was uncompromising in his demand for full understanding of the reasons for his demand for perfection—there were no short cuts, and no one was allowed to treat his work as a hobby or pastime.

Those of us who were young architects began to know the significance and the process by which the great Art of Byzantium, the Middle Ages, primitive areas, and the great early periods of the Renaissance came to be one big, continuous book of revelations. Our new understanding of color was tenfold more than any art students anywhere were acquiring, and he knew more about architecture through the ages and down, more than most university professors. The understanding of the nineteenth century—so-called Victorian architecture—was an entirely unusual thing in the days when it was ignored, despised, and fast being destroyed. About 1931 he showed me extraordinary things in Waco—and that was more than any native of that town could have done.

So—here we wonder how this man can be gone—here we feel a big measure of regret for not hearing more from him—and some shame that his words and work have been poorly recorded. Some of us who owe him so much feel some sadness that we didn't seek him out when we knew he was alone. It seems to me that only those tennis-playing friends saw him pretty regularly—even to the last day he lived.

We say good-bye to the lectures, admonitions, criticisms he gave to those who were seriously interested, but what we remember is endless—and our memories. How I wish I could

FIGURE 20. O'Neil Ford, Richard Colley, Arch Swank, Sam Zisman, et al.; Arthur Berger and Marie Berger, landscape architects, Texas Instruments Semiconductor Components Division Building, courtyard, Dallas, 1958. Ceramic panels by Tom Stell.

remember—and wish I had written—all those stories of his boyhood in Cucro. I wish I were sure I could remember all the stories about his family, particularly his father. And he had some good stories about another gifted Cuero boy, Buck Schivetz. I am deeply grateful that I did have visits with his father—and I am glad to remember that I have known Buck since 1926.

I don't know how to say good-bye—or why we should try. Tom Stell will be with us in our hundreds of differing ways as long as we all will live. He, like my brother, Lynn, who was Tom's friend, probably fell victim to compromise of any kind fewer times that any men I have ever known. They are a forever part of our knowledge and our conscience—will give us a jerk and a happy shock when we unexpectedly think of things he told us. So now a man who put his mind and hand and voice to creating and knowing and making and explaining beauty will speak no more. But Tom Stell was something profound and lasting—like a great mountain or river—or old live oak tree. Nothing he did or said was perfunctory or whimsical or expedient.

Any man who loved beautiful things, children, Dixieland music, and knew of them so well, was very significant in our lives. He was, in my opinion, the best mosaic artist on this earth, and an extraordinary painter and draftsman. He was very quiet about it, never sought, or got, much credit for being a great artist and great influence on all who listened to his words or saw his works.

1982

Foreword to *David R. Williams, Pioneer Architect*

Muriel Quest McCarthy's book on David R. Williams was pub-
lished after Ford's death but included the foreword the architect
had written for it shortly before he died. Ford praised his mentor's
intense appreciation of the ways buildings are linked to and shape
a sense of place and recalled the excitement of being at the center
of the cultural efflorescence that swirled around Williams in the
1930s. Ford recalled two projects that Williams, in his capac-
ity as an administrator of the National Youth Administration,
had directed to him: the design and construction of a community
in Pine Mountain Valley, Georgia, from 1934 to 1936, and the
restoration of La Villita in 1939. Both works combined plan-
ning, architecture, craft, and negotiating complex social, politi-
cal, and cultural challenges. Of the La Villita commission, Ford
wrote that it "changed the whole direction of my life. I was in the
place I loved—San Antonio." In 1960 Williams told the Jury
of Fellows of the American Institute of Architects in a letter, "I
consider O'Neil Ford far and away my greatest contribution to
Architecture." As Williams himself recognized, Ford was ulti-
mately the more consequential of the two architects, but Ford's
admiration for his mentor remained steadfast.

The initial thought of a foreword to a book about Dave Williams
brought memories exploding into a vast cloud of vagueness
that dissolved into a myriad of specific details. The incredible
variety of good times, hard times, discoveries, as well as all the
work done between 1926 and 1941, came sharply into focus.
Then there was the conflict between the feeling that I could

Reprinted from *David R. Williams, Pioneer Architect*, by Muriel Quest
McCarthy (Dallas: Southern Methodist University Press, 1984), ix–xii.

and should write a large volume to describe the amazing succession of adventures, projects, and learning experiences of this period and the knowledge that most of this and more had already been done—and carefully done—by Mickey McCarthy in this book.

For my part, talking about Dave Williams needs to start on June 23, 1926, when I boarded the interurban from Denton to Dallas. Gathering my courage by presenting my drawings at several architectural offices (and being quickly dismissed at each), I approached the only important one, at 1302 Southwest Life Building. What happened there on that happy day is entirely indicative of the style and habits of Dave Williams and gives a reasonable measure of that remarkable man.

I had written to Williams, explaining that I wanted to work for him. The letter was carefully composed, probably laboriously, as I had no training except the correspondence course provided by the International Correspondence Schools. I wrote that I had a lot of drawings I could present, which were all my own idea of what and how I should draw. Then there were the scrupulously executed plates regularly submitted to and returned from the I.C.S. (usually with good marks—which I now feel might have been suspect).

I was warmly greeted by a thin, Latin-looking gentleman who put me in a fine old Spanish chair and started asking questions. I discovered he was Mr. Williams, and was baffled by his rambling talk—which scarcely touched the subject of architecture. He was so neat in his linen suit and starched shirt; his scholarly courtesy was almost overwhelming, frightening. Shortly, a man much like the dapper Mr. Williams but loosely dressed and obviously pressed by something pressing burst into the room. The contrast was astonishing. He was Dave, the architect, and twin brother of Dan, the writer, who had been passing time with me while awaiting Dave's arrival.

After I was introduced to Dave, I made some clumsy remark about having written to him, hoping he had received the letter, etc. He asked if I had drawings and, while taking a cursory look through them, explained that he had no time to answer letters and where had I been? Within five minutes he assigned me a space and proposed $13 a week as starting salary.

I didn't hear anything else. I was well above ordinary elation and only wanted to get out and tell someone and decide whether I was terrified or just happy. I suppose I went home to get some clothes, but it was only hours before I was back, wearing a new smock (a mark of high status as a draftsman) and getting myself placed in very low rank between Ed Bliss and Ted Stueber.

About the fourth day I was there, a big handsome man named Dent burst in and was in the process of upbraiding Dave about delays in designs for his lighting fixtures. Dave calmly came to me, asked for my folder, and pulled out my drawings of several copper lanterns. He handed these to Dent, who looked quite as surprised as I did. They were the sort of colored glass and flat copper and rivets that the William Morris era had produced many years before, but it was a triumph for me. That day, after the others had gone, Dave showed me some of his own early drawings and explained that he too was a "graduate" of the I.C.S. That was the day I knew I was working with a friend.

We worked together, lived in cheap rented rooms together, traveled together, and moved from one place to another together for years. Now, as I look at the frequency with which we did move around, I realize that it was all a little frantic and actually quite intense, as far as experiences go.

The Architectural Club (a beautiful building designed by Ralph Bryan) was on Pacific Avenue, across from the Medical Arts Building (designed by our dear friend Todd Dale), and there we set up shortly after the club folded. The elegant lounge, with its fine, Spanish-style furniture, fireplace, kitchen, ballroom, and tiny sleeping places: all were ours. There was no drafting room, but then we didn't have much drafting to do. We had some jobs in Wichita Falls and a few small houses to work on, and I was the "force."

We did, however, have a sudden explosion of social life, as most of the Dallas architects continued to visit our big lounge (the ballroom was rented to a dancing teacher). We got to know a lot of girls, too. That was when I met Jerry Bywaters, and Tom Stell appeared one winter in a coonskin coat and hat. Dave saw to it that I became associated with the cultured bohemian set, and bold talk and brave discussions were our principal occupations (girls filled in the empty places).

Also, Dave introduced me to Ralph Bryan, who conducted a sketching tour every Sunday. Rice Nelson, the dancing, singing club cook and launderer, was our keeper: his ingenuity in the acquisition of food was extraordinary. He did give us the only class we could muster, as he always wore black trousers and a starched white jacket.

Jerry introduced me to the intelligentsia, as they called themselves, at S.M.U., and Tom Stell filled us with fine prejudices about everything—a great teacher. There were fancy and plain restaurants galore, three or four theaters downtown, bookstores, some shady places called "clubs," and very personable bootleggers.

I must say that we had started big homes in Corsicana before we moved to Pacific Avenue, so Dave and I made many trips down that rough road in his new secondhand Packard Straight Eight. He also conspired with me to buy tools and start my brother, Lynn, carving big beams for the Drane house in Corsicana, and he set Tom Stell to work painting the walls of the Drane library. Dave bought all the furniture for the Stroube house, and we designed rugs and doors, hunting everywhere for materials. This was my first experience in the search for and use of native stone (even old slabs of stone from Galveston sidewalks), and we began to design all the gates, grilles, lighting fixtures, mantels, and some furniture. This was entirely out of the stream of custom and practice in those days. We gathered craftsmen, and soon Dave's nephew Bub Merrick joined us.

Now, where and how we lived still remains pretty cloudy, but I suppose it was as vague then because we were working the way we wanted to work. The idea of regular salaries had disappeared, and Dave just collected when he could and divided the money.

We moved from Pacific Avenue to Pearl Street, where we occupied a three-story, most unusual "modern" stucco building that looked much like an early Lescaze or Corbusier effort. There again was a great lounge with a room behind it for Dave's bed, a drafting table, and his collection of fine books and bric-a-brac. This collection was the only thing that was always there when he later lived in several places in Washington, D.C., and in the house in Lafayette, Louisiana. Those books and artifacts were a great mark of continuity for me, as all the memories were somehow associated with them.

Life at the Pearl Street house was partly work (not very much) and partly working out ways to survive. The depression had just about stopped all building. We teamed up with several others and did decorations for the Terpsichorean Club and the Idlewild balls—and after the days and nights rented tailcoats and went to the balls! We then began to gather an amazing crew, who shared and sang and had parties (when funds were available) together: Denys Nettleton (Oxford), adventurer and writer Horace McCoy (*They Shoot Horses, Don't They?*), the brothers Marcel and Emile Robin from France, Buck Winn from Celina, Bub Merrick, cartoonist Ed Reed, and Harrison Stevens, the accomplished piano player; and I was there with the wonderful old etching press Dave had bought for me.

I began to have closer ties with Jerry Bywaters, Henry Smith, Lon Tinkle, and John McGinnis. Gangsters were in the neighborhood, and several accomplished beer makers were nearby. One could buy an old Lincoln or Packard for $250. Sonny, Rice Nelson's son, had joined us because he had no job but liked us all. Credit at Gallagher's Restaurant on McKinney at Fairmount was a great convenience, and now and then McCoy sold a story to *Black Mask Magazine* for four or five hundred dollars. Horace did allow us to drive his green Hudson Speedster when we had to see a client, and Dave got a second racy Packard touring car.

What is left out of this compressed account is so much that was near tragic, so much that was hilarious, and so much that was inspiring experience and real creativity. I had seen some South Texas towns in 1924 and barely remembered their real nature, but as early as 1926 Dave and I had made several wide-ranging trips to all those places and to San Antonio and East Texas and New Orleans; and we had begun serious study of indigenous building, history, and materials. Dave wrote excellent articles for *Southwest Review* and a local art magazine, and we began to feel the sense of native things and the respect for climate, and the development of a kind of style just grew. Dave kept pressing for understanding of these values and suppressing the idea that we, or anyone, should copy the old buildings and develop a new "ranch style." All this had an enormous effect on all of us, and I presume to say there is evidence enough that it shaped the thinking of a lot of other architects.

Dallas had been a real clutter of eclecticism during the opulence before the depression. About the time I was setting out for myself, and work was becoming even more scarce, Dave was at work on the Elbert Williams house on McFarlin. This one he did his own way and quite alone. I had participated in the design of the Clark house on St. Johns in Dallas, as well as the Corsicana houses, and we were finally not sure who was the originator of certain ideas. Dave never allowed any such distinction, and, of course, I felt great comfort in the lack of hard discipline or dominance by "the boss." This was all just a natural way of working; no one was praised and no one was blamed.

Then came very much harder times, about 1932, and Dave took a position with the government. The excellent description of this period by Mickey McCarthy eliminates any necessity of my retelling this story. I entered the Williams scenario again, having had no great success with my own practice.

Dave was set up in Washington with Aubrey Williams's office and put in charge of Rural Industrial Communities. So he called me to come to Austin, where we set up a planning office. I was back and forth between Austin and Trinity County, where the first community was planned and built. On this occasion I was made the head man and was lifted to a $250 a month salary. Dave shuffled all over the country and Alaska on these projects, and I raced by Pierce-Arrow roadster down into the piney woods a lot of times. Dave then got my brother to open a furniture shop at Woodlake Community. We were solvent.

I left this job to take a position in New Orleans, but after nine months of little sleep and rather exhausting high life, I got a call. Dave Williams said he had a terrible job in a worn-out valley between mountain ranges in a depressed place in Georgia called Pine Mountain Valley. He started describing the rough nature of the ten thousand acres. I stopped him and said I'd leave in the morning to meet him in Atlanta. So I was given a task considerably beyond my experience. We set up offices at the WPA headquarters in Atlanta, and it was back and forth to Hamilton—planning, working out drainage, building roads, and even counseling the three hundred applicants for homesteads. This was a most difficult assignment—in the face of the eroded valley, the poverty, the adamant prejudices so rampant then—but we did get it done, and Dave and I had the great pleasure of taking our plans to Washington to present to President Roosevelt. This project demanded and provided knowledge of all kinds of management and diplomacy, as well as no small measure of toughness. Dave stuck by me during some explosions between the state officials and me and my crew.

I moved back to Dallas after working a short spell for the National Youth Administration in Washington. Dave had now become a real force in this splendid program for indigent youth all over the United States.

Now again I was back in private work in Dallas, but Dave put me on some jobs at the Centennial Exposition there. That done, and two years later came another call from the old boss. At Hugh Drane's penthouse atop the Adolphus Hotel, he told me I was to take on the restoration job at La Villita. This changed the whole direction of my life. I was in the place I loved—San Antonio—with all the surrounding old towns we knew so well. Then, too, working with Dave's flamboyant classmate Mayor Maury Maverick was something one could never match. Then I met Wanda Graham, got married, and here I am.

I believe no untrained young person was ever given the free rein Dave gave me, and as I remember a hundred incidents that were good (and as many that were bad) I suddenly realize that we never once had a quarrel. I believe this is entirely pertinent, as I am positive about my contentions and so was Dave. Arch Swank, who knew Dave quite well and was my partner for years, also observed that the relationship was remarkable—but then I don't think Arch and I ever quarreled, either.

One of our last adventures was the trip to San Francisco when Dave and I were awarded fellowships in the American Institute of Architects. Arch and I had both helped assemble the material to support Dave's nomination, and I told the Institute that I could not accept mine if Dave's was denied. So much for nobility: he told them the same about me.

I have often heard the phrase "the Dave Williams myth." It was no myth. It was a great association of dedicated and devoted friends. Had I not known Dave, how would I ever have met such great ones as John H. McGinnis, Al Powers, Frederick Charles Cowderoy-Dale (Todd Dale), Ida Oran, Maury Maverick, Ladine Martin, Phyllis Berglin, President and Mrs. Franklin D. Roosevelt, Colonel Lawrence Westbrook, Hugh Drane, Tom Knight, Crystal and Lewis Dabney, the Robin brothers, and the great Louisiana Givens clan?

Dave Williams's work was important for a lot of reasons, and way up on the list was the bond he saw—and expressed in his work—between design and place. That his place was the Southwest was lucky for us, since he also tied place to a lot of other things, including people. Dave had this gift for getting diverse people to work together, and talk and drink and play monstrous practical jokes together—to express, with him, a kind of wild joyousness in life. That vitality went into his architecture, and there was enough to spill over into all our lives.

Acknowledgments

My deepest thanks go to the children of O'Neil and Wanda Ford, for their kindness to me and their enthusiasm for this project. On the Fords' wedding anniversary in 2017, Wandita Turner, Linda Ford and Michael Howard, and Michael Ford shared their memories and perspectives with me over lunch at El Mirador. It was delightful.

Many in San Antonio's architectural community have encouraged me in this research. I especially thank Carolyn Peterson for sharing her recollections and for her support. Michael Guarino has been a vital interlocutor and coconspirator. I thank him particularly for making available the archives of Ford, Powell & Carson to me and my students. The encouragement and models of advocacy that Rick and Jane Lewis provided in the early phases of my research on Ford were invaluable. Mary Carolyn Hollers George's generosity and comradeship have been especially meaningful.

At the Alexander Architectural Archives I am enormously grateful to the incomparable Nancy Sparrow, who embraced this project, tracked down and shared documents and images, and made easy the countless logistical aspects of realizing it. I thank Lauren Feltner of the Edith Garland Dupré Library at the University of Louisiana at Lafayette and Katie Dziminski of the DeGolyer Library at Southern Methodist University for their assistance in locating texts. At the Coates Library at Trinity University, I heartily thank Maria McWilliams, as ever. Several years ago, Amy Roberson dug up a trove of old photographs in Special Collections and Archives at Coates Library that opened up Ford's work for me in new ways. I am very grateful as well to Lisa Endresen and Denise Wilson in the Department of Art and Art History at Trinity University for their expert logistical support.

My research has benefited from three invitations to lecture on Ford. I am most grateful to the Texas Society of Architects, and especially Brantley Hightower, for including me in their Design Conference on craft several years ago. I thank Docomomo US and the Southeastern Chapter of the Society of Architectural Historians for the opportunities they provided to talk about Ford's work with their members.

In 2012 Trinity University President Dennis Ahlburg sponsored a symposium on O'Neil Ford that brought together four fantastic scholars and friends, who changed the way I think about Ford: Julia Walker, Kathryn Holliday, Stephen Fox, and Alice T. Friedman. I thank them all most warmly. Remarks by Boone Powell and Vincent Canizaro at that event were enlightening and inspirational.

I am extremely grateful to Kenneth Hafertepe and an anonymous reader for their wise suggestions for improving the manuscript. Curtis Swope has, as always, helped in countless ways small and large. Anadelia Romo provided a critical push at a key moment in developing the book and steadfast cheerleading throughout. At the University of Texas Press, Editor-in-Chief Robert Devens was a joy to work with; I am extremely grateful, as well, to Sarah McGavick, Lynne Chapman, and Gloria Thomas for their assistance in preparing the manuscript.

My students at Trinity University have been the most enduring and important sources of inspiration. Over many semesters, in class and in long-running conversations about their own projects and beloved campus, or in our shared research, we have learned about Ford together. Those students, now alumni, to whom I am particularly grateful are Larsen Andrews, Jason Azar, Anh-Viet Dinh, Anne Ferguson, Andreas Jozwiak, Natalie Cap Hugentobler, Fiona Lane, Cole Murray, Brooks Cameron Piper, Monica Stanton, Roha Teferra, and Jane Wilberding. I hope that Ford's words will inspire them and future Trinity students to build lives of service and stewardship.

Finally, I dedicate my parts of this work to my parents, Joanne Edmundson and Terence O'Rourke, who taught me to see the best in Texas.

Image Credits

FIGURE 1. Photograph by Rondal Partridge.
© Rondal Partridge Archive.

FIGURE 2. Photograph by Debbe Sharpe. University of Texas at Austin, School of Architecture Archives: Visual Resources Collection. The Alexander Architectural Archives, The University of Texas Libraries, The University of Texas at Austin.

FIGURE 3. P|A Images.

FIGURE 4. Merritt T. Cooke Memorial Virginia Print Collection, Albert and Shirley Small Special Collections Library, University of Virginia.

FIGURE 5. Photograph by Arthur W. Stewart for the Historic American Buildings Survey. Prints and Photographs Division, Library of Congress, Washington, DC.

FIGURE 6. Trinity University Archives.

FIGURE 7. *Southwest Review.*

FIGURE 8. Orly, Val-de-Marne, France/Bridgeman Images.

FIGURE 9. *Southwest Review.*

FIGURE 10. *The Restoration of La Villita: A Report of Progress, Aims and Historic Significance* (San Antonio: City of San Antonio, 1939).

FIGURE 11. O'Neil Ford Collection, The Alexander Architectural Archives, The University of Texas Libraries, The University of Texas at Austin.

FIGURE 12. Pom². Wikipedia, Creative Commons License.

FIGURE 13. Photograph by Arthur W. Stewart for the Historic American Buildings Survey. Prints and Photographs Division, Library of Congress, Washington, DC.

FIGURE 14. Photograph by Kathryn E. O'Rourke. © FLC/
ADAGP, Paris/Artists Rights Society (ARS),
New York, 2017.

FIGURE 15. Perspectives—The Photography Club,
IIM Ahmedabad. Wikipedia, Creative Commons
License.

FIGURE 16. Trinity University Archives.

FIGURE 17. Photograph by Walter Rawlings.
© 2018 Walter Rawlings/fotoLibra.

FIGURE 18. Photograph by Dorothy Candela.

FIGURE 19. Photograph by Rondal Partridge.
© Rondal Partridge Archive.

FIGURE 20. Photograph by Rondal Partridge.
© Rondal Partridge Archive.

Index

Page numbers in *italics* indicate illustrations.

International Style, 7, 23, 30, 31
Ireland, 21, 146, 159
Islamic architecture ("Moslem"
  architecture), 15, 137. *See also*
  Great Mosque at Samarra (Iraq)
Italian Renaissance, 20, 23, 189
Italy, 226. *See also specific cities
  in Italy*

Jefferson, Texas, 149
Jefferson, Thomas, 17, 18, 19, 24,
  25, 164, 183, 197
Johnson, Lady Bird, 9, 38
Johnson, Lyndon B., 7, 8, 9,
  37, 179. *See also* civil rights;
  segregation/desegregation
Johnson, Philip, 184
Jones, Inigo, 156–157
Jonsson, J. Erik, 32, 36–37, 38.
  See also Skidmore College;
  Texas Instruments

Kahn, Louis, 6, 12, 24, 34, 133,
  151, 152, 153, 154, 155, 156,
  158, 160; Indian Institute of
  Management, 34, 160, *160*
Keck, George Frederick, 104
King, Stewart, 5, 99, 102
Kingston, Jamaica, 194

Lachaise, Gaston, 154
La Grange, Texas, 58
land: deference to, 34, 35, 37–38,
  52; destruction of, 13, 23,
  28–29, 36, 67–68, 103, 108,
  110, 126, 140–141; Native
  American, taken by Anglo
  settlers, 144–145; at Trinity

University, 169. *See also*
  Berger, Arthur; Berger, Marie;
  environmental conservation;
  Johnson, Lady Bird
landscape design, 101. *See
  also* Berger, Arthur; Berger,
  Marie; King, Stewart; Trinity
  University; Wurster, William
Las Vegas, Nevada, 127
Laurie, James, 163, 177
Le Corbusier, 12, 24, 26, 27,
  32, 34, 129, 143, 147, 184,
  251; Notre Dame du Haut,
  (Ronchamp, France), 34, 129,
  143, 147, *148*; *Towards a New
  Architecture*, 32
Leonardo da Vinci, 106
Lescaze, William, 251
lift-slab method. *See* Youtz-Slick
  lift-slab construction method
Lima, Peru, 184
Lincoln, Abraham, 25, 183
Lincoln Logs, 129, 132
Lippi, Filippo, 158
Lisbon, Portugal, 219
London, England, 14, 15, 16, 32,
  85, 124, 137, 141, 153, 213, 219;
  British Museum, 138. *See also*
  England
Los Angeles, California, 92,
  127, 194
Louisiana, 54, 55, 60, 65, 199,
  232, 251, 254

Martin, Brooks, 143
Massachusetts Institute of
  Technology, 94, 167
materials, 3, 4, 6, 15, 19, 23,

Yale University 93, 133, 151
Youtz-Slick lift-slab construction
    method, 6, 17, 31, 32, 85–89,
    93, 95–96, 130, 131, 173, 174
Yucatán, 223–224

Zion, Robert, 34. *See also*
    Paley Park
Zisman, Samuel (Sam), 104;
    father of, 104–105